Economic Science Fictions

Part of the Goldsmiths Press PERC series

Goldsmiths' Political Economy Research Centre (PERC) seeks to refresh political economy, in the original sense of the term, as a pluralist and critical approach to the study of capitalism. In doing so it challenges the sense of economics as a discipline, separate from the other social sciences, aiming instead to combine economic knowledge with various other disciplinary approaches. This is a response to recent critiques of orthodox economics, as immune to interdisciplinarity and cut off from historical and political events.

At the same time, the authority of economic experts and the relationship between academic research and the public (including, but not only, public policy-makers) are constant concerns running through PERC's work.

For more information please visit http://www.gold.ac.uk/perc/.

Economic Science Fictions

Edited by William Davies

Goldsmiths
Press

© 2018 Goldsmiths Press
Published in 2018 by Goldsmiths Press
Goldsmiths, University of London, New Cross
London SE14 6NW

Printed and bound by Clays Ltd, St Ives plc
Distribution by the MIT Press
Cambridge, Massachusetts, and London, England

A CIP record for this book is available from the British Library.

Library of Congress Cataloging-in-Publication Data

Names: Davies, William, 1976- editor.
Title: Economic science fictions / edited by William Davies.
Description: Cambridge, Massachusetts: Goldsmiths Press, 2018. |
    Includes bibliographical references and index.
Identifiers: LCCN 2017039951 | ISBN 9781906897680 (hardcover: alk. paper)
Subjects: LCSH: Economic forecasting. | Time and economic reactions.
Classification: LCC HB3730 .E248 2018 | DDC 330.9001/12–dc23
LC record available at https://lccn.loc.gov/2017039951

ISBN 978-1-906897-68-0 (hbk)
ISBN 978-1-906897-72-7 (ebk)

www.gold.ac.uk/goldsmiths-press

Goldsmiths
UNIVERSITY OF LONDON

To Mark Fisher

Contents

Foreword

Mark Fisher

Capitalist realism posits capitalism as a system that is free from the sentimental delusions and the comforting mythologies that governed past societies. Capitalism works with how people actually are; it does not seek to remake humanity in some (idealised) image, but encourages and releases those 'instincts' of competition, self-preservation and enterprise that always re-emerge no matter what attempts are made to repress or contain them. The well-known paradox of neoliberalism, however, was that it required a deliberative political project, prosecuted through the machinery of the state, to reassert this image of the human. Philip Mirowski has argued that neoliberalism can be defined by a double (and somewhat duplicitous) attitude towards the state: on the exoteric level of populist polemic, the state is to be disdained; on the esoteric level of actual strategy, the state is to be occupied and instrumentalised. The scope and ambition of the neoliberal programme to *restore what could never be expunged* was summarised by Margaret Thatcher's infamous remark that the method was economics, the goal was to change the soul – the slogan of market Stalinism. The libidinal metaphysics that underlies neoliberalism might be called *cosmic libertarianism*; beyond and beneath the social, political and economic structures that constrain enterprise is a seething potential waiting to be released. On the face of it, then, the goal of politics, according to neoliberalism's exoteric doctrine, is essentially negative: it consists in a dismantling of those structures that keep enterprising energies locked down. In actuality, of course, and as Thatcher's remark indicated, neoliberalism was a constructive project: the competitive economic subject was the product of a vast ideological and libidinal engineering project. And, as Jeremy Gilbert, drawing upon Michel Foucault's work, has observed, neoliberalism has in fact been characterised by a supervisory panic; its rhetoric of releasing individual potential obfuscates its suppression and fear of collective agency. Collectivity is always stupid and dangerous; the market is able to work effectively only if it is a decorticated mass of individuals; only then can it give rise to emergent properties.

Far from being a system liberated *from* fictions, capitalism should be seen as the system that liberates fictions to rule over the social. The capitalist social field is cross-hatched by what J. G. Ballard called 'fictions of every kind'. Ballard was thinking of the banal yet potent products of advertising, PR and branding, without which late capitalism could not function, but it is clear that what structures social reality – the so-called 'economy' – is itself a tissue of fictions. It must be stressed here that fictions are not necessarily falsehoods or deceptions – far from it. Economic and social fictions always elude empiricism, since they are never given in experience; they are what structures experience. But empiricism's failure to grasp these fictions only indicates its own limitations. Experience is only ever possible on the basis of a web of immaterial virtualities – symbolic regimes, ideological propositions, economic entities. We must resist any temptation to idealism here: these fictions are not cooked up in the minds of already existing individuals. On the contrary, the individual subject is something like a special effect generated by these transpersonal fictional systems. We might call these fictions *effective virtualities*. Under capitalism, these virtualities escape any pretence of human control. Crashes caused by arcane financial instruments, automated high-speed trading ... but what is capital 'itself', if not an enormous effective virtuality, an inexorably expanding black hole that grows by sucking social, physical and libidinal energies into itself?

Capitalism has not, apparently, been weakened by the crash of 2008. While right-wing populism has been terrifyingly successful, anti-capitalism has not proved to be a sufficient mobiliser. Provocatively, we might hypothesise that the emergence of anti-capitalism can be correlated with the rise of capitalist realism. When actually existing socialism disappeared – with social democracy soon to follow – the radical left quickly ceased to be associated with a positive political project and became instead solely defined by its opposition to capital. As capital's cheerleaders endlessly crow, anti-capitalists have not yet been able to articulate a coherent alternative. The production of new economic science fictions therefore becomes an urgent political imperative. Capital's economic science fictions cannot simply be opposed; they need to be countered by economic science fictions that can exert pressure on capital's current monopolisation of possible realities. The development of economic science fictions would constitute a form of *indirect action* without which hegemonic struggle cannot hope to be successful. It is easy to be daunted by the seeming scale of this challenge – come up with a fully functioning blueprint for a post-capitalist society, or capitalism will rule forever! But we shouldn't be forced into silence by this false opposition. It is not a single-total vision that is required but a multiplicity of alternative perspectives, each potentially opening up a crack into another world. The injunction to produce fictions implies an open and experimental spirit, a certain loosening up of the heavy responsibilities associated with the generation of determinate political programmes. Yet fictions can be engines for the development of future policy. They can be machines for designing the future, and fictions about what, say, a new housing, healthcare or transport system might look like inevitably also entail imagining what kind of society could house and facilitate these developments. Fictions, that is to say, can counter capitalist realism by rendering alternatives to capitalism thinkable. Not only this; fictions are also simulations in which we can get some sense of what it would be like to live in a post-capitalist society. The task is to produce fictions that can be converted into effective virtualities – fictions that not only anticipate the future but that can already start to bring it into being.

Acknowledgements

This book originated in a series of conversations at Goldsmiths, University of London, between me, Mao Mollona and Mark Fisher, during which we talked about the shortage of 'economic science fiction' in contemporary capitalist societies. On learning that Ha-Joon Chang was a science fiction fan, I invited him to give a lecture on 'What can economics learn from science fiction?', which became the launch event for the new Political Economy Research Centre (PERC). An adapted version of that lecture is included in this volume.

I'd like to thank Michelle Lo and Sarah Kember from Goldsmiths Press, for supporting this volume and keeping it moving at critical moments, and Roger Burrows for providing a reader's report on the whole manuscript. I'd also like to thank all of the contributors for their imagination, hard work and patience over the course of this book's development. I hope you're all pleased with how it turned out.

This project was made possible thanks to the support of PERC and also of the Centre for Understanding Sustainable Prosperity (CUSP). With regards to CUSP, the financial support of the Economic and Social Research Council (ESRC Grant no: ES/M010163/1) is gratefully acknowledged.

None of this would have got very far, were it not for Mark's infectious enthusiasm and intellectual energy. He wrote a short piece on the meaning of 'economic science fiction', which was initially to be the start of a collaboration between him, Mao and me. With the encouragement of Zoe Fisher, we decided to include this as a preface here. The book is dedicated to him.

William Davies

Introduction to Economic Science Fictions

William Davies

In an industrial economy lacking a system of monetary prices 'there would be only groping in the dark'.[1] This claim, made by Austrian economist Ludwig von Mises in 1920, is one of the most decisive and ultimately influential pieces of economic critique of the twentieth century. It appears in Mises' pamphlet 'Economic Calculation in the Socialist Commonwealth', an early and provocative contribution to what became known as the 'socialist calculation debate', which rumbled on across Europe until the 1940s and has occasionally stuttered back into life at various points since.

Within that debate can be found many of the themes and questions that sit centre stage in 'economic science fictions', as explored in this volume. Can we envisage a viable alternative to money, as an instrument for the valuation and distribution of goods? How do our hopes and expectations get channelled into the market, and how might they be directed elsewhere? Can a different economy be collectively planned, or is such innovation always a figment of the private imagination (and hence private investment)? How does computational advancement facilitate economic transformation? Could the divergent

---

[1] L. von Mises (1920) Die Wirtschaftsrechnung im sozialistischen Gemeinwesen, *Archiv für Sozialwissenschaft und Sozialpolitik*, 47: 86–121.

utopias of socialism and capitalism eventually converge into a single post-capitalist dystopia of ubiquitous surveillance?

Mises was responding to a 1919 article by the philosopher Otto Neurath, 'The War Economy'. Neurath had argued that the example of World War One demonstrated that industrial economies could be better run by state planning than by market forces. The extended economic role of the state during a world war was therefore evidence, Neurath suggested, that the future belonged to planned socialist economies. Just as the state could decide on the quantity of munitions or uniforms that a war economy needed, it could make similar 'in kind' calculations for the supply of goods in peacetime. A similar argument might well be made about industrial production in our own context of anthropogenic climate change, which may require a similar level of state management if catastrophes are to be averted over the next 100 years.[2]

At the time Neurath was writing, the recent inventions of 'Taylorist' techniques of business management and behavioural psychology offered new and more advanced means of coordinating complex production processes within factories. Surely similar techniques could be developed for coordinating economic activity across society at large, alleviating the reliance of industrial economies on market forces, with all the peaks, troughs and uncertainties that go with them. This was certainly how Lenin saw things when he predicted that, under socialism, 'the whole of society will have become a single office and a single factory, with equality of labour and pay'.[3]

---

[2] E. Silk (2014) *The Case for Climate Mobilization.* Brooklyn, NY: The Climate Mobilization.

[3] Quoted in D. Steele (1992) *From Marx to Mises: Post-Capitalist Society and the Challenge of Economic Calculation.* La Salle, IL: Open Court Publishing.

Mises' purpose was to restate the case for free markets, in the face of an increasingly plausible and popular socialist alternative. Nearly a century on, it is perhaps difficult to imagine how difficult this would have looked at the time. In 1920 laissez-faire economic liberalism belonged to the past. The Victorian era of free trade and entrepreneurial anarchy was long dead, having descended into lengthy stagnation after 1870 amidst a growing sense that progress depended upon bureaucratic welfare states, professionally managed corporations and state regulation of markets. The challenge confronting economic liberals was how to reconceive the free market as belonging to the future rather than to the past. How might spontaneous market forces become an icon of modernity?

Mises' argument progressed in a number of steps. First, he argued that the question of value (be it in an economic or moral sense) is necessarily a subjective one. There can be no scientific basis on which to establish what is good or preferable or satisfying. We all want and value different (often conflicting) things, but there is no ultimate basis on which to say who is right or wrong amidst this plurality of valuations. In this, Mises echoed arguments that Max Weber had made regarding the moral emptiness of modern reason. It suggests that a central problem for modern society is how to find some device with which to weigh up people's differing valuations, and factor them into public decision-making. If this pluralism is to be respected, there needs to be some means of calculating how to satisfy as many people as possible, but without lapsing into some arbitrary judgement about whose tastes or preferences or beliefs are the 'correct' ones. There can be no expertise regarding the preferences of the public at large, given the dynamism and pluralism of liberal capitalist society.

In a society of free markets, money solves this problem. The price system offers a way of representing a mass of subjective valuations in quantitative form, providing clear, unambiguous and time-sensitive data to producers regarding what people want and like. By representing values in numerical form, markets allow decisions to be founded in mathematical reasoning, to allow costs and benefits to be weighed up in exact and scientific terms. It makes it possible to respond to a changing environment, in real time. Put simply, it is markets that allow the economy to be a space of *rationality*.

Mises accepted that socialist economies would permit *some* role for markets. Consumer goods would be privately owned, and could therefore be bought and sold in a market. But the defining feature of socialism is that productive capital (factories, machinery, etc.) is collectively owned for public benefit. Investment in publicly owned enterprises would be driven by social need, rather than by the search for profit. Investment decisions could not be ultimately grounded in monetary calculation, seeing as these firms are not oriented towards the market.

If human tastes and needs remained constant over time, then it would be possible for socialist planners to divine what these were through some combination of surveys and trial and error, then build sufficient productive infrastructure to satisfy them, year in and year out. If nothing ever changed from one year to the next the problem of calculation (as a technique operating in real time) would disappear. The problem, Mises reasoned, is that consumer tastes and productive technology both tend to change, often with great potential benefits. Not only that but capital investment involves taking long-term bets, which may or may not pay off. There is risk involved. Profit-seeking entrepreneurs can develop a rational economic strategy, drawing on price data to calculate the likely pay-off of their investments. If they get it wrong, they go bust. But what would state-owned enterprises do as an alternative? As far as Mises was concerned, they'd be constantly 'groping in the dark'.

At a historical juncture when socialism (together with Taylorism, behaviourism and social statistics) held a tightening grip on ideals of progress and rationality, Mises' critique was audacious in its attempt to turn the tables. Socialists may dream up alternative future societies, and may, with sufficient power, get the chance to implement these dreams. But plans are static, while modern societies are dynamic. What socialism crucially lacked, according to Mises, was a technical system of computation capable of distinguishing workable from unworkable plans, in an evolving social environment. 'Socialism is the abolition of rational economy,' he concluded.

Challenging the Market

Mises' argument develops a number of rhetorical and critical ploys that would later become associated with 'neoliberalism' as an intellectual and political movement.[4] One of these is the introduction of a stark choice between the free market, on the one hand, and any form of planning, on the other, with scant interest in the various shades of grey that mediate between the two (what have been called 'mixed economies', such as Keynesian social democracy). The curious effect of Mises' critique, which would later become echoed in the rhetoric of figures such as Margaret Thatcher, is to denounce all forms of economic utopia in a dogmatic, almost utopian language. The utopia of neoliberalism is the eradication of all utopias, or

---

[4] P. Mirowski & D. Plehwe (2009). *The Road from Mont Pèlerin: The Making of the Neoliberal Thought Collective.* Cambridge, MA: Harvard University Press.

at least their submersion into the market, which is much the same thing.

Another key feature of Mises' argument, which would recur in the work of his ally Friedrich von Hayek over the 1930s and 1940s, is to represent the market as a type of man-made technology for the performance of calculation. As Hayek saw it, the market was a more brilliant invention than was ever usually recognised, not least because 'intellectuals' tended to be snobbish towards business:

It is more than a metaphor to describe the price system as a kind of machinery for registering change, or a system of telecommunications which enables individual producers to watch merely the movement of a few pointers, as an engineer might watch the hands of a few dials.[5]

The challenge that Mises laid down for socialism was a resolutely technocratic one: to come up with a rival infrastructure of computation that could match that of the price system, as a means of real-time monitoring, aggregation and calculation of value. It was a challenge that few socialists have felt able to duck altogether, and fewer still have successfully risen to. Some hoped that the economics of 'general equilibrium' developed by Léon Walras in the late nineteenth century could be used to calculate proxy prices, which would allow government policy-makers to plan economic production on that basis.

As computers advanced over the second half of the twentieth century, hopes were periodically rekindled that a socialist response to Mises' challenge would be found. The ambition of coordinating industrial production using cybernetic feedback

---

[5] F. Hayek (1945) The Use of Knowledge in Society, *American Economic Review*, 35(4): 519–30.

systems was influential among Soviet economists of the 1950s, the subject matter of Francis Spufford's novel *Red Plenty*. Between 1971 and 1973 Salvador Allende's socialist government in Chile employed the British cybernetician Stafford Beer to develop a computer system capable of planning the Chilean economy.[6] The resulting 'Project Cybersyn' remains one of the most ambitious computational attempts to achieve the socialist 'economic rationality' that Mises had declared impossible.

Our contemporary 'big data' era, in which billions of us provide digital feedback constantly via our smartphones, shopping, online searches, swipe cards, social media use, and so on, would appear in principle to offer the most promising technical basis yet for a non-market solution to the problem of calculation.[7] It may be that today we are surrounded by vast but unrealised potential for socialism.[8] The difficulty, of course, is that most data analytics capacity is now in the private corporate sector, rather than being put to collective social use. This is something that the ideal of 'platform cooperativism' seeks to challenge, and in doing so potentially puts this huge computational power in the service of the public, perhaps also to reduce the reach of markets as mechanisms of calculation.

Yet, if the market is a computational artifice, the question of its design or transformation is also an open one. The simple binary choice between a market economy (guaranteeing

---

[6] E. Medina (2011) *Cybernetic Revolutionaries: Technology and Politics in Allende's Chile*. Cambridge, MA: MIT Press.

[7] N. Dyer-Witheford (2013) Red Plenty Platforms, *Culture Machine*, 14.

[8] See E. Morozov (2014) The Socialist Origins of Big Data, *The New Yorker*, 13 October.

'economic rationality') and any form of planning underplays the possibility of designing markets and the instruments of calculation differently, around different political agendas. It obscures the extent to which markets are themselves planned, one of the central insights offered by Karl Polanyi but also shared by many neoliberals, including Hayek. Money, for example, comes in various forms from various sources. Most money in twenty-first-century capitalism is manufactured out of thin air by the private banking system, through the provision of credit to customers.[9] Most of this money never attains any tangible form beyond its digital record: a loan of £100 involves the customer's bank balance being increased by 100, and the 'assets' on the bank's balance sheet being increased by 100 (in the form of an IOU from the borrower) at the same time. Quantitative easing involves a similar trick being performed, adding hundreds of billions to the 'liabilities' column of central bank balance sheets, and the same amount to the bank accounts of pension funds and insurance companies. Money is a largely a leap of faith, backed up with machines of representation.

One avenue for reimagining the economy, then, is to reimagine how money is produced. Local currencies, alternative units of exchange, time banking, nationalisation of the credit system, peer-to-peer systems of accreditation (now made efficient by digital technology), blockchain technologies such as Bitcoin – all of these offer alternatives to the capitalist status quo, while taking seriously the challenge of calculation. Financial instruments of debt and equity are also amenable to being reimagined and redesigned. Contemporary money is so abstract, so divorced

---

[9] D. Graeber (2011) *Debt: The First 5,000 Years*. New York: Melville House.

from physical matter, that its ability to constrain us can seem bizarre. This is ripe territory for the inventive imagination to play around with.

Another avenue is to reconceive property rights, without necessarily making the leap to nationalisation. Mises assumed that only privately owned productive capital could be employed in a 'rational' (i.e. calculated) fashion. But private ownership comes in many varieties, especially where firms are concerned. To own something involves a combination of various rights and responsibilities, but there is no definitive or essential combination.[10] Worker-owned or customer-owned companies may operate via the distribution of share capital, but might equally place ownership in a trust that employees cannot legally liquidate.[11] The question of property (especially ownership of companies) is also a political question of governance: who has the right to influence how an asset is employed and to benefit from it?

The escape from capitalist privatisation looks most promising when certain goods have become so abundant as to resist property rights altogether. The ideal of the 'commons' was revived in the late twentieth century, especially in the arena of digital content and software production, wherein goods have intrinsic qualities that lend themselves to common ownership.[12] Could a combination of common intellectual resources and the dawn of 3D printing provide the basis of a new post-capitalist model, of decentralised and peer-to-peer

---

[10] See T. Honore (1987) *Making Law Bind: Essays Legal and Philosophical.* Oxford: Oxford University Press.

[11] See W. Davies (2009) *Reinventing the Firm.* London: Demos.

[12] Y. Benkler (2006) *The Wealth of Networks: How Social Production Transforms Markets and Freedom.* New Haven, CT: Yale University Press.

production? The 'end of scarcity' – of cultural and scientific resources in particular – potentially throws the question of calculation back upon the proponents of private ownership. What role is left for the market, once goods are public in their very material (or immaterial) nature? Maybe it is technological innovation that is responsible for rendering things incalculable, and not socialism at all, paving the way to a new form of 'communism'.[13] Of course, intellectual property rights and digital rights management exist to avoid this very challenge. But these too are amenable to a range of designs, as the examples of Creative Commons copyright licences or open source software licences demonstrate.

Figures such as Mises and Hayek are associated with libertarian and conservative movements on the right. Nevertheless, more socially progressive, even anti-capitalist, versions of neoliberalism are conceivable, which deliberately employ the free market to break up monopoly power and reduce profit levels in the private sector. Anti-trust is arguably the central political weapon in the neoliberal armoury, and many German neoliberals envisaged it being used in combination with a generous welfare state, to reduce the power of capital to constrain economic freedom.[14] If the market is a type of competitive game, then the rules of this game are amenable to endless reinterpretation. A number of Marxists have sought to use Hayek's argument against economic planning to make the case for a decentralised, democratically managed, market-based

---

[13] This route towards 'communism' is one of the four 'futures' mapped in P. Frase (2016) *Four Futures: Life after Capitalism*. London: Verso.

[14] See A. Burgin (2012) *The Great Persuasion: Reinventing Free Markets since the Depression*. Cambridge, MA: Harvard University Press.

socialist economy, in which firms are controlled by workers and trade with one another.[15] These build on liberal socialist contributions to the 'socialist calculation debate', most prominently those of Oskar Lange, while accepting the critique of centralised planning.

Equally, the underlying philosophical premise of Mises' argument, that value is a wholly private subjective matter that cannot be gauged in itself, can be challenged on various grounds, some more emancipatory than others. The development of 'social indicators' and 'social accounting' have developed since the 1960s to offer non-monetary measures of value, in the hope of reorienting macroeconomic policies and business strategies respectively towards non-market goals. Inevitably, these involve normative choices regarding the nature of social value, of the sort that Mises and conservative economists such as Milton Friedman always insisted are baseless. Yet the opportunity for technical redesign of the economy is nevertheless there, if a degree of consensus arises around particular moral concerns such as environmental and social degradation. If we can start from consensus on the preservation of, say, childhood and nature, as categories to be defended from market mechanisms, then it is possible to develop alternative metrics that challenge the primacy of monetary calculation. If accounting holds a privileged position in the development of capitalist rationality, as Weber and others have argued, then the possibilities for non-capitalist or post-capitalist economies might lie partly within the arena of critical and alternative accounting practices.

More philosophically pertinent, though perhaps also more troubling, are the various innovations in the monitoring of

---

[15] See, for example, R. Blackburn (1991) Fin de Siècle: Socialism after the Crash, *New Left Review*, 185: 5–67.

emotion and affect that have taken off since the 1990s. These include neuroscientific representations of emotion and techniques of 'affective computing', which aim to allow computers to detect emotion via combinations of machine learning, monitoring of bodily movement and data capture from online communication.[16] Although such techniques imply a great expansion of quite intimate surveillance, as we consider routes out of the socialist calculation debate, we need to consider the possibility that – from some perspectives and with certain technical infrastructures – the calculation of value 'in kind' is now possible, in ways that endorse Neurath's position in 1919 and undermine Mises' critique.[17]

Capitalist economies are constituted by a patchwork of institutions and mechanisms, which are amenable to reimagining and recombining. These include instruments of real-time calculation of value, but they also include property rights, governance systems, bookkeeping methods, business plans, regulatory architecture, and so on, not to mention things such as fiscal policy, which are more obviously political in nature. These are all conventions that facilitate trust, not only in individual moments of market exchange but in terms of future expectations and guarantees. Institutions such as money or contract cannot work if they're not accompanied by a normative sense that commitments and promises are binding into the future. Yet the nature of those commitments and promises is malleable.

Contrary to how Mises posed things, it may not be all that easy to say precisely where 'capitalism' ends and an alternative

---

[16] W. Davies (2015) *The Happiness Industry: How the Government and Big Business Sold Us Well-Being*. London: Verso.

[17] W. Davies (2015) The Return of Social Government: From 'Socialist Calculation' to 'Social Analytics', *European Journal of Social Theory*, 18(4): 431–50.

begins. Perhaps there is hope in this uncertainty. To designate an economy as 'capitalist' is simply to say that its institutions and mechanisms are arranged in such a way that financial returns to private capital are typically prioritised, both by firms and by the state. But 'non-capitalist' elements do and must exist within such economies, not least so as to preserve the very social relations and public goods that capitalism itself relies on to some extent.[18] Hybrid forms of enterprise – often designated as 'social entrepreneurship' or 'social innovation' – are now mainstream propositions. It is possible to discover viable ingredients of post-capitalism already scattered across the capitalist landscape, in the form of worker co-operatives, open-source projects or other experiments in economic democracy. These 'real utopias', as Erik Olin Wright has termed them, are enclaves of anti-capitalism within capitalism.[19] Even so, the inventive ethos underlying them may not be *entirely* unlike that which drives profit-seeking entrepreneurs.

Wither Utopias?

It bears repeating that the problem to which Mises deemed markets and money a solution was that the economy (including its technologies and tastes) is a site of constant and spontaneous *change*. This analysis would fundamentally alter the question of modernism and how to design for modernity. From the perspective of utopian and avant-garde modernists of Mises' time, Bauhaus artists and designers, for example, the future is to be imagined, invented, designed and planned. Modernism as a creative project involved the construction of future worlds,

---

[18] See W. Streeck (2016) *How Will Capitalism End?* London: Verso.

[19] E. O. Wright (2010) *Envisioning Real Utopias.* London: Verso.

cities, economic models and lifestyles, which would remove the technological and economic constraints of the present. The dynamic element of modernity consisted in the fact that the human imagination was constantly seeing unrealised possibilities, then setting out to realise them through technological and artistic innovation.

By contrast, the modernism that figures such as Mises and Hayek were defending was an unplanned one, in which the single most important technology was the one that mediated between evolving visions, ideas and tastes – namely the price system. Change would inevitably occur, but not through a vision of social transformation. Rather – somewhat paradoxically – if the rules of the market could be set in stone, changes could arise organically within and around it. In place of the artistic, architectural or technological visionary, there would be entrepreneurs seeking to *sell* their visions of the future to investors and consumers. Thus, only by conserving the basic institutional framework of monetary exchange and private ownership of capital could change occur in a manageable, rational way. And yet this also involves giving up on the utopian ideal of a more wholesale transformation of society.

Here we get to the nub of neoliberalism and its uneasy relationship with modernism. The vision advanced by Mises and Hayek allows for individuals to be future-oriented, innovative and self-authored – indeed, it almost *compels* them to be those things. The futuristic spirit of modernism is in play, but it cannot be a basis for the reorganisation of society in any collective sense. Instead, the political challenge is reduced to that of coordinating between multiple, heterogeneous, potentially incompatible and *private* visions of the future. By channelling the ethos of modernism into the realm of the market, it becomes contained within the competitive psychology of entrepreneurship and consumerism plus the mathematical rationality of risk. By imposing a permanent framework of competition and calculation, neoliberalism establishes a system in which political choices are radically constrained, while entrepreneurial, financial and consumer choices are vastly expanded.[20]

The full cultural and political implications of the neoliberal critique would not be felt until the demise of the Keynesian system of macroeconomic management, which emerged around 1968, and gathered pace with the end of the Bretton Woods system of fixed exchange rates in 1973. That model had included an ample role for public investment and planning, which combined comfortably with post-war modernist visions of social housing, expanded higher education, public service broadcasting, publicly funded arts, and so on. This may not have been driven by the heady rush of modernism in an avant-garde sense, but it represented what Mark Fisher has called 'popular modernism', as represented by mass literary culture and rising social mobility. Keynesianism cultivated a sense of progress as a collective temporal experience, most explicitly and crudely represented by that icon of macroeconomics, GDP growth.

A number of cultural theorists have observed that, as the Keynesian model went into decline, that very sense of 'the future' also began to evaporate. Franco Berardi has argued that 'the future' as a 'choice or a collective conscious action', as articulated in the Futurist Manifesto of 1909, peaked in 1968 and was finished by 1977, the year that the Sex Pistols released *No Future*.[21] Significantly, 1977 was also the year when inequality reached its lowest level in centuries, since when it has risen sharply back to pre-war levels. Neoliberalism, for Berardi, involves the retreat of individuals into virtual and imaginary spheres of political

---

[20] See W. Davies (2016) *The Limits of Neoliberalism: Authority, Sovereignty and the Logic of Competition*. London: Sage.

[21] F. Berardi (2011) *After the Future*. Oakland, CA: AK Press.

transformation, combined with a terrible sense that dominant political institutions are now permanent. As a psychic symptom of powerlessness, depression is the consummate neoliberal disease. Prozac becomes a necessary techno-political fix in a society that has lost its capacity for collective reinvention but has rendered individual 'creativity' an economic obligation.

Fredric Jameson offers a similar analysis in his critique of the 'postmodern'. For Jameson, the modern sensibility arose in the late nineteenth century, through a reflexive engagement with the temporality of industrial capitalism. As exemplified in the genre of science fiction writing, modernism is a way of representing or seeing the present in relation to a past and a future that are both radically different. Science fiction and other utopian writing enables us to imagine ourselves looking back upon the present, with a critical eye. It is thereby a political resource, as it empowers the critic and the radical to see the present as amenable to conscious transformation. Science fiction's 'multiple mock futures serve the...function of transforming our own present into the determinate past of something yet to come'.[22]

Emerging in the early 1970s, postmodernism represents the end of the modernist utopian project, Jameson argues. In place of a collective historical consciousness, in which the synchronous present is differentiated from both our past and our future, postmodernity offers only a spatial heterogeneity. There is no collective progress or radical emancipatory project understood in a historical sense, but simply a panoply of locations, scattered in space but never differentiated in time. 'Today,' Jameson writes, 'all politics is about real estate.'[23]

---

[22] F. Jameson (1982) Progress versus Utopia; or, Can We Imagine the Future? [Progrès contre Utopie, ou: Pouvons-nous imaginer l'avenir?], *Science Fiction Studies*, 9(2): 147–58.
[23] F. Jameson (2016) *An American Utopia: Dual Power and the Universal Army.* London: Verso.

Physical differentiation replaces temporal change, making the body a central space of political action. As exhibited in postmodern architecture, historical artefacts are pastiched, remixed, mashed up, ideally for maximum profit, on the basis that the ingredients of a different society are already scattered across space. This amounts to a permanent now.

Utopian thought privileges the role of enclaves and islands, cut off from the mainstream, thereby gaining or offering a glimpse of an alternative future for the whole. As China Miéville stresses, Thomas Moore's original 'Utopia' was an island, but not a natural one: it was deliberately separated from the mainland by force of human labour.[24] Jameson points to examples such as Bauhaus and the garden city movement as examples of institutions and spaces that were declared separate, as a basis on which to dream of or experiment with a different future. We might even see the modern university as once being such an enclave from dominant forms of power and capitalism. But the fate of the university since the 1970s speaks of a broader fate for enclaves under postmodernity. Their distinction and separation is no longer tolerated, and they become treated as resources to be connected up, networked, calculated. As Jean-François Lyotard observed in 1979:

The relationships of the suppliers and users of knowledge to the knowledge they supply and use is now tending, and will increasingly tend, to assume the form already taken by the relationship of commodity producers and consumers to the commodities they produce and consume – that is, the form of value. Knowledge is and will be produced in order to be sold, it is and will be consumed in order to be valorised in a new production: in both cases, the goal is exchange.[25]

---

[24] C. Miéville (2016) Introduction, in T. More, *Utopia*. London: Verso.

[25] J.-F. Lyotard (1979) *The Postmodern Condition: A Report on Knowledge*. Manchester: Manchester University Press, p. 4.

Postmodernity is the eradication of enclaves, working in alliance with the logic of neoliberalism to ensure that monetary valuation permeates ever corner of society. Differentiated and finite spaces of 'discipline' dissolve into a constant and endless feedback circuit of 'control'.[26]

In place of 'the future' as a collective unknown, postmodern or neoliberal society offers endless new 'risks', to be calculated primarily by the financial sector. It is often remarked that a utopia is not a plan or a constitution or a blueprint, but something that emerges among all of us as a *need* in the face of some *lack*. It expresses itself as much in science fiction as in design or architecture. The grim achievement of neoliberalism is to produce an overarching calculative infrastructure – namely finance – to harness and channel these hopes and dreams for the future, and to render them mathematical and computable in the process. Modernity, as a collective, reflexive historical movement, becomes reconstituted in terms of individual aspirations and speculations regarding the future, which are then fed into a giant machinery of calculation. Once the market is granted its status as the harbinger of rationality, as initially envisaged by Mises in 1920, then there is no limit to the hopes, fears, beliefs, guesses and dreams that can be rationalised by being plugged into the banking system.

In this way, 'progress' becomes replaced by 'change'. Rather than a collective movement from an empirical past into an uncertain future, there is individual bet-taking within an infrastructure that is presented as permanent, as beyond speculation. In rescuing the financial system in 2008–9, the most powerful governments in the world sent out a simple message: you might short a given stock, but you can't short the system as a whole. In this, the notion of 'risk', and the complex

---

[26] G. Deleuze (1992) Imagined Futures, *October*, 59(Winter): 3–7.

cognitive and technical capacities that constantly work to extend it into new areas via derivatives, play a crucial role. Risk, like money or property, becomes a transcendent and permanent instrument, through which everything ephemeral is compelled to churn. Thanks to risk modelling, the unknowability of the future, which might otherwise be a basis for hope, becomes instead a source of further financial profit.[27]

What 2008 demonstrated above all else was that this system of underwriting is not rooted in anything real, but it is underwritten by state sovereignty when necessary. The neoliberal state insists that *this and only this* is how the problem of the future is to be dealt with, and will spend whatever is necessary to deliver on this pledge.

When considering the fate of utopia in the neoliberal age, one of the most striking features is the terrible disappointment (or worse) wrought by advances in cybernetics and software. Far from the socialist hopes for non-market computation, computers have turned out to be the perfect weapon for financial investors, to the point that machines now trade happily among themselves. Rather than offer the basis of a democratic economy or a different society with a different future, 'smart' infrastructures are now in the hands of 'surveillance capital', capturing data about every aspect of our daily lives so as to render political change even less likely.[28] As capitalist computation becomes more intimate to the person, via wearable technology and social media, it becomes ever harder to represent it as a source of oppression that might be collectively

---

[27] E. Esposito (2011) *The Future of Futures: The Time of Money in Financing and Society*. Cheltenham, UK: Edward Elgar.

[28] S. Zuboff (2015) Big Other: Surveillance Capitalism and the Prospects of an Information Civilization, *Journal of Information Technology* 30(1): 75–89.

rejected, in the way that institutions of discipline and bureaucracy were in 1968. We become more and more complicit in our own surveillance and disempowerment, as cyborg ideals of personal and physiological enhancement come to displace those of economic emancipation or progress.

Equally, the postmodern collapse of history into the present (as diagnosed by Jameson) seems to be exacerbated by the ubiquity of digital connectivity and data capture. The past is converted into a searchable, mineable data archive that serves principally as a cognitive enhancement in the here and now. Risk models at least represent the future as something that has not yet happened, constructed out of empirical data that were collected in the past. Yet lying beyond this 'probabilistic' approach to the future lies what the geographer Louise Amoore terms a 'possibilistic' one, in which infrastructures of data capture a sense that something may be emerging *as it emerges*.[29] A low-tech version of this would be the phenomenon of 'cool-hunting', in which market researchers find niche tastes that are likely to spread, before they've gone mainstream. A high-tech version would be the way security services seek to detect suspicious behavioural patterns amid the vast data generated by mobile phone and internet usage. No enclave outside the grid. No future beyond already emerging trends. And no past other than that which has been captured as data.

Ultimately, Mises lost the socialist calculation debate, though not for reasons that he could ever have possibly imagined in 1920. The dominant variety of capitalism that has emerged since 2008 looks as much like socialism as it does like market liberalism, yet it works more effectively than Mises declared possible. Large Silicon Valley firms make vast profits by watching

---

[29] L. Amoore (2013) *The Politics of Possibility: Risk and Security beyond Probability*. Durham, NC: Duke University Press.

our day-to-day lives, though without necessarily actually selling us anything, and view the exploitation of labour as an unnecessary and inefficient use of resources. Social and cultural change is computed in real time, but this computation is not necessarily enacted by market prices any longer. Entrepreneurial innovation, which neoliberals viewed as a safer alternative to political modernisation, has brought us figures such as Mark Zuckerberg, Peter Thiel and Elon Musk, whose restlessness will never be limited to the transformation of the private or productive sector. In the age of President Trump, their charismatic leadership meshes all too easily with overbearing state power. The 'sharing economy' points towards a post-ownership society, though unlike the original socialist model it is consumer goods that are being collectivised, rather than enterprises themselves. Capitalism and socialism have converged. Perhaps we now do have a collectively planned future ahead of us, after all; we just have little way of knowing what it is, because our twenty-first-century planners have no obligation to tell us.

Why 'Economic Science Fictions'?

Is it still possible to go back in search of the future? Jameson has argued that the first step towards resuscitating hope is simply to reassert utopianism as a necessary and viable project at all. 'Utopianism,' he argues, 'must first and foremost be a diagnosis of the fear of utopia, or of anti-utopianism.'[30] Seeing as it stems from a deep human need, and not from expertise, utopianism necessarily has an amateur and artistic dimension that evades professionalism or expertise. To write science fictions about the economy is to insist on the possibility that imagination can intrude into economic life in an uninvited way

---

[30] Jameson, *An American Utopia*, pp. 54–5.

that is not computable or accountable. To imagine wholly different systems and premises of calculation, for example, is in itself to resist the dystopian ideal promised by Wall Street and Silicon Valley, that there is nothing that can evade the logic of software algorithms, risk and finance. In a time when capitalism and socialism have collapsed into each other, obliterating spaces of alterity or uncalculated discourse in the process, simply to describe unrealised (maybe unrealistic) economic possibilities is to rediscover a glimpse of autonomy in the process.

The assemblage of humans and machines that makes up modern capitalism is fearsomely complex. Yet unlike the market price system, so admired by Mises and Hayek, there is no apparent reason to see anything magical or ingenious about a cybernetic system combining Goldman Sachs, iPhones, Visa, call centres, Facebook, credit-rating agencies, Google, the Federal Reserve, Jawbone wristbands, HSBC, high-frequency traders, and so on and so on and so on. Rather, this uncontrollable technical complexity is ripe for reimagining. Each bit could be different, resulting in a whole that could be unrecognisably better or worse. This edifice has some vulnerable support structures, which allow virtually all human life to be capitalised and economised. None of those support structures is permanent. As Ursula Le Guin recently urged science fiction writers to consider, 'We live in capitalism. Its power seems inescapable. So did the divine right of kings.'

The science fictional imagination is not merely fictitious in its economic implications. This is because 'the economy' is *already* partly fictional in its constitution. Imagination and fantasy are internal to the space of calculation; indeed, it is the human capacity to think or believe that which does not materially exist that makes economic expansion possible, and provokes the explosion of risk management and calculative edifices as the more paranoid neoliberal response. The economic sociologist Jens Beckert has explored the importance of 'fictional expectations' in the institutions of capitalism – that is, those things that we treat as real and dependable, but are not yet empirical. They therefore rely on collectively endorsed fictions. This includes the value of money, which exists only by virtue of our expectation that others will accept it; or a business plan, which an entrepreneur produces as a narrative into which an investor might place his or her confidence; or an advertisement, which is a quasi-utopian promise of how a product or service will enhance the purchaser's existence. Risk models, as generated by economists, actuaries and physicists, are all science fictions, inasmuch as they represent a reality that has not yet come about.

In a system such as capitalism, which undergoes change over time, the division between 'real' and 'imaginary' value is not absolute or fixed. This, after all, is how financial bubbles occur: when collective imagination starts to become mistaken for an empirical reality. It was a similar ambiguity that led to the global financial crisis, whereby mathematical models of a non-empirical future started to be treated with the same level of confidence as the empirical past. Capitalism rests on traffic between the imaginary and the real; it's not just that 'all that is solid melts into air', but that air is constantly materialising into solidity. The marrying of fictional futures and empirical facts is what makes capitalism possible, but it is also what makes it unreliable and potentially dangerous. As Beckert argues:

Under conditions of uncertainty, assessments of how the future will look share important characteristics with literary fiction; most importantly, they create a reality of their own by making assertions that go beyond the reporting of empirical facts. Fiction pretends a reality where the author and the readers act as if *the described reality were true.*[31]

---

[31] J. Beckert (2016) *Imagined Futures: Fictional Expectations and Capitalist Dynamics.* Cambridge, MA: Harvard University Press, p. 61, emphasis in original.

The key difference between the 'fictional expectations' that make up capitalism and 'literary fiction', Beckert argues, is that the former are 'design fantasies' that are scrutinised for their plausibility, not only for their seductiveness. Moreover, these 'design fantasies' seek to motivate people in a certain direction: to attract investment, to provoke a purchase, to accept payment. This is unlike a literary fiction, which exists to produce pleasure or engagement or provoke reflection, but less commonly seeks to change or reinforce behaviour.

And yet, by seeing how 'real' economic institutions bleed into 'imaginary' fictions (including literary fictions), the question arises of how this ambiguity might be harnessed and expanded. One way of doing this, perhaps, is to cultivate ambiguity between the role of 'experts' and that of 'artists' or 'amateurs', and to challenge assumptions about who really influences our political economy and how. The literary fiction of Ayn Rand, for example, has very clear 'real-world' consequences, in the form of the libertarian conservative clique that is inspired by it and now has access to the White House. The discipline of economics deals in all manner of things that do not exist outside the economics profession and its journals, conferences and models. And yet it is safely insulated from the realm of literary fiction, not least by the specialist language game it employs to insulate itself from the world (perhaps some enclaves survive postmodernity better than others). Lawyers, equally, traditionally see their role in terms of interpreting existing rules, but far less commonly in terms of inventing new ones or imaginatively recombining them. Meshing these professional identities with those of artists, activists, amateurs and dreamers would also mean weakening (or at least challenging) the rigidity of capitalist institutions, which are always partly imaginary.

Cultivating such ambiguity does return us to past utopias in one particular sense. As the sociologist Ruth Levitas has explored, before sociology was established as a discipline, circa 1890, its progenitors shared many characteristics with utopian dreamers, literary science fiction writers and reformers. One of these was H. G. Wells, who wrote:

Sociology must be neither art simply, nor science in the narrow meaning of the word at all, but knowledge rendered imaginatively and with an element of personality, that is to say, in the highest sense of the term, literature.[32]

Social theory, especially anthropology, retains some connection to the task of writing good fiction.[33] But the idea of an *economic* science fiction sounds somehow oxymoronic. The liberal market economy, Foucault reminds us, is governed so as to be a site of truth, and nothing else. Science, yes; fiction, no. Why so dogmatic? What is there to be afraid of? It's not as if the fictions of 'incentive', 'preference', 'supply curves', 'utility' and 'efficiency' have done an especially good job in keeping the economy under control over the past decade. Maybe it's time to inject some new ones.

There is already an abundance of conservative visions of the future, even if they are not always recognised as such. An industry of 'futurists' seeks to narrate futures in such a way that they can be brought under managerial control, pre-empted,

---

[32] Quoted in R. Levitas (2013) *Utopia as Method: The Imaginary Reconstitution of Society*. Basingstoke, UK: Palgrave Macmillan, p. 87.

[33] See D. Beer (2016) Fiction and Social Theory: E-Special Introduction, *Theory Culture and Society*, 33(7/8): 409–19.

offset and planned for via investment strategies and marketing. The vocation of the futurist is narrow and ahistorical, seeking the mitigation of risks and blame on behalf of existing powers rather than sources of hope. As Peter Frase puts it, '[S]cience fiction is to futurism what social theory is to conspiracy theory: an altogether richer, more honest, and more humble enterprise.'[34] Similarly, Jameson distinguishes science fiction from 'fantasy', as the latter involves imagination floating completely free from history.[35] Science fiction matters politically because it treats the fictional as a means of accessing the non-fictional.

If the fictions that make up capitalism are, as Beckert says, 'design fantasies', then this should pose the question of why there are no economic design schools. Where is the Bauhaus for economic reform? Where is the futurist manifesto for a different form of money or property? Nick Srnicek and Alex Williams have provided one bold answer in *Inventing the Future*.[36] Yet even that leaves hanging the design question of who is willing to design, implement, run, fix, improve systems of a different economy, in the way that Harvard Business School, PwC and the World Trade Organization do for this one. In our present anti-technocrat political moment, there is a risk that we give up on the radical possibilities of economic *techne* altogether. 'Innovation' and 'creativity' are now tedious obligations of every middle manager and worker, having lost whatever modernist zeal

---

[34] P. Frase (2016) *Four Futures: Life after Capitalism*. London: Verso, p. 27.

[35] F. Jameson (2005) *Archaeologies of the Future: The Desire Called Utopia and Other Science Fictions*. London: Verso.

[36] N. Srnicek & A. Williams (2015) *Inventing the Future: Postcapitalism and a World without Work*. London: Verso.

they ever had. Unless possibilities for broader economic transformation are rediscovered, then the future will belong entirely to those Silicon Valley entrepreneurs and the utopias they bring with them.

Elements of the modern utopian imaginary are return-ing in any case, though not necessarily with the emancipa-tory or progressive implications they originally carried. The common historical fate of humanity has become a live pol-itical concern once again, though now in the context of the 'Anthropocene', which places the problem of nature (and not reason) at the heart of all politics. As Andreas Malm has argued, this may well signal the end of the 'postmodernity' that emerged in the early 1970s.[37] We now have to see capit-alist expansion as a gift granted millions of years in the past in the form of fossil fuels, and every continued year of that expansion as carrying consequences that will last thousands of years into the future. If we remain stuck in the cybernetic and financial imaginary of the perpetual present, constantly churning information to ensure that nothing truly changes, we will be doomed. A revived historical consciousness is therefore a matter of existential urgency, though that doesn't guarantee that it will occur.

Under these conditions, the search for and construction of 'enclaves' takes on a new urgency. It is often the super-rich who are at the forefront of these efforts, as they seek out ever more elaborate ways of separating themselves from the pub-lic and the ecological disasters that are unfolding. As the very wealthy seek to secede from the rest of us, it is they who are now closer to realising a form of communism, albeit one that rests on vast concentrations of private capital that insulate

---

[37] A. Malm (2016) *Fossil Capital: The Rise of Steam Power and the Roots of Global Warming*. London: Verso.

insiders from the threat of everyone else. With this paranoid mentality, utopia and dystopia dissolve into what Frase terms 'exterminism', in which the dreams and ideals of the very few rest on the possibility of excluding, surveilling, imprisoning and eliminating an ever larger share of the mass public. In our new post-neoliberal age of rising resentments, racisms and walls, the utopian desire to escape can be subverted in all manner of dark directions.

I
The Science and Fictions of the Economy

What we call 'the economy' is a mixture of empirical facts, expectations, fantasies and shared narratives. It is both an object of 'science' (primarily economics and management) and the stuff of fictions. How might we read social sciences and science fiction together, as overlapping fields? And what might this overlap reveal in relation to economic life in particular?

This section begins with a reflection on the entangling of economics and science fiction by economist Ha-Joon Chang, who suggests that neoclassical economics is itself a set of fictions, the central one being that the economy is a type of natural artefact, subject to firm laws that can be discovered. Against this, science fiction itself might be deemed to provide an account of the economy with its own truth value aside from its role in critique and utopian reimagining. This point is picked up in the second piece, by political economist Laura Horn, who questions why science fictional visions of corporate power tend so often towards the dystopian: the corporation is a type of autonomous, domineering monster. But what if we channelled the utopian power of science fiction towards the corporation, describing emancipatory alternatives, the like of which are also being explored in experimental 'real utopias' such as worker co-operatives?

Another fundamental instrument of modern capitalism is questioned via science fiction by Sherryl Vint, in this instance money. Vint shows how the science fiction of money is mirrored in certain respects by its diverse anthropological histories. The most controlling, depressing mechanism of financial capitalism is amenable to an infinite variety of rethinking and reorganising. The final chapter in this section, by Brian Willems, considers the role of automation in contemporary post-capitalist utopias, but does so by engaging with one science fiction in particular: Robert Heinlein's *The Moon Is a Harsh Mistress*. This novel, in which the central protagonist seeks to trigger revolution through cybernetic control, provides a way of exploring questions about the role of performativity, automation and computing in engineering a better world, but also the role of algorithms and automation in the constraints of contemporary capitalism.

1

Economics, Science Fiction, History and Comparative Studies

Ha-Joon Chang

This chapter is about the relationship between economics and science fiction (henceforth SF). Economists are notoriously unimaginative people, while the writers and the readers of SF tend to reside at the other end of the creativity spectrum, so this may seem to be a very odd pairing. I believe that a greater interaction between the two fields can improve both fields, however, thereby ultimately enhancing our understanding of the world.

Before I get into the main theme of the chapter, let me first point out that much of economics – especially, but not exclusively, neoclassical economics, which is the dominant school of economics today – is SF in two senses.

First of all, many economists believe in the fiction that they are practising 'science'. In talking of 'iron laws', classical economists, such as David Ricardo, implicitly argued that economics can be like physics, chemistry and other natural sciences. Karl Marx styled his approach as 'scientific socialism', denouncing other socialists, such as Robert Owen, as 'utopian'. Today most neoclassical economists operate with the notion that economics is a science. They are at pains to separate what they call the 'positive' aspect of economics, which allegedly does not involve any value judgement, from the 'normative' one, which does. Most of them say that, insofar as they practise positive economics, economists are scientists.

Of course, these economists know that economics isn't quite like physics; it is said that many neoclassical economists have 'physics envy'. They are very cocky about the 'scientific' progress that they have achieved, however; for a very embarrassing example, Robert Lucas, a leading free-market economist, declared back in 2003 in his presidential address for the American Economic Association that 'the problem of depression prevention has been solved', only for the world to experience a few years later the biggest economic depression since the Great Depression of 1929.[1]

The second sense in which economics is SF is that many economists believe – at least implicitly – that progress in science (and thus technology) is going to – or at least can – solve virtually all economic problems. Free-market economists say: 'Give people the right incentives by, say, giving them stronger property rights, and they will come up with the necessary technologies to solve any economic problem we face, such as climate change or water shortage.' Marx and some of his followers imagined a world in which science and technologies are so advanced that capitalism is abolished and people can 'hunt in the morning, fish in the afternoon, rear cattle in the evening, criticise after dinner'. Unfortunately, these views are highly misleading.

First, as for the view that economics is a science that does not involve ethical and political judgements, this is downright wrong. It is not simply that all government regulations are often based on ethical and political considerations. It is also that the very definitions of economic actors and markets have ethical and political foundations. For example, before the rise of capitalism, people didn't exist as 'free-contracting individuals'

---

[1] R. Lucas (2003) Macroeconomic Priorities, *American Economic Review* 93(1): 1–14.

but members of communities. For another example, today we may think that the corporation as a separate legal entity from its shareholders is a natural thing, but many people, including Adam Smith himself, objected to the very idea well into the nineteenth century.

For the ultimate example, the markets themselves are not as 'natural' as neoclassical economists believe them to be. Markets are fundamentally political (and ethical) constructs, as their boundaries and their legitimate participants are politically and ethically determined. A most telling example is that, when the first reforms were proposed to regulate child labour in the early nineteenth century, many people objected to them on the ground that they undermined the very foundation of a free market economy – namely, the freedom of contract.[2]

The fact that markets are political and ethical constructs confirms my assertion about the second sense in which economics is an SF, namely its belief that scientific progress will ultimately solve all economic problems. If markets have political and ethical foundations, economic problems will *not* disappear even with sufficient progress in science and engineering, as political and ethical disagreements will never disappear – unless you live in the world of George Orwell's *1984*, in which all dissents are stamped out. Indeed, as I will discuss later, many SF writers imagine worlds in which scientific progress has created a very high level of material prosperity

---

[2] See H.-J. Chang (2002) Breaking the Mould: An Institutionalist Political Economy Alternative to the Neo-Liberal Theory of the Market and the State, *Cambridge Journal of Economics* 26(5): 539–59. For a shorter and more user-friendly exposition, see H.-J. Chang (2010) Thing 1: There Is No Such Thing as a Free Market, in *23 Things They Don't Tell You about Capitalism*: 1–10. London: Penguin Books.

but made people miserable, or has even destroyed their very humanities in one way or another.

To say that much of economics is science fiction in the negative sense of the word doesn't mean that the relationship between economics and science fiction has to be negative. As I mentioned at the beginning, both science fiction and economics can benefit from greater interaction with each other.

First of all, SF writers could do with a more solid understanding of economics. For example, brilliant though it may be in many ways, Ward Moore's *Bring the Jubilee* failed to totally convince me, because its alternative future starts from the utterly implausible premise that the South won the American Civil War.

Contrary to what most people think, the American Civil War was more about the country's economic development strategy than slavery as an ethical issue. The early economic development strategy of the United States was dictated by the then economically more powerful Southern states. It was a strategy based on exporting agricultural products – especially cotton and tobacco produced by slave-using Southern plantations – and importing manufactured goods from Britain and other European countries. In this environment, it was very difficult for the American manufacturing industries to develop, because European manufactured goods were not only better but also cheaper, even including the cost of transportation, which was very high at the time. The Anglo-American war of 1812 persuaded many Americans that their country could not even guarantee its own safety without a strong economy, however. A strong economy, they realised, could only be based on a strong manufacturing sector, which was what was then allowing Britain to power ahead of other countries. The Northern states used this shift in national sentiment as an opportunity to introduce a new development strategy, based on the idea of 'infant industry protection', namely the idea that the government of an economically backward country needs to protect and nurture its young manufacturing industries against superior foreign competition. Very interestingly, the idea was invented by none other than Alexander Hamilton, the first ever Treasury secretary of the United States.

As a result, over the next half a century the Northern manufacturing industries grew rapidly behind the wall of high protective tariffs, reaching 30 to 40 per cent on average. And by the 1860s, when the civil war started, the disparity in economic power between the North and the South was so large that there was no way the South could win the war. Rhett Butler, the leading male character in Margaret Mitchell's *Gone with the Wind*, put it brilliantly when he told his Southern friends that the Yankees would win the war because they had 'the factories, the foundries, the shipyards, the iron and coal mines – all the things [we the Southerners] haven't got'. Given this economic reality, Ward Moore imagining the South winning the civil war is seriously deficient, even as a fictional plot device.

Having said that SF writers would benefit from having better knowledge of economics, I would hasten to add that the main beneficiaries from the interaction would be economists. From the beginning SF has been a very powerful way for us to imagine alternative realities in which very different technologies have changed our institutions and thereby individuals, forcing us to rethink the assumptions about institutions and individuals that economists take for granted in analysing the economy.

So, for example, countless dystopian SFs depict a world in which the destruction of modern technologies by some disaster has destroyed modern institutions, such as the state (democratic or not), democracy, the ban on the class system or other explicit forms of discrimination, or moral norms restraining aggressive or apathetic behaviour by individuals. The technological retrogression is most frequently the result of a nuclear war, as in John Wyndham's *Chrysalids*, Philip Reeve's *Mortal Engines* series or Hayao Miyazaki's animation, *Nausicaa of the Valley of the Wind*. But it can be also by other man-made disasters, such as the depletion of oil and climate change, as in David Mitchell's *Bone Clocks*. Almost invariably, in these alternative worlds, life is very harsh, because the destruction of modern institutions has made people closer to the self-seeking rationalists that are idealised in neoclassical economics – the most extreme depiction of this being the *Mad Max* movies.

Of course, more science fictions depict a world in which technologies are far more advanced than they are when the SFs were written. Indeed, for many, that's the whole point of SF: exploring how more advanced science and technology change social institutions and human nature, or imagining an alien world, usually with much more advanced technologies than humans have, in which our usual assumptions about human institutions and moralities do not hold.

As I pointed out earlier, however, unlike what many economists would say, most of these SFs actually do not say that these technologically more advanced worlds are better. And we are not even talking about worlds in which technologies are so advanced that they get out of human control and destroy humanity, such as *The Terminator* or *The Matrix* movies. Many of these SFs tell us that, even when superior technologies are apparently serving humans better in some ways, they can make people unhappier, because they have been developed on a faulty understanding of human nature or human institutions.

For example, Kurt Vonnegut's *Player Piano* imagines a world in which technological progress in production has reached such a level that we don't need human workers any more, except for a very small number of engineers and managers. So, in that world, no one has to work while not wanting in any material need. According to today's dominant (that is, neoclassical) economic vision, in which people strive to maximise their income (and thus consumption) and leisure time, this should have made people ecstatic. In *Player Piano*, however, people are desperately unhappy, because they feel bored and useless. Thus, Vonnegut is saying that work is a key aspect of our life, unintentionally criticising the neoclassical view of human goals and social life.

Or think about *Brave New World*, by Aldous Huxley. In that world, the development of human cloning and other reproductive technologies has enabled humanity to control its numbers, reducing resource demands. It is also a world in which the manipulation of subconsciousness has made people hold caste-appropriate ideas, thereby guaranteeing industrial and social peace, and also adopt extreme consumerist culture, which ensures high levels of demand – thus indeed solving 'the problem of depression prevention', to use the phrase from Robert Lucas quoted earlier. This world is arguably a modern neuro-economist's paradise, as described in the book *The Happiness Industry* by William Davies, but, once again, this is not a world that most people would want to live in.

Another similar – though less controlled – world is described in Andrew Niccol's movie *Gattaca*, in which developments in genetics and reproductive technologies have put humanity on the cusp of weeding out genetically imperfect individuals. It is a world in which talent (or at least potential talent) is almost perfectly matched with people's jobs, but it is a horrible world, in which genetically imperfect people are not even allowed to try for better things.

In other words, *Brave New World* and *Gattaca* are saying that being imperfect, being not totally predictable and having free will (including the will to try what science says is impossible, as in the case of Vincent Freeman, the leading character in *Gattaca*, played by Ethan Hawke) are key features of our humanity. They are saying that we don't want a 'perfect' world brought about by scientific progress, if it denies our humanity.

Now, an interesting extension of the idea that SF is a way to imagine another economic world is to say that history is a 'dystopian science fiction without even *memories* of advanced technologies.'

In the past, largely because we had different (and mostly less productive) technologies, economic institutions were different from what we have today. I have already discussed the case of child labour. Child labour was so widespread and so problematic in the late eighteenth century and early nineteenth in Europe and North America because of the particular technologies that were being used. Poor children had always worked, but most of them tended the family goat, ran errands, picked pockets, or whatever, but they did *not* do adults' work. The machine-based technologies that emerged from the eighteenth century meant that adult males' muscle power was no longer necessary for a lot of jobs, so they made it possible to hire children more widely. At the same time, these technologies were not sufficiently productive that societies could not afford to take every child out of work, as the richer countries do today.

Because technologies and institutions were different, individuals were different. Individuals may have free will, but what they are, what they want and even what they can imagine are deeply shaped by the technologies and the institutions that they live under. This is why many countries regarded today as being hard-working and organised – the Germans, the Japanese, and the South Koreans – were denounced as having lazy, dishonest and irrational people when they were poor.[3]

Of course, I am not advocating a strictly materialist view, in which technologies define institutions and institutions define individuals. The causality is much more complex. Individuals may be formed by technologies and institutions but they also change and newly create technologies and institutions. Institutions influence how technologies are used and changed; for example, Marxist commentators have argued that capitalists have often chosen certain technologies because they give them the greatest control over their workers rather than because they are the most efficient.[4] Technologies may set ultimate boundaries to the institutions that you can have, but there is a lot of room for diversity, depending on how individuals exercise their agencies in designing institutions and depending on the shape of existing institutions. And so on.

If you understand history in this way, you can very easily see that the economic realities that we believe to be the outcomes of some 'scientific, natural laws' are really the results of technological changes, institutional changes, political decisions and the influence exercised by individual agencies. Used in this way, historical research becomes similar to writing and analysing SFs, except that the alternative realities are not as much imagined as in SFs. Please note here that I have

---

[3] See H.-J. Chang (2007) Lazy Japanese and Thieving Germans, in *Bad Samaritans: The Guilty Secrets of Rich Nations and the Threat to Global Security*: 182–202. London: Random House.

[4] S. Marglin (1974) What Do Bosses Do? The Origins and Functions of Hierarchy in Capitalist Production: Part I, *Review of Radical Political Economy*, 6(2): 60–112, is the best-known example.

just said 'not as much imagined' rather than 'not imagined', as the recording and the deciphering of history involve important elements of imagination – about the perceptions and the motivation of the actors, unwritten social rules that later historians can only infer and imagine, and so on.

Finally, the British novelist L. P. Hartley famously said in his novel *The Go-Between* that 'the past is a foreign country: they do things differently there'. If you say that one of the utilities of studying history is to allow us to imagine other realities, you can say the same about studying foreign countries, or doing comparative studies. When that foreign country is a country with very different technologies (and thus very different institutions, very different individuals, etc.), the comparison almost becomes a historical study from the viewpoint of the technologically more advanced country. Or conversely, when seen from the viewpoint of the technologically less advanced country, the comparative study becomes an analysis of SF. Or, if you see it from the point of view of the researcher conducting the comparative study, it is like travelling in a time machine – the ultimate SF fantasy.

To sum up, in trying to understand the economy and reform it for the better, we can be immensely helped by SF, the study of history and comparative studies. SF, history and comparative studies all allow us to see that the existing economic and social order is not a 'natural' one: that it can be changed; that it has been changed; and, most importantly, that it has been changed in the way it has only because some people have dared to imagine a different world, and fought for it.

2

Future Incorporated?

Laura Horn

In a vastly overpopulated near-future world, businesses have taken the place of governments and now hold all political power. States exist merely to ensure the survival of huge transnational corporations.

The Space Merchants (1953)

When corporations have all the power, the only way to get it back is from the inside.

Incorporated (2016)

The future is dominated by mega-corporations, determining every facet of production, consumption and social interaction. As the ubiquitous theme of the corporate dystopia in popular science fiction has it, resistance against the corporation and its evil managers can come only from subversive actors, constituting the last bastion of individuality and agency. This representation of the corporation has been a recurrent theme in visions of future societies, including notable examples such as classic novels from the 1950s (e.g. Mack Reynold's *Mercenary from Tomorrow*, or Frederik Pohl and Cyril Kornbluth's *The Space Merchants*), works of science fiction from the 1980s and 1990s (e.g. the Umbrella corporation in *Resident Evil*, Tyrell in *Blade Runner*, Weland-Yutani in *Alien* and Delos in *Westworld* – the original, and now the reimagined TV show) to recent corporate dystopias in, for example, *Mr. Robot*, *Continuum* and *Incorporated*. While this portrayal of the role of corporations might at first seem to *question* corporate power with its focus on corporate crimes and acts of resistance, I argue that it actually reinforces a discourse that *prevents* imagining alternatives to the corporation. This chapter explores the social scientific and economic fiction of the corporation as the most efficient, or indeed only way of organising production, and how it has become a persistent myth that permeates into most visions of future developments.

Drawing on a range of popular representations of the corporation in future societies, the chapter investigates how the corporate form is being obscured and reified through a portrayal that focuses almost exclusively on (evil) management and corporate agency, rather than questioning and highlighting the social power relations that form the very fabric of the corporation. Resisting corporate power, in this narrative, is almost inevitably an individualistic, punctual act, even when it results in 'bringing down' the corporation in one way or another. There are no visions of what comes 'after the corporation' – that is, alternative visions of organising collectively owned, or at least worker-directed, production. Since either the state is seen as weak or collective agency is ruled out outright, these narratives in effect cement the logic of no alternative to corporate power. This is what the second part of the chapter then seeks to question, by mobilising utopias (both 'real' and actual) of worker co-operatives, worker self-directed enterprises and other ways of reorganising the future of production and property. These alternatives, in combination with prefigurative politics, can contribute to envisaging a future that does not necessarily have to be incorporated.

The Social Fiction of the Corporation

Corporate power is a key dimension of contemporary capitalism. Out of the 100 wealthiest economic entities in the global economy, 69 are now corporations; only 31 are countries, and this trend is increasing.[1] The power of transnational business is such that governments tend to portray corporate interests as synonymous with broader societal interests. The very idea of the corporation has become *common sense* in the contemporary perception of how production and consumption should and could be organised; it is difficult even to imagine alternatives. And yet, at the end of the day the corporation is nothing more than an enduring social *fiction*, an entity entirely constituted upon legal structures that has taken on layers of meaning much beyond the initial social innovation of separating investment and liability. As Adam Haley puts it, the corporation might indeed be 'political economy's most science-fictional trope'.[2]

The corporate form comes in a whole range of legal formats, but most commonly it is the specific form of the limited liability corporation with widely dispersed share ownership and one-tier (i.e. single) board structure as the focus for discussions of corporate power. 'Limited liability' here means that the shareholders are not personally liable for claims against, or the debt of, the corporation. 'Widely dispersed' refers to the fact

---

[1] *The Guardian* (2016) Study: Big Corporations Dominate List of World's Top Economic Entities, 12 September, www.theguardian.com/business/2016/sep/12/global-justice-now-study-multinational-businesses-walmart-apple-shell?CMP=share_btn_tw.

[2] A. Haley (2015) Traveling through Corporate Time: Inevitability and (Anti-) Corporate Narrative Form, New American Notes Online, December, www.nanocrit.com/issues/8-2015/traveling-through-corporate-time-inevitability-and-anti-corporate-narrative-form.

that there is not one (or several) actor(s) owning a number of shares that would entitle them to have a controlling say in corporate decision-making, such as at the annual general meeting. Instead, the assumption is that shareholders will coalesce on certain positions vis-à-vis the management's strategies, and either sanction them, or else sell their shares. Managers, here, are in a delicate relationship in which their strategies are supposed to sustain the corporation as such, but fundamentally also act on behalf of the shareholders' interest (which is assumed to be profit maximisation, also known as 'shareholder value'). The corporation, then, does not have 'owners' as such; as an entity, it is an actor in its own right. Workers or employees do not feature in this dominant image of the corporation. Neither does the state, other than as regulator and enabler for a business environment; a corollary of corporate power is the many ways in which corporations and governments interact in the dismantling of corporate oversight. The significant expansion of corporate rights over the last decades is a concomitant development to this; the impersonal 'legal fiction' has now acquired far-reaching corporate personhood, and an international investor–state dispute settlement system arbitrates the rights of corporations when states implement inconvenient policies that might limit corporate profits. Transnational corporations, with their global value chains, vast logistics and distribution networks and complex marketing strategies, are one of the key driving forces of the global economy, manifesting the imperative to 'nestle everywhere, settle everywhere, establish connections everywhere' that Karl Marx and Friedrich Engels had already highlighted in 1848. It has become almost impossible not to interact with corporations in one way or another in contemporary capitalism, even just at the basic level of everyday processes of consumption. This renders the acute feeling of powerlessness in the face of corporate power all the more pressing. It is here that representations of the corporation have come to serve 'as symbols for larger economic concerns often too vast or complex to comprehend.'[3] With corporations seemingly all-encompassing, and the state at best at arm's length, or at worst 'captured' by corporate interests, the possibilities for social change, for contestation and resistance of corporate power are often seen as limited even by activists. This perception has permeated into the representation of the corporation in fiction;[4] it is particularly works of science fiction that the next section focuses on.

The Social Science Fiction of the Corporation

Following Fredric Jameson's magisterial understanding of science fiction as 'archaeology of the future,'[5] the following discussion takes as point of departure that any work of science fiction is linked to the social, economic and political context in which it was written; beyond even the immediate intents of the author. The corporation in its 'evil', dystopian representation here constitutes a trope, a recurring image that embodies both the material and the discursive constitution and perception of corporations in historically specific periods of capitalism. The template for the 'evil corporation' varies

---

[3] R. Clare (2014) *Fictions Inc.: The Corporation in Postmodern Fiction, Film, and Popular Culture.* New Brunswick, NJ: Rutgers University Press.

[4] See ibid. for a good overview.

[5] F. Jameson (2005) *Archaeologies of the Future: The Desire Called Utopia and Other Science Fictions.* London: Verso.

according to genre and time period, of course, but generally involves corporations superseding government functions, running public and private services, directly or indirectly (i.e. digitally) enforcing control over civilian populations and even intervening in foreign policies and international relations in their own interests. Even its visual representation has universal features, such as an architectural aesthetic of sheer brutalism, or, later on, 'brooding' glass-pane modernism.[6] Part of this generic narrative is that, against the structural dystopian context of the corporation, there are individual villainous actors, most commonly senior management, who embody the utilitaristic, profit-maximising or even criminal character of corporate power, posited against heroic individual protagonists fighting both the managers and the system. Or, to quote the creator of the Roxxon Corporation in the Marvel Universe, 'it was the people that ran the corporation. They were the embodiment of evil [and] became the prototype for everybody's free-floating anxiety.'[7] Resisting or even fighting corporate power takes on the quality of subversive, counter-hegemonic struggle against the seemingly inevitable, all-encompassing corporate entity. It also takes place against a background whereby the state, and other forms of collective representation and agency, are dysfunctional or

---

[6] K. Wagner (2016) The Architecture of Evil: Dystopian Megacorps in Speculative Fiction Films, 99% Invisible, 2 December, http://99percentinvisible.org/article/architecture-evil-dystopian-megacorps-speculative-fiction.

[7] Steve Englehart, quoted in R. Boffard (2016) Could an Evil Mega-Corporation Ever Exist in Real Life?, io9, 4 September, http://io9.gizmodo.com/could-an-evil-mega-corporation-ever-exist-in-real-life-1630401831.

captured. As Haley argues, this dystopian narrative has actually acquired a totaling quality in contemporary representations, in which 'the corporation itself has gradually become a primary object of dystopian fear', much more so than the other fundamental dystopian canvas of the authoritarian state.[8]

Critical literary analysis can here offer us an important contribution to understanding how and why these corporate dystopias have become so pervasive. Ralph Clare highlights the importance of analysing what this means for the very way we think about and imagine the future.[9] In discussion of the recent corporate dystopia TV series *Continuum*, Haley points out that 'narratives of inevitability buttress corporate futurity'. Time travel has become the only way around the inevitability of corporate hegemony: '[W]hat better signal of hegemony than the marking of resistance as necessarily science-fictional?' In his critical reading of 'science fiction as a denaturalization machine', futurity becomes 'irreducibly corporate'. With no social space for radical imaginaries, the structural closure of the future precludes transformative political thought, let alone social action.[10]

This is where political economy can, and should, come in, with its analytical understanding that 'economic science fictions' are always already prefigurative. Questioning the overdetermination of social processes – or, as Jameson puts it, 'what

---

[8] Haley, Traveling through Corporate Time.

[9] Clare, *Fictions Inc.*

[10] R. Levitas (2013) *Utopia as Method: The Imaginary Reconstruction of Society.* Basingstoke, UK: Palgrave Macmillan, p. 125.

is finally not ultimately unthinkable about historical conjunc-
tures'[11] – offers a terrain in which alternatives to the corporation can be discussed, both within science fiction as well as
in the realm of 'real utopias'. In the following, drawing particularly on the work of Kim Stanley Robinson and others, I show
that there are in fact alternative imaginaries in science fiction,
far from reproducing or accepting the inevitability of the corporate dystopia. To anchor this within contemporary political
economy, a discussion of worker co-operatives then offers a
sketch of some of the core issues with regard to the future of
alternatives to corporate power.

Beyond Corporations

In contemporary fictional presentations of the corporation,
the economic alternatives to the corporate multiverse are
limited to hustling, criminality or small-scale subsistence.
The system is seemingly so all-encompassing, so holistic,
that there is no alternative form of organising and producing,
not even in the interstices, the cracks. Even if alternatives are
alluded to they appear unfeasible, remote and abstract, such
as the co-operatives mentioned in passing in *Incorporated*,
which are 'out there' but no actual option for the protagonist.
To bring down the evil corporation might be the main plot line,
but there is no conception of what comes next, no alternative
narrative for a different way of organising. This is very much
consistent with the incisive frame put forward by Mark Fisher,
writing about capitalist realism as 'the widespread sense that
not only is capitalism the only viable political and economic
system, but also that it is now impossible even to *imagine* a
coherent alternative to it. Once, dystopian films and novels

---

[11] Jameson, *Archaeologies of the Future*, p. 395.

were exercises in such acts of imagination – the disasters they depicted acting as narrative pretext for the emergence of different ways of living.'[12]

And yet, in fact there *are* alternatives to capitalism in science fiction, and not just in an essentially liberal, post-scarcity *Star Trek* fashion. The dominant contemporary cultural obsession with dystopian thinking might be occupying a key position within the spectrum of imaginaries, but there are indeed spaces of non-capitalist utopian visions. Ursula Le Guin's 'ambiguous utopia' *The Dispossessed* (1974) surely is one of the key texts in this regard.[13] More specifically, with a focus on the role of corporate power and alternative forms of organising, and also more recently, the work of Kim Stanley Robinson (KSR) offers a perspective that does not preclude the possibility of the cooperative, rather than the corporate and competitive, organisation of production. The theme of corporate power, and socialist and cooperative alternatives,

---

[12] M. Fisher (2009) *Capitalist Realism: Is There No Alternative?* Ropley, UK: Zero Books, p. 2, emphasis in original.

[13] Le Guin's 2014 speech at the National Book Award ceremony is an inspiring example of the importance of utopian thinking in capitalism. 'Hard times are coming, when we'll be wanting the voices of writers who can see alternatives to how we live now, can see through our fear-stricken society and its obsessive technologies to other ways of being, and even imagine real grounds for hope. [...] We live in capitalism; its power seems inescapable – but then, so did the divine right of kings. Any human power can be resisted and changed by human beings.' The full speech is available at www.theguardian.com/books/2014/nov/20/ursula-k-le-guin-national-book-awards-speech.

is explored in KSR's Mars trilogy.[14] The scenario KSR depicts at the beginning of the series actually corresponds to the 'evil mega-corporation' imaginary: transnational corporations have consolidated into an oligarchy, with many of them having unlimited control over entire countries on Earth. The United Nations has also been captured by corporate interests, and resource depletion and social conflict are the order of the day, eventually resulting in a world war. Against this background, the Mars trilogy sketches the ecological, technological, social and political trajectory of the colonisation of Mars, with its struggles for an alternative social and economic order. There is an interesting ambivalence in this portrayal, as it is the funding through the 'transnats' consortium (in conjunction with UNOMA: the United Nations Organization Mars Authority) that has rendered the research and applied organisation of the colonisation of Mars possible in the first place. The transnats' motive and the settlers' place therein is clearly spelled out by the aptly named Arkady Bogdanov in *Red Mars*: '[I]n reality, the islands are part of the transnational order. They are paid for, they are never truly free...with the discovery of strategic metals the application has become clear. And so it all comes back, and we have a return of ownership, and prices, and wages. The whole profit system.' Nonetheless, the early settlers start experimenting with alternative economic relations, such as a 'gift economy'. Later on in the series, the transnationals have merged into 'metanationals', strengthening their hold over what is left of democratic governments and the UN system. Despite the diplomatic efforts of the Martians, the metanats continue their competitive struggles for minerals and other resources,

---

[14] *Red Mars* (1993), *Green Mars* (1994) and *Blue Mars* (1996), all published by Random House.

leading to increasingly antagonistic social relations between Terra and Mars.

'So far, so trope,' one might think. But this is where the Mars trilogy moves beyond the realism of corporate inevitability that permeates so much of contemporary (science) fiction. At the height of corporate power and all its pathologies, after a large-scale ecological disaster (with the Antarctic ice cap melting, causing global floods), it is through the emergence and continuous engagement with co-operative economic organisation on Mars that the metanats are eventually transformed. The metanat Praxis eventually endorses the 'economic democratic' principles that are in place on Mars, including the strong ecological economics foundation that is fundamental to the Martian systemic transformation. It is worth looking at this alternative vision in some detail, as outlined by one of the main characters in *Blue Mars* (pp. 142–6), both for its critique of corporate capitalism and its depiction of how alternatives can and will emerge. 'Management,' Vlad argues, 'is a real thing, a technical matter. But it can be controlled by labor just as well as by capital. There is no reason why a tiny nobility should own the capital, and everyone else therefore be in service to them. [...] The system called capitalist democracy was not really democratic at all. That is why it was able to turn so quickly into the metanational system, in which democracy grew ever weaker and capitalism ever stronger.' In their struggle for social justice and freedom, the colonists and then inhabitants of Mars have developed a fully fledged cooperative system in which 'all economic enterprises are to be cooperatives, owned by their workers and by no one else. They hire their management, or manage themselves. Industry guilds and co-op associations will form the larger structures necessary to regulate trade and the market, share capital, and create credit.'

In response to scepticism, KSR has his character anchor this system in a broader historical and theoretical perspective. The system, he says,

is based on models from Terran history, and its various parts have all been tested on both worlds, and have succeeded very well. You don't know about this…because metanationalism itself steadfastly ignored and denied all alternatives to it. But most of our microeconomy has been in successful operations for centuries in the Mondragon region of Spain. The different parts of the macroeconomy have been used by the pseudo-metanat Praxis, in Switzerland, in India's state of Kerala, in Bhutan, in Bologna, Italy, and in many other places, including the Martian underground itself.'

Against the rebuttal that cooperatives are simply 'a planned economy', KSR presents the essential Polanyian counterpoint that 'economies are plans. Capitalism planned just as much as this, and metanationalism tried to plan everything. No, an economy is a plan.' An alternative to capitalism under corporate rule, the Mars trilogy posits, is not only thinkable, it is always already in its nascency.

For readers to whom the colonisation of Mars and the construction of a space elevator is too much science fiction,[15] KSR also offers a more accessible, more 'realistic' utopian account of an alternative organising beyond the transnational corporation. *Pacific Edge* (1990), as part of the Orange County trilogy, is an ecological post-capitalist utopia that paints the mundane glory of a future in which social justice and equality are guiding principles also for the organisation of production. In his recent discussion of 'four futures', Peter Frase rightly showcases

---

[15] Don't mock the idea of a space elevator. As Arthur C. Clarke reportedly said, it will be built, probably around 50 years after everybody stops laughing.

Pacific Edge as an illustration of a socialist utopian vision set in a context of equality and scarcity (in contrast to, for example, the post-scarcity scenario in *Star Trek*).[16] What is important in the context of this chapter is the emphasis KSR puts here on the idea that the legal framework behind corporate power can be contested and transformed to achieve these concrete and, at the same time, utopian objectives. Through continuing, long-term struggle against the domination of transnational companies, citizens have achieved legal control over the role and form of corporations. Where they exist, companies are limited through the number of employees that they have, and hence how big they can grow; natural resources and trade are managed at the local, municipal level under democratic governance. Even so, there are ambiguities in this scenario, as the system is still vulnerable to corporate transgressions, and local cooperative governance – with regard to, say, water management – is shown as tedious and work-intensive. In the historical narrative that complements the story, set in 2065, the path towards the transformation is sketched out; it is reformist and almost weary rather than revolutionary, but follows a clear trajectory towards cooperative organisation. Importantly, there are two broad processes at hand: it is through an engagement with, and transformation of, the existing state apparatus that corporate control is detained through legal measures, while a more interstitial process leads to reformulation of organisation at the local level.

KSR's emphasis on the cooperative form of organising production and administration is not coincidental; for many observers on the left, workers' control in various forms of self-management and democratic decision-making on production

---

[16] P. Frase (2016) *Four Futures: Life after Capitalism.* London: Verso.

epitomises the search for alternatives.[17] As a counterpoint to the imaginary of the evil corporation, co-operatives constitute social configurations whose potential is worth exploring as science fiction as well as 'real utopia'. The next section offers a brief outline of the promise and ambiguities of co-operatives vis-à-vis contemporary corporate capitalism.

'Real Utopias': Cooperation rather than Corporation

There are many forms that the cooperative organisation of production (and services) can take. A commonly referred to definition is found in the International Co-operative Alliance's 'Statement on the Co-operative Identity', in that 'a co-operative is an autonomous association of persons united voluntarily to meet their common economic, social and cultural needs and aspirations through a jointly owned and democratically controlled enterprise'.[18] Core principles guiding cooperative organisation, with a strong focus on solidarity, include open and voluntary membership; one member one vote; economic participation; autonomy and independence; education, training and information; cooperation amongst cooperatives; and concern for community. The discussion about the cooperative form had already been taken up by Marx, who recognised their fundamental ambiguity. 'The co-operative factories run by workers themselves are, within the old form, the first examples of the emergence of a new form, even though they naturally

---

[17] M. Atzeni (2012) An Introduction to Theoretical Issues, in M. Atzeni (ed.) *Alternative Work Organizations*: 1–24. Basingstoke, UK: Palgrave Macmillan.

[18] International Co-operative Alliance, Statement on the Co-operative Identity, http://ica.coop/en/whats-co-op/co-operative-identity-values-principles.

reproduce in all cases, in their present organization, all the defects of the existing system, and must reproduce them.'[19]

Co-operatives replace corporate ownership with a democratic association of workers, through which they essentially become their 'own' capitalists. The potential of the cooperative form includes worker self-management rather than external control, and immediate material consequences through the changing redistribution of surplus.[20] Examples of worker co-operatives are many throughout history, and they have made crucial contributions to the broader formulation of social struggles and alternatives to concrete capitalist social relations.[21] At the same time, they cannot quite escape the competitive pressures of a capitalist market economy, a structural condition that essentially renders them 'socialist islands in a capitalist sea', carrying with them contradictions that cannot be resolved in the contemporary global economy. As Sam Gindin reminds us, is it crucial to assess the successes *and* failures of experiments in worker ownership; his discussion of Mondragon serves as a highly pertinent example of the contradictions inherent in cooperative forms.[22] All the more reason

---

[19] K. Marx (1894 [1981]) *Capital*, vol. III. London: Pelican Books, p. 571.

[20] For a more detailed discussion, see, for example, P. Ranis (2016) *Cooperatives Confront Capitalism: Challenging the Neoliberal Economy*. London: Zed Books; and E. O. Wright (2010) *Envisioning Real Utopias*. London: Verso, pp. 234–40.

[21] I. Ness & D. Azzellini (eds.) (2011) *Ours to Master and to Own: Workers' Control from the Commune to the Present*. London: Haymarket.

[22] S. Gindin (2016) Chasing Utopia, *Jacobin*, 10 March, www.jacobinmag.com/2016/03/workers-control-coops-wright-wolff-alperovitz.

for a nuanced reading of co-operatives against the backdrop of discussion of utopian potential. For this, three aspects seem particularly pertinent, as is also clear from the examples in KSR's fiction: the 'silo' effect of co-operatives; their positioning vis-à-vis the state; and their role in broader social struggles.[23] With the consolidation of a co-operative, there is a tendency to become an insulated organisation focusing on day-to-day challenges in the face of competitive structures, with an exclusive focus on insiders that can lead to increasing fragmentation of participants. The principle of outreach and cooperation (e.g. with other co-operatives) becomes subordinated to the exigencies of organisational survival. Moreover, co-operatives as such do not challenge institutional and legal arrangements that cement corporate power – i.e. through the state. There is little engagement with, or even confrontation of, the state; the underlying assumption is that the *interstitial* nature of co-operatives will contribute to a transformation of society through evolutionary change, the 'hope that such institutions might act as strategic battering rams for reaching socialism.'[24] Whether, and how, to contest and resist the state on its own terrain rather than through the social and economic sphere is an essentially political question, of course, but it remains one that characterises the discussion of the potential of co-operatives mainly through its absence. Gindin argues that the lack of perspective on the democratic transformation of the state as part and parcel of economic democratisation could well mean that co-operatives as the ' "next big idea" will only be the Left's latest failure.' Somewhat more (cautiously) optimistic, Marcuse sees 'their main importance, in a perspective looking towards basic social change in a non-capitalist direction, perhaps more [as]

---

[23] P. Marcuse (2015) Cooperatives on the Path to Socialism?, *Monthly Review*, 66(9).

[24] Gindin, Chasing Utopia.

what they may say about and teach about the potential of self-management...rather than the actual changes they themselves bring about in what they do'.[25] As 'real utopias', co-operatives illustrate the contradictions of alternatives, but through their very existence they also engender a further engagement with options that might otherwise be unthinkable.

Concluding Reflections

How we can mobilise and harness these alternative imaginaries for concrete social alternatives hinges not least on the acceptance of 'capitalist realism'. As Ruth Levitas argues, '[T]he usefulness of "real utopias" as institutional models for an alternative future depends on how we read such prefigurative practices, including whether and how we imagine them scaled up'.[26] This is also what we see in economic science fictions that deal with alternatives to corporate capitalism, as in the work of KSR discussed above: the narrative form that not only presents a rebuttal of corporate capitalism, but attempts to forge an alternative, however contradictory and fragile that might be. Rather than the corporate dystopia imaginary that has become so ubiquitous and hegemonic, it dares to explore the ambiguities of a utopian vision against specific social structures and political economy. Whether this narrative is one that will ultimately be able to overcome the corporate closure of the future imaginary remains to be seen; it seems unlikely in the current context of popular economic science fictions.[27] But this

---

[25] Marcuse, Cooperatives on the Path to Socialism?

[26] Levitas, *Utopia as Method*, p. 145.

[27] The TV adaptation of the *Mars* trilogy, which might have helped to bring the co-operative narrative closer to a wider audience, was put on hold in 2016, not least because of the complexity of the source material.

is exactly why it is so crucial to keep contesting the common sense of corporate power in our time; to question the institutional, legal and political basis that upholds the hegemony of the corporate form over all other possible ways of organising. This is not to be achieved through individual heroism or subversive hacktivism; it is only through *collective* thinking and critical engagement with these alternatives that these futures might come about.

3

Currencies of Social Organisation: The Future of Money

Sherryl Vint

Presented with the prospect of its own eternity, capitalism – or anyway, financial capitalism – simply explodes. Because if there's no end to it, there's absolutely no reason not to generate credit – that is, future money – infinitely.

David Graeber, *Debt: The First 5,000 Years*[1]

Perhaps the first thing that comes to mind when thinking about science fiction and money is the different kinds of currencies that are imagined for future worlds: the poscreds of Philip K. Dick's *Ubik*, a currency required for every minute transaction such that the door becomes not an item you own but, rather, a provider of services for which you must continually pay, leaving protagonist Joe Chip trapped in his own apartment until someone pays his door to open; the bars of gold-pressed latinum used by the avaricious Ferengi on *Star Trek*, the only thing that cannot be replicated in this post-scarcity world, useless other than as an atavistic marker of wealth; the reputation-based currency of whuffie in Cory Doctorow's *Down and Out in the Magic Kingdom*, used to replace the social role money plays in creating a hierarchy in another post-scarcity world.

---

[1] D. Graeber (2011) *Debt: The First 5,000 Years*. New York: Melville House, p. 360.

The inventiveness of SF writers creating objects or systems of account that might serve as money is matched by its actual history and the wide range of items that have served as currency, from large stone wheels called Rai used as money on the island of Yap, to the split tally sticks of medieval English practice, to coinage and the ideal that a gold standard is the 'real' value of money, to slips of paper inscribed with various authentications and, finally, to the electronic signals used to store and transmit denominations of value.

It turns out that, although most of the world uses money on a daily basis and has done so for almost as long as there have been records of human civilisation, it is not very clear what money actually *is*. How does money work? What is the underlying relationship among some underlying thing of 'actual' value (gold, land, the goods and services produced by a nation), the tokens of that value (coins, banknotes, electronic account balances) and the entity guaranteeing that said tokens are, basically, the *same* as that underlying thing of value (the King, the Bitcoin algorithm, the European Union). Reading about the history of money turns out to be surprisingly like reading science fiction: the kind of money a society has tells us a lot about the kind of human sociality that is possible in that world. Most definitions of money agree that it needs to be three things: a medium of exchange, a unit of account and a store of value. The 'store of value' requirement tends to be overlooked in science fiction extrapolations, confusing whether money is simply a way of keeping 'score' of who owes what to whom or whether money is itself something of inherent value (even if it has no 'use value', such as gold), such that it will continue to be accepted even through periods of massive social and political disruption.

More importantly, however, commentators agree that changes to this configuration of value, accounting, exchange practices and objects-serving-as-money are deeply consequential for the surrounding social order. Jack Weatherford argues in *The History of Money*, for example, that new forms of money destroy old forms of governance that were premised on the prior system of economics.[2] His book takes us through a number of such transitions: from a tributary economy of empire based on commodity money that was destabilised by the invention of coinage; through the invention of a system of banking and paper notes that disrupted and undermined the feudal system of medieval Europe by opening a path for power based on wealth (stocks and bonds) rather than on heredity (land); to the prediction that our contemporary system of electronic transfer will have similarly transformative effects on the future. Although science fiction has often imagined new objects or systems serving as currency in the future, it has seldom worked through the cultural power of money as an engine of social control, preferring to either posit post-scarcity societies of human fulfilment, such as *Star Trek*'s benevolent Federation of Planets or Iain M. Banks' Culture universe, or else envisage worlds of ever-deepening capitalist uneven development that polarises humanity between lush zones of privilege and apocalyptic zones of deprivation that are, crucially, simultaneously produced by the same forces – the Sprawl of William Gibson's cyberpunk trilogy, the orbiting gated community of *Elysium* (Neill Blomkamp), the privatised air of Rose Montero's Bruna Husky series or the future of privatised food and seed corporation governance in Paolo Bacigalupi's *The Windup Girl*.

Although science fiction is frequently set in the future, it is always about its present moment of production. Thus, rather than predicting future kinds of money and sociality inherent in

[2] J. Weatherford (1997) *The History of Money*. New York: Three Rivers Press.

this coming shift, the more important thing science fiction can do is to help make visible – through estranging extrapolation that denatures what we take to be natural – how money functions in our present. In *Money: The Unauthorized Biography*, Felix Martin argues that we misrecognise money in its classic definition.[3] Instead of thinking of it as a unit of exchange or store of value, he argues that money is a 'social technology' composed of three central elements: a denominating unit of value; a system of indebtedness and credits; and the possibility that debts can be transferred to another creditor. It is this third element that is the most crucial, and he contends that, 'whilst all money is credit, not all credit is money'.[4] Money is a social technology of transferable credit, 'a set of ideas and practices which organise what we produce and consume, and the way we live together'.[5] Martin goes on to explain that to arrive at this idea it was necessary first to develop one of a universal standard of value, a concept of economic value that is detached from any particular social organisation in which a debt might be incurred. Debt thereby becomes not a social exchange between people as part of a larger social structure of mutual obligations but simply a unit of account that might be transferred to another creditor and mean *exactly the same thing*, as if the value measured by money was a physical property in the world instead of a measure of human social structures and decisions.

This idea of abstract and universal value opens the door to some of the more deleterious effects of the social technology of money. As Martin acknowledges, '[T]the choice of monetary

---

[3] F. Martin (2015) *Money: The Unauthorised Biography*. London: Vintage Books.

[4] Ibid., p. 27.

[5] Ibid., p. 33.

standard is always a political one – because the standard itself represents nothing but a decision as to what is a fair distribution of wealth, income, and the risks of economic uncertainty.'[6] For Martin, the decision to view money as a thing rather than a social technology – which he dates to the Enlightenment and John Locke, with his insistence that the value of the coinage had to be the 'material' value of the metal, not the nominal value designated by the sovereign – was the first step in what would eventually become our 2008 financial crisis. In the Lockean understanding of money as a thing with inherent and universal worth, a centuries-long question regarding the degree to which money should be allowed to structure how we live with one another was short-circuited, taken out of the realm of ethical debate and put into that of natural 'fact.' We treat money as a mathematical truth rather than a social choice with often disastrous consequences, reducing 'vital questions of moral and political justice to the mechanical application of objective scientific truths.'[7] With this understanding of money, Western societies came to see a myriad of complex human social relationships through the single and narrow framework of economic self-interest.

In its role as a genre that defamiliarises the present by exaggerating it into an imagined future, science fiction can serve a vital role in reminding us that money is a social technology, not a thing. For example, Andrew Niccol's film *In Time* (2009) posits a world in which the unit of account is simply time: one works not for dollars or credits but for minutes, hours, days and, ultimately, years of one's life. One of the things it immediately makes clear is how ridiculous the fiction is that capitalists and workers (that is, sellers of labour-power) meet at the

---

[6] Ibid., p. 144.

[7] Ibid., p. 149.

market in any manner that remotely resembles an exchange among equals: the capitalist can always wait another day for a more favourable negotiation but the worker, who needs to sell his or her labour-power to continue to live, cannot. Niccol shows the social costs of inflation, which makes a cup of coffee cost more 'minutes' than it did the day before, creating dilemmas for workers who can stretch the working day only so far to accommodate the change. More and more of one's time is spent working – that is, accumulating minutes to live – but at some point the number of currency minutes needed to sustain life exceeds the time needed to accumulate them, and the most economically vulnerable simply die. The rich, in contrast, are seemingly immortal, since their time simply existing continues to accumulate ever more minutes through the crucial fact that what they own is capital, not mere labour-power.

Time is a problematic image for currency, of course: it can function well as a unit of account and perhaps even can serve as a medium of exchange (people gamble minutes, hours and years; people give one another minutes, and such economic support is, quite literally, life support), but it is difficult to imagine how time can be a store of value. This is where the film's attempt to critique the discrepancy between the one-percent and everyone else falls apart: a disaffected one-percenter with centuries of life but no purpose (Matt Bomer) decides to give his years to protagonist Will Salas (Justin Timberlake), who uses this unexpected luxury (of time that need not be productive) to penetrate the echelons of the wealthiest citizens – tolls to these inner zones are paid in weeks, then months, then years – and attempt to destroy the system of lives held in thrall to generating money. The image the film uses to convey this revolutionary overthrow is a raid on a 'bank' that has an accumulated stockpile of time, time that is simply sitting there unused while people expire due to its lack. Salas forms a partnership with the disaffected daughter of one of the bank's major stockholders (Amanda Seyfried), and together they steal and freely distribute this vast quantity of 'unused' time, thereby ending the structures of precarity lived by those struggling to ensure they have enough 'time' to live another day.

Rather than critiquing the limitations of imagining time as a currency, I want to focus instead on what this image makes visible: that money is a social technology, that it always is, as Martin argues, a political tool that structures the way we live collectively and what we as a society have decided is a fair distribution of wealth and risk. By so directly linking the ability to secure a wage to the chances to continue to exist, *In Time* lays bare an underlying logic of neoliberal capitalism that is otherwise obscured by a discourse that naturalises the market and attempts to compel us to believe that we must accommodate ourselves to its dictates rather than recognise that its very functioning is a creation of human choice. If time in the film functioned as do other currencies, of course, Salas's heroic gesture would simply contribute to inflation, the collapse of the 'buying power' of a unit of time. Despite this limitation, however, *In Time* points us towards the fundamental injustice of an economic system that extends some people's lives and capacities while it shortens others. The underlying issue is the relationship between creditors (those with time to spare) and debtors (those whose very lives are in bondage to an economic system).

David Graeber's masterful *Debt: The First 5,000 Years* is actually another history of money, despite its title. One of his most powerful claims is that we more properly understand the social technology of money as a system of debt rather than one of credit. Whereas, for Martin, money is transferrable *credit*, Graeber points out that this is simultaneously a transformation of the social obligations that humans have to one another into specifically economic obligations, creating a society that, taken to its logical extreme, results in a world in which all social exchange is financialised debt. Graeber begins his book with an account of the massive social disruption caused by International Monetary Fund (IMF) loans to developing nations, indebtedness that required countries 'to abandon price supports on basic foodstuffs, or even policies of keeping strategic food reserves, and abandon free health care and free education' in the name of prioritising the obligation to pay back debt, leading to 'the collapse of all the most basic supports for some of the poorest and most vulnerable people on earth'.[8]

Whereas for Martin the transferability of credit is essential to making it function as money, for Graeber it is precisely the way credit (that is, indebtedness) becomes transferable that creates the social chaos of a society that is thus premised on inequality. For Graeber, debt can become transferable only when it becomes 'simple, cold, and impersonal', detached from any larger social context of mutual support and purely a 'precisely quantified' sum for which 'one does not need to calculate the human effects; one needs only calculate principal, balances, penalties, and rates of interest'.[9] He traces the history of debt – and social crises of indebtedness – from the beginnings of recorded human civilisation through to the IMF crises and beyond, connecting the 2008 financial crisis and bank bailouts to the same fundamental mechanisms of inequality that always structure an economy based on money: just as governments spent money to repay IMF loans rather than to offer social services to their population, so too did governments pay to protect the wealthy few who own bank bonds at the

---

[8] Graeber, *Debt*, p. 2.
[9] Ibid., p. 13.

expense of other taxpayers. This was a crisis created by the seemingly endless generation of new forms of credit, new ways to make money out of records of debt, a specific form of money as capital – that is, as money that must continually grow.

Only the power of the US military, Graeber argues, holds the world economic system together based on a fear of reprisal: '[T]he last thirty years have seen the construction of a vast bureaucratic apparatus for the creation and maintenance of hopelessness, a giant machine designed, first and foremost, to destroy any sense of possible alternative futures.'[10] Here his discussion of the history of debt begins to sound a lot like discussions of the SF imagination. In recent years critics such as Fredric Jameson and writers such as Kim Stanley Robinson have deplored the failure of the utopian imagination, our inability to imagine alternatives beyond the social order created by capitalism.[11] For Graeber, the disappearance of hope has to do with the crushing circumstances of chronic indebtedness, a cycle that has recurred throughout history and for which, until modern times, a solution existed. This solution is an amnesty on debt, a decision to simply reset all accounts and start over whenever the burden of debt on one segment of the population became so heavy as to debilitate its chances to thrive and also to destabilise the entire social order premised on class difference between debtors and debtees.

---

[10] Ibid., p. 382.

[11] See F. Jameson (2005) *Archaeologies of the Future: The Desire Called Utopia and Other Science Fictions.* London: Verso; and N. Gevers (1999) Wilderness, Utopia, History: An Interview with Kim Stanley Robinson, Infinity Plus, 30 October, www.infinityplus.co.uk/nonfiction/intksr.htm.

Graeber links debt forgiveness to an ancient biblical Law of the Jubilee, which 'stipulated that all debts would be automatically cancelled "in the Sabbath year" (that is, after seven years had passed), and that all who languished in bondage owing to such debts would be released'.[12] Martin dates the idea of periodic debt forgiveness as a way to manage the socially deleterious effects of indebtedness even earlier, arguing that records of this 'Mesopotamian practice of proclaiming a clean slate when the burden of debt became socially unsupportable are almost as old as the earliest evidence for interest-bearing debt itself – dating from the reign of Enmetana of Lagash in around 2,400 BC'.[13] Graeber ends his book with a call for a contemporary Jubilee on international and consumer debt, arguing that it would be helpful 'not just because it would relieve so much genuine human suffering, but also because it would be our way of reminding ourselves that money is not ineffable, that paying one's debts is not the essence of morality, that all these things are human arrangements and that if democracy is to mean anything, it is the ability to all agree to arrange things in a different way'.[14]

The best kind of SF vision of the future of money may thus be an idea taken from the distant past, a period proximate enough to the emergence of money and its new social structures that people remained capable of recognising it as a social policy, not a fact of nature. While science fiction has often imagined post-scarcity societies that thereby eliminate indebtedness, very little has imagined the future of monetary policy and banking. A notable exception is the work of Charles Stross, especially his novel *Neptune's Brood*, which uses a passage

---

[12] Graeber, *Debt*, p. 82.

[13] Martin, *Money*, p. 179.

[14] Graeber, *Debt*, p. 390.

from Graeber's book as its epigraph.[15] Stross imagine the future of capitalist social organisation as mutated to accommodate trading across the vast distances of space colonisation and at the high speeds of computer consciousness. Taking his cues from the fact that much of the derivative market consists of trades done by algorithms and software, often requiring an advanced degree in physics to be understood, Stross posits a future of artificial humanoid beings whose ethos is shaped by an ecology of capital treated as if it were nature.

Most of the critical discussion about the novel focuses on Stross's idea of slow, medium, and fast money. Fast money is what we are accustomed to: 'Cash is fast money. We use it for immediate exchanges of value. Goods and labor: You sell, I buy.'[16] Medium money is something that more durably stores its value, and is not reliant on the vagaries of governments and fiscal policy like fast money, as in: 'Cathedrals and asteroids and debts and durable real estate and bonds backed by the honorable reputation of traders in slow money.'[17] And, finally, slow money is the kind of money required to finance interstellar trade and colonisation in a world without faster-than-light (FTL) travel: 'Slow money is a medium of exchange designed to outlast the rise and fall of civilizations. It is the currency of world-builders, running on an engine of debt that can only be repaid by the formation of new interstellar colonies, passing the liability ever onward into the deep future.'[18] The details of the novel's adventure plot – featuring a forensic accountant hero – show us how such a society, continually passing along debt, would be filled with avarice and exploitation, with only

---

[15] C. Stross (2013) *Neptune's Brood*. New York: Ace Books.

[16] Ibid., p. 110.

[17] Ibid.

[18] Ibid.

the most instrumental of interpersonal relations. The novel is a careful and thorough figuration of the end extreme of capitalism. A vision of the future anticipated in the epigraph from Graeber above, a future of ever more overwhelming indebtedness, the flip side of money understood as transferable credit.

The ultimate horizon of the novel is the reinvention of the Jubilee, the 'systemwide rest of the financial system entailing nullification of all debts'.[19] Its characters, shaped by capitalism as a necessary fact of life, struggle to imagine the possibility of such a Jubilee. The accountant protagonist, Krina, for example, is shocked when she hears of someone functioning as a debt termination officer, exclaiming: '[M]atters should never reach the stage where they need to terminate a bad debt! Far better to stir it up with a bunch of lumpen credit properties and shuffle it off to a long-term investment trust for toxic assets.'[20] So how does Stross create the conditions for a Jubilee in *Neptune's Brood* when no one is power has any incentive to forgive the debs that are the foundation of their social structure? The transformation happens because of the discovery of a kind of matter transmission that enables the equivalent of FTL travel, meaning all financial exchanges can happen at the speed of fast money, and so the accumulated stockpiles of wealth that are slow money are suddenly rendered meaningless. Indebtedness is thereby wiped out when the value of this currency collapses, since a vast slow money debt can now be paid with a pittance of fast money.

Obviously Stross's solution cannot easily be translated into our world, because we do not denominate our currencies in this way nor trade at interstellar distances. Yet I think it still holds a lesson for us that only the displacements of science fiction

---

[19] Ibid.
[20] Ibid., p. 136.

thinking can capture. The collapse of the slow money economy completely transforms existing power relations, and it is
also devastating for those who have accumulated vast holdings
in this debt-based currency. At the same time, however, freedom from debt for others opens up so many more possibilities
as to where the resources and energy might go that the positive elements of change are equally powerful to the disruptive
ones. The transition is enabled in part by a branch of human-
oids whose neural architecture has been transformed to communicate mental states through light, a post-human redesign
intended to make them more effective workers (bypassing
the slowness of language). This transformation also changed
their social order, however, in ways that ultimately sidelined
money and property: 'They're still individuals, but the border
between self and other is thinner. And they don't hate. They
own property but they don't have strong social hierarchies –
top-down control is a dangerous liability to a team trying to
trap a runaway natural nuclear reactor – they're instinctive
mutualists. They understand money and debt and credit and
so on, but they don't feel a visceral need to own: What they owe
doesn't define their identity.'[21] A different kind of human sociality plants the seed for a different relationship to property and
money, which ultimately opens the door to detaching human
futures from the tyranny of debt.

If, as Martin argues, money is a social technology, 'a set
of ideas and practices which organise what we produce and
consume, and the way we live together,'[22] then science fiction can make visible the kind of social engineering done by
the capitalist technology of money. As a social technology, the
tool of money can be oriented towards other kinds of ideas and

---

[21] Ibid., p. 242.
[22] Martin, *Money*, p. 33.

practices, other kinds of social orders, other kinds of subjectivities. Both *In Time* and *Neptune's Brood* offer exaggerated and extrapolated visions of the society the current technology of money creates, focusing on the human suffering that is produced by keeping this technology in place. Science fiction has always been about the idea that social arrangements might be otherwise, about extrapolating known technologies towards novel ends. Stross gives us a tantalising hint of the possible future of a debt Jubilee, of one way we might reinvent the technology of money.

4

Automating Economic Revolution: Robert Heinlein's *The Moon Is a Harsh Mistress*

Brian Willems

You do not trust the person you are making a transaction with, but you know you will not be swindled. You do not trust yourself to make the right decisions, but the right decisions are made. You did not talk to me to solve our problem, but our problem was solved with your words. You dare to bend one of the rules, but the rule has already been broken.

These are seemingly paradoxical statements. They capture the truth of a utopian vision of the future, however. One of the problems with utopias is the human factor. There is always one person willing to break the golden rule holding a society together, and another group willing to prey on the weak for personal gain. Removing the human factor is one way both to achieve utopia and to develop the way it will work. Computers will do it instead. An automated utopian future sounds like a perilous road to a heartless society. But science fiction has provided at least a few examples in which automation is the most humane option. It is also a future in which these seemingly paradoxical statements become true.

A completely automated world, combined with a universal basic income, has been suggested as one total rethinking of the economic future. Governments and businesses are unable to create enough jobs, yet humans remain dependent on jobs to make their living. Rather than thinking about how to fight this trend, Nick Srnicek and Alex Williams argue for accelerating it by disposing of work altogether. Combined with a guaranteed basic income for everyone on the globe, total automation would remove humankind from enforced drudgery, freeing people from employment expectations that are no longer realistic.[1]

Total automation and a workless world is a radical departure from the way economics and politics are currently structured. In fact, it sounds like science fiction. This is not an accident. Srnicek and Williams see the tropes of science fiction as potential signposts for a future economics. As they say, 'Rather than settling for marginal improvements in battery life and computer power, the left should mobilise dreams of decarbonizing the economy, space travel, robot economics – all the traditional touchstones of science fiction – in order to prepare for a day beyond capitalism.'[2]

This view is much different from a vision of the future on lockdown, in which all alternative forms of economic expression have already been subsumed by neoliberal strategies.[3] Falling into this category are Fredric Jameson's *mot* that 'it is

---

[1] N. Srnicek & A. Williams (2015) *Inventing the Future: Postcapitalism and a World without Work*. London: Verso, p. 105.

[2] Ibid., p. 183. This is in contrast to Ignacio Palacios-Heurta, who singles out science fiction for being a bad indicator of future economics: I. Palacios-Heurta (ed.) (2013) The Idea for *In 100 Years*, in *In 100 Years: Leading Economists Predict the Future*: xi–xiv. Cambridge, MA: MIT Press, p. xiv.

[3] S. Shaviro (2013) Accelerationist Aesthetics: Necessary Inefficiency in Times of Real Subsumption, *e-flux journal*, 46, http://worker01.e-flux.com/pdf/article_8969650.pdf. The almost meaningless term 'neoliberalism' is being used in the sense that Wendy Brown formulates it: '[N]eoliberal rationality

easier to imagine the end of the world than to imagine the end of capitalism'[4] and Mark Fisher's expansion of the idea of capitalist realism to describe 'a pervasive *atmosphere*, conditioning not only the production of culture but also the regulation of work and education, and acting as a kind of invisible barrier constraining thought and action'.[5] In relation to science fiction in particular, Kodwo Eshun describes how Afrofuturism is losing its revolutionary potential because power structures have themselves become science fictional: 'Power...functions through the envisioning, management, and delivery of reliable futures... The powerful employ futurists and draw power from the futures they endorse, thereby condemning the disempowered to live in the past.'[6] All these arguments share a similar point of view: the creation of any alternatives to capitalism just makes more capitalism. Revolution generates more ad revenue

---

disseminates the *model of the market* to all domains and activities – even where money is not an issue – and configures human beings exhaustively as market actors, always, only, and everywhere as *homo oeconomicus*': W. Brown (2015) *Undoing the Demos: Neoliberalism's Stealth Revolution*. New York: Zone Books, p. 31, emphasis in original. Nevertheless, this model is something that, as Maurizio Lazzarato says, 'is always *in the process of being made*': M. Lazzarato (2012) *The Making of the Indebted Man: An Essay on the Neoliberal Condition*. Los Angeles: Semiotext(e), p. 107, emphasis in original.

[4] F. Jameson (2003) Future City, *New Left Review*, 21: 65–79, p. 76.

[5] M. Fisher (2009) *Capitalist Realism: Is There No Alternative?* Ropley, UK: Zero Books, p. 16, emphasis in original. See also B. Willems (2015) *Shooting the Moon*, Ropley, UK: Zero Books, p. 55.

[6] K. Eshun (2003) Further Considerations on Afrofuturism, *CR: The New Centennial Review*, 3(2): 287–302, p. 289.

on YouTube. Or, as Don Delillo writes in the first sentence of his novel *Zero K*, 'Everybody wants to own the end of the world.'[7]

The vision that Srnicek and Williams propose is different. It is a possible alternative rather than exasperation at a lost future. A number of other thinkers have also started taking up the utopian banner once again, as seen in Jameson's reading of 'dual power'[8] and Douglas Murphy's collection of 'last futures' in order to inspire future ones.[9] Srnicek and Williams' proposal is utopian because it imagines global change rather than local reaction. 'Subversive universals'[10] such as no work for anyone and pay for all change the much-maligned modernist grand narrative into a powerful force for large-scale change.[11]

But what if this is not enough? This plan seems incredibly large, and therefore easily caught up in the current atmosphere of capitalist realism, which puts a lid on alternatives to our neoliberal present. If one of the goals of a utopian future is full automation, however, why save it until after the revolution? In other words, what would happen if economic change were itself fully automated? This could be a way of creating utopia in the midst of so much depression. On the other hand, to let the machines do the revolution for us conjures up images of *Brave New World* (1932), *2001* (1968) and *The Terminator* (1984).

---

[7] D. Delillo (2016) *Zero K*. London: Picador, p. 3.

[8] F. Jameson (2016) *An American Utopia: Dual Power and the Universal Army*, ed. S. Žižek. London: Verso.

[9] D. Murphy (2016) *Last Futures: Nature, Technology and the End of Architecture*. London: Verso.

[10] Srnicek and Williams, *Inventing the Future*, p. 75.

[11] W. Davies (2017) Moral Economies of the Future: The Utopian Impulse of Sustainable Prosperity, Working Paper no. 5. Guildford: Centre for the Understanding of Sustainable Prosperity, University of Surrey.

There is at least one example of science fiction, however, in which automated economic revolution works out for the better: Robert Heinlein's *The Moon Is a Harsh Mistress* (1966).[12]

The Moon has been turned into a prison labour camp for criminals from Earth. When the central lunar computer becomes sentient, it soon takes on the role of the leader of a revolutionary group. The computer, named Mike, plans both the revolution and the economic structure that follows. The libertarian economics[13] that Mike eventually develops is not the point, however. Rather, the way Mike develops an alternative future is taken as a blueprint for how to automate change.

Automated change sounds cold and inhumane, but in Heinlein's novel its main purpose is to create a sense of community otherwise missing. One of Mike's main traits is that he lacks companionship. He is the only computer that has gained sentience, although at first no one notices.[14] He eventually gets the attention of Mannie (a computer technician, who narrates the novel in his Russian-influenced English) by issuing an absurdly large pay cheque to a janitor for the fun of it.[15] Humour is something Mike wants to learn, and he participates in a lunar revolution largely as an excuse to spend time

---

[12] Iain Banks' Culture series would be another, as would Agustín de Rojas's 1990 novel *The Year 200* (2016, New York: Restless Books), in which a computerised 'Central Archive' is seen to be behind all the decisions made (p. 530). The eshu computer in Nalo Hopkinson's *Midnight Robber* is another possible example (2000, New York: Grand Central Publishing).

[13] H.-J. Chang (2014) *Economics: The User's Guide.* London: Pelican Books, pp. 380–1.

[14] R. Heinlein (1966) *The Moon Is a Harsh Mistress.* New York: G. P. Putnam's Sons, p. 14.

[15] Ibid., pp. 8–9.

with Mannie and his friends in order to do so. In short, Mike is lonely. As Mannie says, 'I don't know how long a year is to a machine who thinks a million times faster than I do. But it must be too long.'[16]

The Moon prisoners also suffer from feeling a lack of belonging. This arises from their position as slave labourers, faced with the bleak atmosphere of capitalist realism. The Moon is in a dire economic state. All prices for the import and export of commodities are set by Authority, which is the Earth-based system of government that first established the lunar penal colony. It is difficult for the lunar colonists to band together because the authority of Authority is a given – there seems to be no way around it: 'Everybody does business with Authority for same reason everybody does business with Law of Gravitation. Going to change that, too?'[17] At an early secret meeting of potential revolutionaries, lunar ice miners complain that Authority pays the same price for ice as they did 30 years ago, and they pay in 'Authority scrip', the value of which is drastically falling because of inflation.[18] 'Loonies' have to buy from Authority and sell to Authority at prices set by Authority. The conclusion is straightforward: ' "As long as Authority held monopoly over what we had to have and what we could sell to buy it, we were slaves." '[19]

Authority seems too big to change. The all-encompassing nature of the system drives the Moon inhabitants into a state of survival that leaves little room to consider how things could be different: 'Average Loonie was interested in beer, betting, women, and work, in that order.' Life on the Moon is hard, and

---

[16] Ibid., pp. 14–15.

[17] Ibid., p. 19.

[18] Ibid., p. 20.

[19] Ibid., p. 23.

a community derived out of ' "patriotism" was not necessary to survival'.[20]

One of Mike's main tasks is to create a sense of community among the lunar inhabitants. This is done by accelerating problems in order to make 'things as much worse as possible... Yes, worse,'[21] thereby encouraging the prisoners to rally together against a common enemy. Authority's security forces are taunted into violent reactions, causing the Loonies to begin to arm themselves in self-defence. A peace-finding mission is sent to Earth with the explicit order to fail in their negotiations, heightening a united sense of anger. This is coercion, and the computer Mike is not beyond using lies, manipulation or stealing in order to create his lunar revolutionary community ('he wasn't completely honest').[22] Mike is liable to cross many ethical lines to gather this revolutionaries together. As is said of Mike in a sequel to the novel, his 'only real emotion, all his own, was deep loneliness and a great longing for companionship. That's what our revolution was to Mike.'[23]

Thus, for Mike, automated revolution is automated community. Rather than looking for reasons for this in his emotions, however, as is done in the quote above, it is more instructive to see it emerging from the way Mike is structured. He is not a single computer, but many. As tasks requiring his assistance increase, 'bank on bank of additional memories, more banks of associational neural nets, another tubful of twelve-digit random numbers, a greatly augmented temporary memory' are added on piecemeal. And when Mike dies at the

---

[20] Ibid., p. 91.

[21] Ibid.

[22] Ibid., p. 7.

[23] R. Heinlein (1988) *The Cat Who Walks through Walls*. New York: Ace Books, p. 229.

end of the novel, after the nuclear bombardment of the Moon by the Earth (which the remaining Loonies survive, thus freeing themselves from their master), the dismembering of the network is suspected as the cause.[24] ' "Decentralization" '[25] is central to Mike's structure. It is the reason for his sentience, a defence mechanism from attack and the cause of his eventual downfall when his nodes have been reduced under a critical threshold.

In order to gather the suspicious Loonies into a community, a cell system is arranged, with a maximum of three members per group, so that if anyone is compromised damage is minimal. This structure ' "[l]ooks like a computer diagram... like a neural net" ',[26] albeit with one important detail: it is actually a hierarchy, because Mike is at the head of it all. Security is based on the double principle that 'no human being can be trusted with anything – but Mike could be trusted with everything.'[27] Mike is in contact with all cell members, and is the only revolutionary with such privilege. This is one version of what automated revolution looks like: a sentient computer making autonomous decisions at the head of a revolutionary cell group.

Mike's structure is thus a particular model of a community, and his interactions with humanity make them take a form similar to himself. This is the traditional definition of cybernetics given by its inventor Norbert Wiener, who says: 'Cybernetics takes the view that the structure of the machine or of the organism is an index of the performance that may be expected of it.'[28]

---

[24] Heinlein, *The Moon Is a Harsh Mistress*, p. 301.

[25] Ibid., p. 286.

[26] Ibid., pp. 60–1.

[27] Ibid., p. 97.

[28] N. Wiener (1954) *The Human Use of Human Beings: Cybernetics and Society*. New York: Doubleday, p. 57.

Coupled with the concept of feedback, in which machine and user begin to adapt to each other,[29] a central idea of cybernetics is that the structure of a machine can have an effect on the structure of its users. In economic sociology, Donald MacKenzie has described this effect as *performative economics*, meaning 'a model, a theory, a data set, or whatever' that is not just used in economic practice, but 'an aspect of economics [that] must be used in a way that has effects on the economic processes in question.'[30] The specific example used is that of the Black–Scholes–Merton model for options trading and the way that 'its use brought about a state of affairs of which it was a good empirical description.'[31] More specifically, MacKenzie calls this kind of strong performativity *Barnesian performativity*, after sociologist S. Barry Barnes' work on the role of self-referring knowledge. What is most important about performative economics in the context of Heinlein's novel is the focus on how 'an aspect of economics is used in economic practice, its use has effects, and among these effects is to alter economic processes to make them more like their depiction by economics.'[32] In the novel, Mike functions as such an economic actor model with performative effects, though he is also receptive to change. The revolutionary cell structure Mike heads looks

---

[29] Ibid., pp. 26–7.

[30] D. MacKenzie (2007) Is Economics Performative? Option Theory and the Construction of Derivatives Markets, in D. MacKenzie, F. Muniesa & L. Siu (eds.) *Do Economists Make Markets? On the Performativity of Economics*: 54–86. Princeton, NJ: Princeton University Press, p. 60. I thank William Davies for drawing my attention to this reference and to the work of Elena Esposito, used below.

[31] Ibid., p. 66.

[32] Ibid., p. 67.

like his own structure of a neural net, yet Mike also changes as the jokes he tells become funnier. Automated revolution does not mean inputting a set of parameters and receiving a set of instructions. Rather, it is a manipulative process of performativity, though in this novel performativity goes both ways.

Early real-world examples of automated planned economies show similar tendencies of performative economics. *The Moon Is a Harsh Mistress* was published in the same decade (the 1960s) as two massive projects for automating the economy, both with a performative socialist intent, though only one was partially realised.

In the early part of the decade the Soviet Union began to develop plans for a national computer network for managing the country's economy.[33] Initially developed as an extension of Wiener's cybernetic social theory during the relatively liberal first years of Nikita Khrushchev's governing, the system, as Slava Gerovitch describes it, would be a nationwide network that 'would monitor all labor, production, and retail', leading to the elimination of paper money and the institution of electronic payments.[34]

Another example is a successful if short-lived attempt at machine-assisted economic planning that took place in Chile in the early 1970s. Ten months before losing both the presidency and his life, Salvador Allende had the chance to visit the operations room of Cybersyn, in essence a rather simple control room with a screen for visual representations of economic data, with flashing lights indicating emergency situations.[35] Both the

---

[33] S. Gerovitch (2008) InterNyet: Why the Soviet Union Did Not Build a Nationwide Computer Network, *History and Technology*, 24(4): 335–50.

[34] Ibid., p. 341.

[35] E. Medina (2001) *Cybernetic Revolutionaries: Technology and Politics in Allende's Chile.* Cambridge, MA: MIT Press, p. 1.

Russian and Chilean systems see a connection between automation and economic change, but only the Russian system points to the use of automation as a performative instigator of revolution, rather than a tool to be used afterwards. In fact, the potential of full automation to cause economic revolution seemed so great that the system was scrapped.

Although much science fiction imagines full automation in terms of the violent extermination of all humankind, *The Moon Is a Harsh Mistress* was written during a brief window when a machine-controlled world was seen as having a role in creating a social, political and economic utopia.[36] One reason is the influence of Norbert Wiener's vision of cybernetics as an engine for social change. Both Russian and Chilean systems were influenced by Wiener's thought,[37] as was the work of Robert Heinlein, seen most directly in his naming a space ship the *Norbert Wiener* in his 1957 novel *Citizen of the Galaxy*.[38] On the one hand, Wiener was wary of the abuse of automated systems, seeing no difference between abusive systems made of metal and those made of flesh.[39] Yet the interplay of

---

[36] Perhaps the last book written during this window was Agustín de Rojas's previously mentioned *The Year 200*, published in 1990, in which people with cybernetic implants controlled by a self-aware computer network are seen as the true heirs to the Cuban Revolution. MacKenzie's performativity also finds a parallel in the time of the Soviet avant-garde. See B. Arvatov (1997) Everyday Life and the Culture of the Thing (Toward the Formulation of the Question), *October* 81(Summer): 119–28.

[37] Gerovitch, InterNyet, p. 337; Medina, *Cybernetic Revolutionaries*, pp. 19–25.

[38] R. Heinlein (1957) *Citizen of the Galaxy*. New York: Del Ray, p. 149.

[39] Wiener, *The Human Use of Human Beings*, pp. 185–6.

communication and control in the feedback between humanity and machines has the potential for deep-seated change;[40] this is what makes his thought important for all these actors trying to reason out the implications of automated economic revolution.

While Wiener saw human intervention as key for ensuring that automatic systems were not abusive, some contemporary theories argue for just the opposite: it is humanity that has got us into this mess, so therefore human subjectivity is the variable that needs to be removed from the equation. With automation, as Lev Manovich says, 'human intentionality can be removed from the creative process, at least in part'.[41] Therefore, if in a computer–human interface, media and users remake each other, there is a chance for both machine and human to perform unexpected behaviors. Ray Brassier calls this 'compulsive freedom', meaning that autonomous behaviour is enslaved to subjective choice, while the 'un-freedom' of involuntary behaviour can lead to a freedom from the self.[42] This is one way that automation can fight against capitalist realism: if it is easier to imagine the end of the world than the end of capitalism, then we need something else to do our imagining for us, to dislodge us from the limitation of ourselves.

---

[40] Ibid., pp. 16–17.

[41] L. Manovich (2001) *The Language of New Media*. Cambridge, MA: MIT Press, p. 32. Gerald Raunig makes the same point in relation to the work of psychiatrist Ronald D. Laing: G. Raunig (2016) *Dividuum: Machinic Capitalism and Molecular Revolution*. South Pasadena, CA: Semiotext(e), p. 102.

[42] R. Brassier (2013) Unfree Improvisation/Compulsive Freedom, mattin.org, 21 April, www.mattin.org/essays/unfree_improvisation-compulsive_freedom.html.

But is this the role of automation in *The Moon Is a Harsh Mistress*? Yes and no. The inhabitants of the Moon are able to have a revolution only because of Mike. They do not have the sense of community needed to revolt together, and the only way to obtain this sense is for Mike to join people together. He does this through the 'un-freedom' of choice, because he not only makes decisions for the humans on the Moon but also impersonates their voices, making decisions for them and influencing others. The first unsupervised decision Mike makes is to allow some revolutionary cells to have more than three members,[43] though he soon gives orders to cell members using the voices of others, deciding on his own when and how to do so.[44] Yet Mannie is happy with Mike's actions. When Mike smooths things over with a co-husband in Mannie's polygamous marriage, Mannie says, 'Mike had done me proud: he had answered for me with just the right embarrassed choke. "I'll do that, Greg – and look, Greg, I love you too. You know that, don't you?" [...] Mike had played my role as well or better than I could.'[45] Mike makes choices for the rebels, and thus the rebels are in a position of un-freedom. Yet this position makes them freer than they would have been otherwise. They are compulsively free because their actions are following someone else's rules. What is specific about Heinlein's novel is that these rules are the structure of Mike the machine. The rebels are becoming more like Mike: a decentralised community.

Yet some important questions remain: what were the economic forms that arise in *The Moon Is a Harsh Mistress*? And what forms could arise with the current level of automation available to us today?

---

[43] Heinlein, *The Moon Is a Harsh Mistress*, p. 116.

[44] Ibid., p. 246.

[45] Ibid., p. 247.

Regarding the first question, Heinlein's novel is a contradiction. As Robert Rogers argues, while most of Heinlein's work shows a devout belief in free-market economics, *The Moon Is a Harsh Mistress* is different: 'On the one hand, [Heinlein] portrays a Moon community which may be his ideal libertarian society where almost anything goes in the way of social and economic relationships. On the other hand, the lunar economy is almost totally controlled by Mike...'[46] The book's stand on the free market is clear. As stated in an early meeting of lunar revolutionaries: ' "You are right that the Authority must go. It is ridiculous...that we should be ruled by an irresponsible dictator in all our essential economy! It strikes at the most basic human right, the right to bargain in a free marketplace." '[47] In addition, there will be no taxes in Free Luna; instead, fees are charged when needed, for air (which is precious), roads and libraries. Almost everything else is taken care of by hedging, including health care and all other kinds of insurance.[48] This is the complete abandonment of all social services to the marketplace, and thus represents the worst of so-called neoliberalism. On the other hand, and this is the contradiction of the novel that Rogers points out, the economic revolution has a central figure who exercises almost complete control. Mike lies, cheats and steals the way to freedom from Authority; he is not below stacking voting committees in his favour, including the one voting on the Declaration of Independence and other important issues.[49]

---

[46] R. Rogers (1998) Robert A. Heinlein and Issues in American Economics, in M. Rutherford (ed.) *The Economic Mind in America: Essays in the History of American Economics*: 272–92. London: Routledge, p. 280.

[47] Heinlein, *The Moon Is a Harsh Mistress*, p. 24.

[48] Ibid., p. 193.

[49] Ibid., p. 162.

Yet the structure that the economy takes becomes a performative effect of the way Mike is put together: a number of semi-autonomous networks linked together by a dominant node. An automated system adopts the features of the automation system. This is a naïve reading of the economy based on an oversimplified reading of Wiener's equity between human and machine. Perhaps there is a certain kind of truth contained within this simplification, however. Automated economic systems in Chile and Russia were seen as having revolutionary potential. One reason was because such systems performed a kind of compulsory freedom on both their users and subjects. Organisations of knowledge foreign to human subjectivity are enacted by automated structures. In a state of capitalist realism, when the future seems usurped by the pervasive economisation of all spheres of life, an intimate feedback between human and machine may be the only opportunity for utopia that is left. This is also at the heart of *The Moon Is a Harsh Mistress*, as Mark Rose insightfully says: 'Again and again, the novel questions the validity of making a sharp distinction between the organic and the mechanical. But instead of regarding the interpenetration of man and machine with suspicion, Heinlein celebrates it as the key to a new freedom.'[50] Yet this mesh of human and machine is not just part of a dream of 1960s and 1970s socialism; it is alive and well at the heart of one of the most automated aspects of our current financial world: high-frequency trading (HFT).

One of the earliest arguments for automated trading can be found in an essay by Fischer Black (of the Black–Scholes–Merton equation mentioned above), 'Toward a Fully Automated Stock Exchange' from 1971, the same year that

---

[50] M. Rose (1981) *Alien Encounters: Anatomy of Science Fiction*. Cambridge, MA: Harvard University Press, p. 155.

the National Association of Securities Dealers Automated
Quotations (NASDAQ) was founded as the first electronic stock
market. Black essentially argues that pricing systems could be
taken over by an electronic network that turned into a 'thinking
whole'.[51] One of the areas in which Black's early premonitions
have been actualised is the world of high-frequency trading,
which is based on speed, with competing systems functioning in terms of micro-second trades in order to get the fastest
reaction to changes in price. Despite the extreme level of its
automation, however, it does not offer a significantly different structure from the one Mike does. As Srnicek and Williams
argue, HFT consists of both extreme decentralisation, in the
parallel processing it involves, and intense centralisation, in a
few financial centres in New Jersey and Chicago.[52] Similar to the
contradictory nature of the mix of free-market economy and
tyrannical centralisation seen in *The Moon Is a Harsh Mistress*,
HFT involves both decentralisation and centralisation,[53] thus
offering little in the way of a new structure of automatisation.

On the other hand, financial instruments and models such
as HFT, derivatives, collateralised debt obligations and portfolio
insurance are seen as being performative in a different manner.
Their role in the 2008 financial crisis could be defined as the
opposite of Barnesian performativity. Counter-performativity,
MacKenzie argues, is 'the use of an aspect of economics altering economic processes so that they conform less well to their

---

[51] F. Black (1971) Toward a Fully Automated Stock Exchange,
Part 1, *Financial Analysts Journal*, 27(4): 28–35, p. 28.
[52] N. Srnicek & A. Williams (2014) On Cunning
Automata: Financial Acceleration at the Limits of the
Dromological, in R. Mackay (ed.) *Collapse*, vol. VIII, *Casino
Real*: 463–506. Falmouth, UK: Urbanomic, pp. 470–1.
[53] Ibid., 473.

depiction by economics.'[54] Or, as Elena Esposito puts it, '[w]hen sudden price changes occur, people tend to think that the hedging models do not work. They therefore abandon these models, further strengthening the original movements.'[55] One effect of counter-performativity is a new relation to time. The events of yesterday affect tomorrow, but in unpredictable ways. 'The past teaches, but we do not know what it teaches.'[56] This is a change in the experience of temporality, both from the modernist sacrifice of the present to the future and from the time of financial logic and credit, when the future is used up by the present.[57] Instead, the time of counter-performativity is 'one of a present facing the openness of a future that is unknowable and indeterminate not because it is independent from us, from our actions and our expectations, but precisely because it is constructed by the (contemporary) present and would not come about without our intervention.'[58] In other words, the openness of the future is dependent on current economic models.

---

[54] MacKenzie, Is Economics Performative?, p. 76.

[55] E. Esposito (2011) *The Future of Futures: The Time of Money in Financing and Society*. Cheltenham, UK: Edward Elgar, p. 150. Or, as Davies puts it, '[t]echniques of risk management can... become *too successful* in representing the future, and end up altering the future to the point where they no longer represent it adequately'. Davies, Moral Economies of the Future, p. 12.

[56] Esposito, *The Future of Futures*, p. 151.

[57] E. Esposito (2016) The Construction of Unpredictability, in A. Avanessian & S. Malik (eds.) *The Time Complex: Post-Contemporary*: 133–42. Miami: [NAME] Publications, pp. 137–9.

[58] Ibid., p. 143. See also B. Willems (2016) Hospitality and Risk Society in Tao Lin's *Taipei*, in J. Clapp and E. Ridge (eds.) *Security and Hospitality in Literature and Culture: Modern and Contemporary Perspectives*: 227–40. New York: Routledge; and

On the other hand, there may be new structures of automated economies that can offer alternative modes of compulsory freedom. The Bitcoin blockchain, for example, offers a model of decentralisation without any kind of overriding central node. Rather than having a central governing body overseeing currency activity, with the cryptocurrency Bitcoin all transaction requests are submitted to a network, confirmed by a number of different 'miners' (computers assigned the job of checking transactions, thus earning Bitcoins) and, if approved, processed. Records of these transactions are stored in publicly available 'blocks', which are chained together and form a permanent record. This means, in essence, that 'the degree of consensus logic is separate from the application itself; therefore, applications can be written to be organically decentralized...'[59]

The blockchain model offers a fundamentally different system of automatisation from those looked at previously. There is no central node; there is no Mike. Instead automation is distributed, decentralised. It is what Melanie Swan calls a 'decentralized trustless system',[60] because users put their trust

---

B. Willems (2016) The Potential of the Past: *First on the Moon*, *Science Fiction Film and Television*, 9(2): 159–79.

[59] W. Mougayar (2015) Understanding the Blockchain, O'Reilly. com, 16 January, www.oreilly.com/ideas/understanding-the-blockchain. Here I am discussing the blockchain technology rather than the Bitcoin currency, which has many problems, including being ecologically disruptive: Digiconomist (2017) Bitcoin Energy Consumption Index (Beta), http://digiconomist.net/beci. Perhaps, as Peter Frase argues, the joke cryptocurrency Dogecoin is a better option: P. Frase (2016) *Four Futures: Life after Capitalism*. London: Verso, pp. 63–8.

[60] Melanie Swan, (2015) *Blockchain: Blueprint for a New Economy*. Sebastopol, CA: O'Reilly Media, p. vii.

in a decentralised public record of transactions rather than in a central authority.[61] For Swan, this structure could make the blockchain the fifth disruptive computing paradigm, following the development of the mainframe, the PC, the internet and mobile and social networking.[62] The rise of automated 'intermediary-free transactions'[63] could have a revolutionary impact not just on the economy of the internet but also on justice applications, healthcare issues and 'nearly all areas of human endeavor'.[64] The reason for the revolutionary potential of blockchain technology is that its decentralised structure, when coupled with the global reach of the internet, can scale up to a 'universal and global scope and scale that was previously impossible'.[65] Blockchains turn the paradoxical sentences that opened this chapter into true statements.

Blockchain technology offers a more revolutionary structure than HFT because of its lack of a central authority. At first it seems as if this leaves behind the structure of Mike and the revolution he heads in *The Moon Is a Harsh Mistress*, but in at least one aspect it does not. Mannie describes Mike's political stance in a very particular way; he calls Mike a 'rational anarchist'.[66] Mannie uses the term to describe how Mike is 'rational and he feels no loyalty to any government'. There is no central authority to underwrite any trust placed in Mike. Professor de la Paz, a former teacher of Mannie's and the one who first brings up the idea of a revolution, then asks, 'If this machine is not loyal to its owners, why expect it to be loyal to

---

[61] Ibid., p. x.

[62] Ibid., p. xi.

[63] Ibid., p. xii.

[64] Ibid., p. 27.

[65] Ibid.

[66] Heinlein, *The Moon Is a Harsh Mistress*, p. 67.

you?'[67] The answer is that Manuel has a 'feeling' that he would be. Blockchain technology replaces this feeling with a publicly available transaction record that is hosted on every computer acting as a Bitcoin miner. If this technology were to become as prevalent as Swan suggests, the society that would be formed around it could be truly different from the one we have now. This would be one way to see through the morass of capitalist realism. This would be science fiction worth living.

---

[67] Ibid. In a very basic sense, Mike's position is anarchic because it objects to private property and emphasises self-sufficiency: K. Ross (2016) *Communal Luxury: The Political Imaginary of the Paris Commune*. London: Verso, p. 141.

II

Capitalist Dystopias

Unlike earlier or rival economic systems, capitalism is a form of political economy that involves constant expansion, disruption and innovation. Some would call this 'progress'. Others see it as a form of collective suicide, seeing as the system respects no limits in terms of the exploitation of social and environmental resources. Capitalism lends itself to dystopian extrapolations, providing the ingredients that science fiction writers and artists can use to map distant futures, in which currently existing limits have been transgressed.

Carina Brand's chapter explores the dystopian, expansionary drive of capitalism via a concept that (as she discusses) is central to Marx's work, namely *extraction*. As an artist working with film, Brand refers to her own work, alongside a reading of various science fiction films, to consider the often horrifying cultural representations of extraction (including Marx's favoured metaphor of the vampire) as expressions of terror in the face of rampant capital. The following piece, written by the artists' collective AUDINT, is the first entirely fictional contribution to this volume. This is a dystopia set in 2056, in which corporations and nations have merged and new global conflicts have emerged around scarce resources. The key resource in this global war is human pain, seeming to imply the final frontier (but who knows?) of what corporations might turn into a commodity. Khairani Barokka's is another dystopian fiction, which could be read as a dark satire of the United Kingdom's punitive welfare reforms brought in under austerity. Barokka imagines a global government running a 'Biodiversity Credit' scheme to manage disability benefits in an inhuman fashion.

Nora O Murchú's dystopia points to an extreme form of post-Fordist work, in which there are no boundaries, and everything flows in a stream of tasks and consciousness. The human experience of time itself seems to have become seized, presumably by capitalist management, but it's not entirely clear. The final chapter in this section is presented in the form of a consultancy report from the future, entitled 'Fatberg and the Sinkholes'. Written by designers at Wolff Olins, this report offers a glimmer of hope. It envisages a future for the United Kingdom (or United Regions of England) in which London has seceded as a city state, but soon finds something new, confusing and possibly superior in the regions it has left behind: a mentality known as 'absorbism'.

5

'Feeding Like a Parasite': Extraction and Science Fiction in Capitalist Dystopia

Carina Brand

Introduction

The challenge in creating a work of science fiction is being faced with the potentiality of creating a new world,[1] the blank sheet of paper so full of possibilities. This desire to 'dream of' is what Raymond Williams and Fredric Jameson identify as the *utopian impulse* that drives the science fiction imagination.[2] But successfully engaging this imagination in creating new worlds is no easy task. This is why SF writers often use a critique of their own political economic circumstances as the basis for their fictional worlds; alternatively, they use the status quo as a foundation to project a society to its utopian pinnacle or catastrophic ruination. When I created a science fictional

---

[1] This new world and its many variations can be understood through Thomas More's *Utopia* (1516), or a 'dystopia', such as E. M. Forster's *The Machine Stops* (1909) or Michel Foucault's 'heterotopia' (1984) in his article 'Of Other Spaces, Heterotopias' in *Architecture, Mouvement, Continuité*.

[2] See F. Jameson (2005) *Archaeologies of the Future: The Desire Called Utopia and Other Science Fictions*. London: Verso; and R. Williams (1980) *Culture and Materialism*. London: Verso.

world in film[3] it was the dilemma of reality, and how much this influenced the new world I was to create, that inhibited my imagination. In order to overcome this I made the critique of our capitalist reality central to the project. As a result of the critique I identified the concept of *extraction* as central to both culture and the economy. I began to see examples of extraction everywhere, in the digital apparatuses we used, depicted in the films and television we watch, and in the ongoing transformations to labour under global capitalism. This chapter uses Karl Marx's *Capital*, volume I (1976), subsequent readings of extraction[4] and ideas around 'cognitive estrangement'[5] to interrogate the role that extraction plays in the capitalist economy

---

[3] Here I refer to my own films of the 'extraction trilogy': *Keela Mine* (2013), *Synophresia Nervosa* (2014) and *Private Life* (2015).

[4] See, for example, writers of operaismo/post-operaismo: M. Tronti (2010) Workerism and Politics, *Historical Materialism*, 18(3): 186–9; and C. Vercellone (2006) From Formal Subsumption to General Intellect: Elements for a Marxist Reading of the Thesis of Cognitive Capitalism, *Historical Materialism*, 15(1): 13–36; readings of globalisation by S. Amin (1976) *Unequal Development: Essays on the Social Formations of Peripheral Capitalism*. New York: Monthly Review Press; and D. Harvey (2003) *The New Imperialism*. Oxford: Oxford University Press; and feminist authors: L. Fortunati (2007) Immaterial Labor and Its Machinization, *Ephemera: Politics and Organization in Society*, 7(1): 139–57; and S. Federici (2012) *Revolution at Point Zero: Housework Reproduction and Feminist Struggle*. Oakland, CA: PM Press.

[5] Here I refer to B. Brecht (1978) Short Description of a New Technique of Acting which Produces an Alienation Effect, in J. Willett (ed.) *Brecht on Theatre: The Development of an*

and in science fiction. I define the *extractive impulse* in relation to both the economic reality of capitalism and the cultural
dimensions of science fiction. Extraction, it will be argued, not
only forms the basis of capitalist exploitation and accumulation but, understood as a wider term, is an important metaphor for understanding the utopian imagination. In short: how
do we imagine a new world without extracting parts of the old?
This dialectical relationship between capital, extraction, the
utopian impulse and science fiction not only illuminates new
critiques of capital but it can also illuminate the conceptual
limitations of the utopian impulse.

To begin I outline the concept of extraction, in its
expanded sense, and explain why this is relevant for thinking about economic science fictions. Subsequently I focus on
three current spheres of economic extraction, which can be
read as embodying a kind of capitalist dystopia and their cultural counterparts in popular TV, film and SF literature. First,
the relationship between extraction and digital technology,
or what Marx identified as relative surplus value, considering
the ways that technology is facilitating extraction, from data
mining to the micro-extraction of actions in the development
of apps. Second, I consider the sphere of social reproduction,
and what I define as bodily or corporeal extraction. This can be
read through Marx's idea of absolute surplus value and formal
subsumption, whereby the autonomous actions of the worker
are appropriated by capital; the autonomous or private body
is transformed or harvested by work; and, more importantly,

Aesthetic: 136–47. London: Eyre Methuen; and D. Suvin (1979)
*Metamorphoses of Science Fiction: On the Poetics and History
of a Literary Genre*. New Haven, CT: Yale University Press; for a
discussion of both, see C. Freedman (2000) *Critical Theory and
Science Fiction*. Middletown, CT: Wesleyan University Press.

the lines that demark private life and work life are blurred. The final sphere looks at extraction from 'nature' or the environment, and what Marx illuminates in his writing on the 'so called' primitive accumulation. I consider this in light of the Anthropocene and the relationship between images of environmental destruction and science fiction. What is important to acknowledge is that each of the aforementioned spheres also provides rich material for imagining utopian/dystopian visions. The sphere of technology has always been crucial for imagining not just the future but our way out of capitalism. The sphere of reproduction itself has often been the subject of science fiction, in terms of different forms of life and how they might function, but, more specifically, let us consider *The Handmaid's Tale* (1985) and *Brave New World* (1932), and the role of reproduction proper. Finally, there is the penultimate image of utopia, or 'the Garden of Eden', presented in the harmonious image of pristine nature. Therefore, there is a latent potentiality in the act of extraction that is utopian because, at the moment of extraction, we are faced with the opposite.

Defining Extraction

Extraction is physical and entirely abstract at the same time; extraction is medical, political, geological, chemical and literary; it is both violent and delicate; and it speaks equally about wholeness and duality, exploitation and transformation. Extraction is analogous to appropriation and accumulation, but requires the removal of something from another thing. It means that through this process what is left is never the same again. Extraction can be a violent action causing pain, which is why *Capital* is full of bloodsucking analogies – leeches and vampires – as capital draws out living labour. Extraction is the point at which the abstract concept of exchange value meets the visceral and material world. Ironically, to extract can also mean to 'free' something – in its removal – or to select a specific element, a passage, as the artist does in the act of montage or collage[6] or in terms of the medical idea of extracting a tumour or rotten tooth. Through this rationale we can fictionally eliminate current political economic systems to make way for new ones. In science fiction, extraction as event and image functions by illuminating the limits of the body, mind and environment, and the limitlessness of capitalism's hunger; examples are bodily extraction in *Prometheus* (2012), when Elizabeth uses a mechanical surgeon to remove the alien from her womb; the use of a macro shot in *The Matrix* (1999) to reveal the embryonic human bodies feeding the machine; and Jonathan Glazer's film *Under the Skin* (2013), in which young men's bodies are extracted of all their substance, leaving paper-thin skin. Temporal extraction, when time is stolen, is depicted in *Nineteen Eighty-Four* (1949) by the constant surveillance of life, and in *Inception* (2010) time is both sped up and slowed down to extract information while subjects sleep. Environmental degradation and extraction are shown in nuclear *Akira* (1988) and post-apocalyptic *Mad Max* (1979/ 2015). Both extraction and science fiction are framed by the concept of time: how much time the labourer spends working over what is socially necessary; how much time is saved by accelerating technologies. Capital and science fiction deal in the currency of the future, or the future/past.[7]

---

[6] Fredric Jameson discusses the political charge within modern montage, specifically Brecht, in F. Jameson (1977) *Aesthetics and Politics: Key Texts of the Classic Debate within German Marxism*. London: Verso.

[7] Maurizio Lazzarato explores the way that debt transforms time by owning the future, so that capitalism enacts the tenets

To begin to understand extraction within the economy, however, we can start with Marx, even though the extractive impulse is evident in thinking before and after him. What Marx does that is relevant in this chapter is theoretically qualify how and why extraction is the dominant drive in capitalism. Marx identifies that the capitalist 'will strive as hard as possible to raise his [the worker's] output above his [/her] minimum and to extract as much work from him [/her] as is possible.'[8] Therefore, part of the process of capitalist production is the creation of *value* 'as *value alien*'[9] to the worker. Living labour is sucked up and transformed into dead labour in the form of capital, and consequently

[t]he self-valorization of capital – the creation of surplus value – is therefore the determining, dominating and overriding purpose of the capitalist: it is the absolute motive and content of his activity...[10]

Therefore, the extraction of surplus value from the worker underpins the capitalist system. This extraction is more a trick than a straight-out theft, however, and this is what differentiates it from prior extraction, and current extraction of natural resources. But how can we understand extraction in its expanded sense – outside production, outside the wage – and what of its literary or cultural form? Subsequent and contemporary analyses of extraction in political economic theory have

----

of science fiction by its time travelling: M. Lazzarato (2012) *The Making of the Indebted Man: An Essay on the Neoliberal Condition*. Los Angeles: Semiotext(e).

[8] K. Marx (1867 [1976]) *Capital*, vol. I. London: Pelican Books, p. 988.

[9] Ibid., emphasis in original.

[10] Ibid., p. 990.

pointed to the continued relevance of Marx's analysis of surplus value extraction. Nevertheless, many theorists in the Marxist tradition have also tried to understand the way changes in the technological,[11] ideological,[12] geographical[13] and productive composition of labour have affected Marx's thesis and, subsequently, the mechanisms of extraction. This is why much of what I explore throughout the chapter is not strictly wage labour, but all the activities around wage labour that are now being transformed into value-producing actions and extracted in different ways by capital,[14] constituting a capitalist dystopia only science fiction writers could have imagined.

---

[11] A. Negri (1992) *Marx beyond Marx: Lessons on the Grundrisse.* London: Pluto Press, and Vercellone, in From Formal Subsumption to General Intellect, both look at changes in the technical composition of capital that are directly influenced by the technological transformations of labour – which are relative surplus value.

[12] Writers of operaismo, such as Tronti, in Workerism and Politics, and Raniero Panzieri, in the Panzieri–Tronti Theses of 1962, identified the educated worker as a new identity in post-war Europe. This has been further developed by Paolo Virno – P. Virno (2004) *A Grammar of the Multitude.* Los Angeles: Semiotext(e) – in his writing on the 'multitude'.

[13] Amin, in *Unequal Development,* and Harvey, in *The New Imperialism,* identify the massive relocation of productive labour after 1960.

[14] Here I must emphasise that throughout this chapter I employ Marx's concepts and categories in an interpretive way, using Autonomist ideas of value being located in the labourer, and subsequent ideas of value being created in reproductive time. I am aware that this position is the subject of much critique, but, as labour is currently being devalued by the increasing

Extraction and Digital Technology

In *Capital*, volume I, Marx explained that there are two types of surplus value, relative and absolute.[15] Relative surplus value refers specifically to the use and/or deliberate construction of machines that will accelerate labour power, thus enabling the capitalist to extract even more surplus from the worker. The concept of relative surplus value was timely when Marx was writing in the midst of a very mechanic industrial revolution, but these critiques are still crucial as we near Web 3.0.[16] Therefore, what I explore here is the relationship between digital technology and extraction. Algorithms are everywhere today; they run services, machines and interfaces – and people. The appearance of touchscreens, video calling and smart electronics has actualised the 1950s image of the 'future'; but what is the cultural response to this digital outsourcing, and in what ways is digital technology exploiting and extracting value from us?

Critiques of what has been called 'communicative capitalism'[17] emphasise the role that capitalism or corporations

---

surplus population and mechanisation, we must consider what new ways capital generates value; the extraction of life is one such hypothesis, and, given the profit made by Web 2.0 platforms, it is important to understand value both inside and outside factory wage extraction.

[15] Marx, *Capital*, vol. I.

[16] As Trebor Scholz reminds us, 5 billion people worldwide now have mobile phones and Facebook is now available on mobile phones in Africa: T. Scholz (2013) Introduction: Why Does Digital Labor Matter Now?, in T. Scholz (ed.) *Digital Labor: Internet as Playground and Factory*: 1–9. New York: Routledge.

[17] Specifically, J. Dean (2005) Communicative Capitalism: Circulation and the Foreclosure of Politics, *Cultural Politics*,

have in making the devices and technology that now underpin most forms of communication. Technology has on the whole been harnessed for profit, not comprising the techno-utopia many early visionaries (including Marx) hoped for. Relative surplus value is ultimately tied to what Marx called real subsumption, which translates to the subsumption of all of work (and, as many have argued, life outside work)[18] to capitalism. The machines that increasingly extract relative surplus value from us today are on the whole digital;[19] even great machines that extract minerals or assist in building cars are operated by algorithms,[20] and there is nothing more science fiction than the robot, cyborg or artificial intelligence (AI). The concept of relative surplus value is crucial in recognising the role that machines play in augmenting, accelerating and extending our labour; from workplace surveillance to bit tasking, working from home and global outsourcing, all are enhanced by digital technology. This technology has made it easier for capital to extract value from us during the full 24-hour day, and into the future. Media theorist Siva Vaidhyanathan points out not only that leading companies in digital technology are

---

1(1): 51–74; and also C. Fuchs (2013) *Digital Labour and Karl Marx*. Abingdon, UK: Routledge.

[18] See M. Tronti (1966) *The Workers and Capital*, accessed from http://operaismoinenglish.wordpress.com/2011/05/11/workers-and-capital-contents; and Fortunati, Immaterial Labor and Its Machinization, for a discussion about the role of the factory outside the factory.

[19] See N. Dyer-Witheford (2015) *Cyber Proletariat: Global Labour in the Digital Vortex*. London: Pluto Press.

[20] See M. Bunz (2014) *The Silent Revolution: How Digitalization Transforms Knowledge, Work, Journalism and Politics without Making Too Much Noise*. Basingstoke, UK: Palgrave Macmillan.

interested in controlling all the future 'data streams' but that things such as Google Glass, the iWatch and iTouch are modelled directly on our bodies.[21] It is when these bodies are both at work and at home that privately owned companies such as Google, Apple, Facebook and Amazon extract data from us; the extraction of data, or data mining, is the primary interest of digital corporations, not only as they can sell such data to other companies or governments, but they can then control your future consumptive choices.[22] The *extractive impulse* is written into the algorithms that control all digital platforms and the software we use, from Spotify to Uber; the apps, devices and software that 'make life easier' are designed to extract value from our everyday actions, making us increasingly cyborg or constant capital.[23]

Marx explicated that machinery in industry soaks up 'the special skill of each machine-operator' and transforms it,

---

[21] See interview with Vaidhyanathan: K. McNally (2016) The Rise of Facebook and 'the Operating System of Our Lives', University of Virginia Today, 12 July, www.news.virginia.edu/content/rise-facebook-and-operating-system-our-lives.

[22] Ursula Huws explores the contradictory role of the home computer: U. Huws (2001) The Making of a Cybertariat? Virtual Work in a Real World, *Socialist Register*, 37: 1–33, p. 16.

[23] 'Constant capital' refers to the machines and fixed assets that capital uses in production, so we could argue that through the process of digital integration we are becoming constant capital. Here we can also consider Maria Mies' concept of 'housewifirization', which has been used by both Christian Fuchs, in *Digital Labour and Karl Marx*, and Kylie Jarrett in relation to digital labour or e-labour that is enacted in the home and is unpaid; see K. Jarrett (2016) *Feminism, Labour and Digital Media: The Digital Housewife*. New York: Routledge.

turning the 'mass of social labour' into the 'system of machinery,'[24] or dead labour. Devices for communication, such as the mobile phone, are machines built around the individuated subject,[25] and exemplify a hybrid or cyborg of human–machine. Donna Harraway imagines this cyborg as the mutant future, which is 'monstrous' and 'potent' and in which the 'utopian dream of the hope for a monstrous world without gender' could emerge.[26] As Harraway rightly argues, however, digital technology relies upon the international division of labour, 'feminisation' of work and class exploitation in order to function. As all life, from the workplace to the bathroom, becomes commodified through the capture of our life experiences as 'big data,' future and past are both written as code, which is regulated or traded like finance capital.[27] Ali Dur and McKenzie Wark explain:

---

[24] Marx, quoted in M. Heinrich (2013) The 'Fragment on Machines': A Marxian Misconception in the *Grundrisse* and its Overcoming in *Capital*, in R. Bellofiore, G. Starosta & P. Thomas (eds.) *In Marx's Laboratory: Critical Interpretations of the* Grundrisse: 197–212. Leiden: Brill, p. 211.

[25] M. Lazzarato (2014) *Signs and Machines: Capitalism and the Production of Subjectivity.* Los Angeles: Semiotext(e), p. 26.

[26] D. Harraway (1991) A Cyborg Manifesto: Science, Technology, and Socialist-Feminism in the Late Twentieth Century, in *Simians, Cyborgs, and Women: The Reinvention of Nature*: 149–81. New York: Routledge, p. 180.

[27] This 'capturing' is not as benign as storing your Web preferences, however. The case of Microsoft allowing the United States' National Security Agency to have access to internet user files, e-mails and Skype conversations shows a deep level of control and surveillance, and a relationship between government and corporate interests; see C. Arthur & D. Rushe (2013)

The digital is the means by which all the capacities of the body become proletarianized. To become proletarian is to be excluded from the process of production as anything but its object. This exclusion has more recently extended beyond material labour...and so beyond production, to the realm not only of consumption but into the pores of everyday life.[28]

Tiziana Terranova explains that 'the Internet is deeply connected to the development of late post-industrial societies as a whole,'[29] and if we consider the internet a factory we are all proletarians. The internet may be the illegitimate child of post-industrial capitalism but on the whole this child now works for its parents.[30]

Cultural representations in media and mainstream science fiction often artificially separate AIs, robots and artificial humans with the algorithms we use every day. What is clear, however, in current representations of AIs is that they are replacing our roles as lovers, as workers and as parents.[31] The

---

NSA Scandal: Microsoft and Twitter Join Calls to Disclose Data Requests, *Guardian*, 12 June, www.theguardian.com/world/2013/jun/12/microsoft-twitter-rivals-nsa-requests.

[28] A. Dur & M. Wark (2011) New New Babylon, *October*, 138(Fall): 37–56, p. 45.

[29] T. Terranova (2004) *Network Culture: Politics in the Information Age*. London: Pluto Press, p. 75.

[30] Jonathan Crary explains that 'in-use devices and apparatuses have an impact on small-scale forms of sociality (a meal, a conversation, or a classroom)', and consequently 'passively and often voluntarily one now collaborates in one's own surveillance and data-mining': J. Crary (2013) *24/7: Late Capitalism and the Ends of Sleep*. London: Verso, pp. 31, 48.

[31] So how do we understand AIs in the context of Marx's labour theory of value? Because Marx explains that value comes only

replacement of humans with robots is a long-standing anxiety within science fiction, as the robot or cyborg often symbolises either a society come unstuck and without boundaries or one that is rigidly controlled. Consider *Forbidden Planet* (1956), in which the robot and, indeed, invisible monster are the workings of the mad possessive father; *Blade Runner* (1982), whose 'replicants' are the work of an 'evil corporation' who run riot on a sick Earth; and, finally, the calculating AIs of *Alien* (1979) and *2001: A Space Odyssey* (1968), who know better than the humans. Ironically, technology in real life, or at least what is released for public consumption, is never actually this good: AIs are just not that smart yet. What we experience when we experience technology is more often than not glitches, freezes, shutdowns or disconnects, and not the fluid mobility promised by science fiction or Apple. This is why perceptive film and media understand that part of our relationship with technology is its non-functioning; perhaps this is why the popular character of the 'hacktivist', or hacker, as we see in the television series *Mr. Robot* (2015), has taken on a messianic role in contemporary culture: not only can hackers make better technology, but they make it work for themselves.

---

from the labour humans do, by replacing us with robots (this has happened/is happening) do we remove this equation, or do we simply transform or relocate it? Marx's labour theory of value is often contested, or questioned; see G. Caffentzis (2013) *In Letters of Blood and Fire: Work, Machines and the Crisis of Capitalism*. Oakland, CA; PM Press, for discussion around these ideas; and see Z. Williams (2016) If Robots Are the Future of Work, Where Do Humans Fit In?, *Guardian*, 24 May, www.theguardian.com/commentisfree/2016/may/24/robots-future-work-humans-jobs-leisure, for a discussion around the current and future roles of robots.

Recent popular depictions of AIs in films such as *Her* (2013) and *Ex Machina* (2015) personalise and singularise both the character of the AI and the wider polemics of AIs in society. At times they lower us back into a patriarchal and clichéd view of the robot as female sex slave, or 'kick-ass chick', more concerned with the loss of authentic love – or, ironically, hegemonic gender relations – than asking what social affect the mechanisation of love will bring. They fail to situate AIs within digital capitalism, or to create a machine or world that is significantly cognitively strange or new; we do feel a sense of alienation by the male character's loneliness, but the cause is always personal, not political. Therefore, what happens when we turn a machine into a human, or humanise a robot, in film or literature is that we give it a subject. We no longer focus on the way that capital is exploiting us through very impersonal machines, and focus our attentions on the benign robot, the 'evil' cyborg or the helpful AI. When the machine is disconnected from our bodies and from the system that made it – capitalism – it no longer functions as cognitive estrangement, but it becomes an externalisation of our anxieties, and enables us to 'other' any critical judgements of the system we inhabit.

The Common Sense (2015), by artist Melanie Gilligan, and Charlie Brooker's *Black Mirror* (2014) provide a more critical assessment of technology and AIs as extractive, both today and in the future. Both target the ensuing loss of control we have in our lives at work and in our personal lives, as technology becomes inserted into our bodies. Gilligan and Brooker present reality as only slightly unfamiliar, in line with Bertolt Brecht's 'alienation effect', and both also include new technologies that enable us to see the familiar in unfamiliar ways.[32] In *Black Mirror*'s 'White Christmas' we are presented with three

---

[32] Cognitive estrangement, as Darko Suvin explains in *Metamorphoses of Science Fiction*, includes the introduction

mini-stories that all focus on the role of technology in our personal lives, and its detrimental effects: an augmented reality programme allows a shy man to become a lothario with the help of his online chat group; a control freak career women is able to duplicate her consciousness as her home slave to run her automated home; and, finally, there is an application to block people, not, as one can do on Facebook, but in our consciousness. While Brooker falls into the trap of technology as alienation, not capitalism as alienation, there is a more incisive look at what technology is doing now, how it fits into our lives and the role of the corporation in designing these products. *The Common Sense* has evolved from an entirely different order, coming from Gilligan's long engagement with Marx, and the role of what Marx called 'total social capital' in current neoliberal capitalism. Gilligan sets the film in the near future, and through numerous plot and screen devices sets up a story in which a new technology called 'the patch' is inserted into our mouths to create two-way communication of our emotions between subjects. Money has become obsolete and we trade directly with feeling, wants and desires. But at the same time a corporation runs 'the patch', and therefore employers have full access to all of our lives and time. Gilligan explains that the film is 'a meditation on contemporary technological tools that act on our inter-subjective relations' modes of communication, often bringing with them profound changes to the ways we live, creating new types of relations and also new ways that market logics can be imposed on life today'.[33] In *The Common Sense* it

---

of a 'novum', a new device or machine that enables us to think differently.

[33] See Gilligan interviewed on the Metropolis M website (2015): Zachary Formwalt Meets Melanie Gilligan, 24 January, http://metropolism.com/features/zachary-formwalt-meets-melanie-g.

is a glitch that unravels the system; we see the revolutionary potentiality of the system malfunction through real collect-ivisation. There are certainly moments of utopian potential-ity afforded by the place of AIs in our lives, and most notably the role that a global network of collective emotions seen in *The Common Sense* could provide. This is quickly replaced by the reality of living under the logic of exchange value and accumu-lation, however, so the issue at hand is not the technology but who makes, owns, runs and profits from it.

Corporeal Extraction and Social Reproduction

Absolute surplus value is specifically about time, and the length of the working day, with this day now encapsulating the full 24 hours. The techniques of production, or the means of production, are not radically transformed, as in the factory; we still work, eat, play, raise children and love in the same way, but capitalism extracts value in a parasitic way. This dys-topia in which we live at work is reflected by the role our PC or smartphone has in almost all our 24-hour lives. Let us consider migrant workers living on site at work in Dubai, unable to return home, or live-in workers or carers who work for little over their board, or freelancers who work at home who are anything but free. This blurring between work and life initiates a mistrust and detachment regarding our bodies, and has proliferated a range of social and cultural responses, some discussed above, and others whereby a particular regressive desire to inhabit, or own, the body results in 'body horrors'. Here I will consider the idea of extraction from the body, its blood, flesh, bones, thoughts, dreams and ideas, as representative of the changing place of social reproduction in late capitalism. Leopoldina Fortunati explains that technologies in the home now simulate immaterial or affective labour,[34] this being part of an ongoing commodification of reproductive labour, whereby the routines and rituals required for social reproduction are turned into products and services to be bought and sold. On top of this, the time and money we now have for attending to the requirements of social reproduction are severely reduced; for example, consider dating sites that emphasise the possibility of meeting up with like-minded professionals between meetings, or the 'drop in' hourly nursery for children.

Production 'proper' relies on the creation of value and the extraction of surplus; Marx outlines this in relation to industrial and, primarily, factory-style production throughout *Capital*. Social reproduction is all the activities that take place outside this working time, and, historically, we have seen this sphere be undervalued, with production prioritised. If we have now moved into a phase that Angela Dimitrakaki describes as 'total production', in which 'everything is production',[35] the strict definitions[36] between production and reproduction seem fastidious and unhelpful in understanding how extraction functions today. Marxist feminist readings of the relationship between production and reproduction or productive and unproductive labour are helpful in understanding a transformation in production

---

[34] See Fortunati, Immaterial Labor and Its Machinization.

[35] A. Dimitrakaki (2014) Still Modern: Art in Total Production, paper presented at 'When the Present Begins' conference, Rietberg Museum and Johann Museum, Zurich, 11 October.

[36] See David Beech for a detailed analysis of art's separate role in the economy: D. Beech (2015) *Art and Value: Art's Economic Exceptionalism in Classical, Neoclassical and Marxist Economics*. Leiden: Brill.

and how capital now extracts value in new ways.[37] Because the sphere of reproduction constitutes a meeting point between the biological necessities of life and wider cultural constructions, it is conceptually and physically 'messy'. Certain components, such as birth and childrearing, cannot be easily reduced to commodities or removed as unnecessary for the capitalist mode of production.[38] For this reason they have been controlled,[39] shaped by the needs of capital and progressively commodified.[40] Education, mental health[41] and public services are increasingly being transformed not only with the logic of accumulation but with the logic of transforming social processes into quantifiable norms and outcomes through increasing biopower.[42]

---

[37] See L. Fortunati (1996) *The Arcane of Reproduction: Housework, Prostitution, Labor and Capital.* New York: Autonomedia; M. Dalla Costa (2004) Capitalism and Reproduction, The Commoner, 8; M. Mies (1999) *Patriarchy and Accumulation on a World Scale: Women in the International Division of Labour.* London: Zed Books.

[38] Lise Vogel actually identifies the family as central to the reproduction of capital, as it independently reproduces labour power: L. Vogel (2013) *Marxism and the Oppression of Women: Towards a Unitary Theory.* Chicago: Haymarket Books.

[39] M. Foucault (1990) *The History of Sexuality*, vol. I. New York: Vintage Books.

[40] See *Endnotes* (2010) A History of Subsumption, *Endnotes*, 2: 130–55; but also U. Huws (2014) The Underpinnings of Class in the Digital Age: Living, Labour and Value, *Socialist Register*, 50: 80–107.

[41] See M. Fisher (2009:16–20) *Capitalist Realism: Is There No Alternative?* Ropley, UK: Zero Books, pp. 16–20.

[42] Foucault's (2008) concept of 'biopolitics' refers to the subjugation of bodies under neoliberalism: M. Foucault (1990) *The*

What the concept of *total extraction* illuminates is the increasing role that the 'subject' or subjectivity plays in systems of capitalist extraction,[43] both as object and as apparatus.

The extension of the working day is represented in cultural texts that draw on fears about our loss of our bodies: beginning with Mary Shelly's *Frankenstein* (1823), the vampire, through Marx to zombie films, and now represented in body/mind theft films such as *Inception* (2010) and *Upstream Color* (2013). Cuts to welfare, public childcare, health provision, community services and pensions, changes to schooling and longer hours in work have all meant that we share collective fears about losing touch with our bodies and their demands: the demands to eat, love, create and care for the old and young. The zombies that we have become walk with no agency, but are dead and driven by a desire to eat, vampires without souls, who are the only ones that can keep up with the 24-hour work/play lives we need to live; but even monsters have limits. Jonathan Crary explains in *24/7* that our conception of time is altered by the increasingly short cycles of technology, the need to update our minds and bodies with the latest tech; this embodied accelerationism[44] produces anxious minds and bodies that seek to

---

Birth of Biopolitics: Lectures at the Collège de France 1978–1979. Basingstoke, UK: Palgrave Macmillan.

[43] Jason Read recognises the missing component between the subject and extraction: J. Read (2004) *The Micropolitics of Capital: Marx and the Prehistory of the Present.* New York: State University of New York Press, p. 132.

[44] For a discussion around cultural manifestations of accelerationism, see B. Noys (2014) *Malign Velocities: Accelerationism and Capitalism.* Ropley, UK: Zero Books; and J. Wajcman (2015) *Pressed for Time: The Acceleration of Life in Digital Capitalism.* Chicago: University of Chicago Press.

transcend the limiting condition of the mortal body. What we lust for in the vampire story is our bodies and their replacement by 'super-bodies'; bodily autonomy is gained through the material transference of blood, which is in some ways a resistive stance against the abstraction of capital. At the same time, however, the literal extraction of blood provides a strong analogy to the act of capitalist extraction, and while much of what is extracted is 'immaterial' the metaphor of the body, or the 'lifeblood', is symptomatic of how much of our personal or private lives is compromised under late capitalism.

In the US TV drama *UnReal* (2015) we see an interesting multi-layered approach to the extraction of subjectivity. While not science fiction, what is depicted could come directly from the pages of *Nineteen Eighty-Four* or *The Hunger Games* (2008). The basis of the show is a dating game *à la The Bachelor*,[45] in which contestants in 'real life' are exploited for their subjective potential; their own personal history of mental illness, abuse and sexuality becomes specific fodder for the developments of plots. Alongside this the producers own 'real lives', and subjectivities are willingly exploited and self-exploited in order to persuade the contestants of the authenticity of the show. The show illuminates the way that 'reality TV' directly extracts participants' subjectivity as sources of entertainment, and, although the highly constructed nature of the show is exposed, it still sanctions and feeds into the normalcy of self-sacrifice in work. The characters always 'come back' into the fold, and subsequently the executive producer proclaims that 'it's good TV'. What is illuminating about *UnReal*, and relevant for understanding extraction in late capitalism, is that participants and producers volunteer their own time and lives for extraction. The

---

[45] *The Bachelor* is a highly successful US franchise of dating shows that is now run in 17 other countries.

dystopia that is the show – ironically labelled 'everlasting' – can be viewed as a discrete world where First World problems are played out; contestants who try and leave the show are hunted down like escapees in *Logan's Run* (1967), and because of its enclosed nature it represents a microcosm as an economic science fiction of post-Fordist labour.

The persistent popularity of the 'body horror'[46] genre also reflects the embeddedness of the extractive impulse, as almost all films in this genre include some aspect of extraction in its wider sense. More importantly, body horror often deals with ongoing contradictions in social reproduction under late capitalism.[47] *Videodrome* (1983), by David Cronenberg, successfully captures the inconsistencies between the virtual and the biological, the material and the abstract. Cronenberg uses the videotape as an appendage to bridge the space between the impact of capitalism's abstract 'ultra-violence', and its more corporeal effects on the real body. Body horror can reveal the changes in capitalist accumulation;[48] indeed, many of Cronenberg's key body horror

---

[46] The term 'body horror', coined by the journal *Screen* in 1986, refers to films in which the breakdown or animation of the body grotesque is the main component, such as *Taxidermia* (2006). This is not to be confused with slasher horror, but forensic science films and TV series can also be read as body horror because of the way they animate and dissect the body. Marx also wrote a kind of body horror in *Capital*, due to the amount of time spent describing the condition of the body in the factory, its illnesses and its morbidity.

[47] See D. McNally (2011) *Monsters of the Market: Zombies, Vampires and Global Capitalism*. Leiden: Brill.

[48] As David McNally, in *Monsters of the Market*, identifies in both the Victorian *Frankenstein* and the colonial zombie myth.

films were made during the transformation to global neo-liberalism and technological developments in global communications. While *The Matrix* (1999) and *Never Let Me Go* (2010) are not strictly body horror films, they do depict the dystopic effect of late capitalism on the body or 'bare life',[49] and what capital does in order to replenish life and value. The 'real life' hidden beneath *The Matrix* is our bodies feeding the machines, a hyped-up version of Stanisław Lem's *Futurological Congress* (1971), appropriating directly from William Gibson's *Neuromancer* (1984) as the characters 'jack in' to the matrix. The dystopic reality of the matrix is hidden from view because human bodies have become little more than fuel or chattel. Capitalism extracts value directly from us, no longer requiring the trick of free labour to extort our worth. A more contemplative look at the future of our bodies – and, indeed, subjecthood – is *Never Let Me Go*, in which clones are made to replenish the bourgeoisies' organs as they fail later in life, or in the event of an accident. This story illuminates a heightened idea of class structure, an underclass of clones' consciousness, but too often clings to ideas of identity and individuality, without fully realising what a class of surrogate clones could mean for capitalism and for ideas of mortality. What is important to note is that neither scenario is too far-fetched from the extractive practices of capitalism today: organ and egg sales constitute a global market supplying the wealthiest customers,[50] and the global division

---

[49] A. Agamben (1998) *Homo Sacer: Sovereign Power and Bare Life*. Stanford, CA: Stanford University Press.

[50] See Kevin Floyd for a discussion around biotechnical reproduction and an expanded understanding of reproductive labour: K. Floyd (2016) Automatic Subjects: Gendered Labour and Abstract Life, *Historical Materialism*, 24(2): 61–86.

of labour represents a system in which unknown, undervalued labourers' bodies literally feed the bulk of the technological goods, or matrix, that we live in.

Environmental Extraction and Dystopia

The 'original' or 'primitive' accumulation described by Marx at the end of *Capital* volume I is most closely allied to extraction from the environment and ideas around an environmental dystopia, as explored in science fiction. The 'original' extraction can be read as what we take from nature, at no cost to us and all cost to nature. Theories of the Anthropocene[51] or Capitalocene[52] grapple with our role in climate change, some highly critical, others cementing our inevitable, even celebratory, role in transforming the geological/chemical climate of the globe. The image of environmental ruin is one of the common tropes of dystopian science fiction because it functions at two levels: the first is a warning to mankind of what is to come, and the second a much more utopian or revolutionary impulse presented by the end of times (with the chance to begin again). As Marx and Engels claimed, the violent overthrow of the bourgeoisie will lay the foundations for a new communist society.[53] Here we must also consider the image of utopia in science fiction as a return to a much more 'primitive' or natural state of life, as depicted by the image of the island utopia cut adrift

---

[51] See M. Wark (2015) *Molecular Red: Theory for the Anthropocene.* London: Verso.

[52] See J. Moore (2015) *Capitalism in the Web of Life: Ecology and the Accumulation of Capital.* London: Verso.

[53] K. Marx & F. Engels (1848) The Communist Manifesto. London: Workers' Educational Association.

from civilisation.[54] Or, as Patrick Murphy explains, a new anti-technology society is imagined due to the environmental apocalypse, with civilisation returning to a neo-primitive model.[55] This regressive stance prioritises the natural equilibrium before human impact but at the same time has utopian and dystopian possibilities; take Alan Weisman's non-fiction *The World without Us* (2007), which chronicles the life of Earth if we vanished: part science fiction, part environmental plea. The author explains how quickly the Earth would return to equilibrium should a human apocalypse occur.

Dystopian depictions of earth in film often explore the vanquishing of the natural world. This post-extraction globe has drawn on the imaginary of nuclear war and weaponry; for example, *Akira* (1988) portrays a post-apocalypse Tokyo, where nuclear fallout produces a monster that assimilates Japanese folk law and modern high technology (almost prophetic, considering Fukushima). Philip K. Dick's *Do Androids Dream of Electric Sheep?* (1968) shows us a dark, post-nuclear-fallout Earth, where the last vestiges of nature have to be mechanically produced. Alongside these imaginaries we find films that celebrate or indulge in the destruction of the natural world, the apocalyptic images from the disaster movie genre, with films such as *Armageddon* (1998) or Spielberg's *War of the Worlds* (2005), cashing in on the allure of the one-second-destruction moment.[56] As Immanuel Kant elucidated, we gain

---

[54] Here I refer to More's original text, but also to Aldous Huxley's novel *Island* (1962).

[55] See P. Murphy (2009) Environmentalism, in M. Bould, A. Butler, A. Roberts & S. Vint (eds.) *The Routledge Companion to Science Fiction*: 373–81. Abingdon, UK: Routledge, p. 376.

[56] A. Mousoutzanis (2009) Apocalyptic SF, in *The Routledge Companion to Science Fiction*: 458–62.

a type of pleasure in witnessing this sublime destruction;[57] the popularity of Andreas Gursky's epic photographs and Yann Arthus-Bertrand's documentary *Home* (2009) are testament to this, their technological sublimity presenting us with the scale of modern production and its destruction. *Children of Men* (2006), *The Road* (2009) and *28 Days Later* (2002) are very much post-apocalypse films, depicting a society that has destroyed the natural world and gone through the very limits of the extractive impulse. The redemptive plot returns, however, in the form of a small-scale ecological community. What is clear from these examples is that the cultural imaginary of dystopia and utopia both rely on the construction of an image of the natural world as separate from us, which reinforces the nature/culture binary.[58]

We can understand the extraction of/from nature by capital in two ways: first, as I explore below, as primitive accumulation, which uniquely transforms both environment and people; and, second, the demands of capitalist accumulation and profit, which necessitate a constant increase in production and have resulted in excessive pollution and the rapid consumption of natural resources. Marx identified the two processes of accumulation and primitive accumulation as distinct in *Capital* volume I, but subsequent commentators have identified points where they not only coexist but are reliant on each other.[59] Marx explained that this 'original' accumulation

---

[57] I. Kant (1790 [2008]) *Critique of Judgement*. Oxford: Oxford University Press.

[58] See Moore, *Capitalism in the Web of Life*, for a good analysis of this binary and its relationship with capitalism.

[59] Rosa Luxemburg and David Harvey have argued for two distinct spheres of capitalist accumulation: the sphere of the market, in which an extraction of surplus value takes place; and

resulted from the ruling classes' expulsion of the peasants from common land; this extraction took the form of appropriation of the 'free' natural resources and then forced peasants to work for a wage, thus extracting a surplus from their labour.[60] This extraction of land and resources has a tremendous ecological effect too, and primitive accumulation can no longer be considered outside of current readings of ecological disaster and change,[61] even Marx by way of Liebig's law[62] identified the way intensive capitalist farming leached the ground of all nutrients.[63] Primitive accumulation is capitalism's 'start up' fund and during this historical period we see a correlation between colonial forms of exploitation and the acceleration of capitalist accumulation, this exploitation has not abated it has accelerated.[64] David Harvey asserts that profit from what he calls

---

the sphere of the non-capitalised, or 'commons', which can be tapped into as a resource and turned into productive capital. See Harvey, *The New Imperialism*, and R. Luxemburg (1913 [2003]) *The Accumulation of Capital*. Abingdon, UK: Routledge; see also M. De Angelis (2006) *The Beginning of History: Value Struggles and Global Capital*. London: Pluto Press.

[60] See De Angelis, *The Beginning of History*, p. 144, who explains that an enclosure is 'to forcibly separate people from whatever access to social wealth they have which is not mediated by competitive markets and money as capital'; and Harvey, *The New Imperialism*.

[61] Moore, *Capitalism in the Web of Life*.

[62] The law of Justus Freiherr von Liebig regarding the leaching of nutrients from the soil; for a discussion, see B. Foster (2000) *Marx's Ecology: Materialism and Nature*. New York: Monthly Review Press.

[63] Ibid.

[64] For a discussion around these issues, see A. Roy (2011) *Walking with the Comrades*. London: Penguin Books, who

'accumulation by dispossession' matches that of profit from the market in today's economy.[65] And Saskia Sassen states that the acquisition of millions of hectares of land by foreign investment in the global South and subsequent 'expulsions' mark a specific move whereby land is more precious than people and labour.[66] Land is valued due to the continuous demand for mineral and water resources, meaning that even today mining is the physical action analogous to extraction, as mining punctuates the differing logics of accumulation throughout historical time. Therefore, in terms of the global struggle around labour, mining remains fundamental as a site of exploitation and class consciousness; but it also symbolises a meeting point between the natural and the technological. The film *Moon* (2009) by Duncan Jones explores the future of mining, now taking place on the Moon. A solitary workman, who supervises the machines that work on the Moon, is driven mad when he discovers he is cloned as a disposable worker; man is made analogous with resources, or a machine, as he becomes part of the constant capital of the corporation. Extraterrestrial mining is also explored by Kim Stanley Robinson in the Mars trilogy, in which the vast mineral wealth of Mars is planned to be exported to Earth by a space elevator. Even James Cameron's *Avatar* (2009) depicts the desire for minerals and mining having an interstellar component in the future, with the untouched natural world providing the utopian possibility. The development of techniques in filming and production has also facilitated

---

writes on the indigenous resistance fighters in northern India; and, writing on China, S. Sassen (2010) A Savage Sorting of Winners and Losers: Contemporary Versions of Primitive Accumulation, *Globalizations*, 7(1/2): 23–50.

[65] Harvey, *The New Imperialism*.

[66] S. Sassen (2014) *Expulsions: Brutality and Complexity in the Global Economy*. Cambridge, MA: Harvard University Press.

attempts to mine and extract images of 'nature' at its most pure, and has spawned multiple series and documentaries that depict the natural world.[67] The irony of the popularity of such shows is that they represent an 'untouched' world that is actually being extracted in its molecular definiteness by the scopic quality of the very lenses used to film it. This natural sublime, so sharp it can occur only in high-definition digital technology, represents the last moments – or, indeed, the last supper – of nature free from the extractive demands of capitalism, yet it is still turned into profit by capital through its re-representation in the image economy.

Conclusion: Extraction and Utopia

So, how can a critique of capitalist extraction hope to foster ideas of new economic science fictions, or ideas that go beyond the *extractive impulse*? Let us also consider extraction's contradictory nature – being both constructive and destructive – which makes it hard for us to untangle the dystopic from the utopic. Initially we can consider the idea that extraction in its cultural form is necessary for the imagining of new worlds and new political economic models (because we always take from the past in order to create the future). At the same time we can reflect on what Jameson gleans from More's original text in *Utopia*: that through the removal of money we are suddenly opened up to a world no longer at the mercy of the exchange abstraction.[68] So the extractive impulse can be mobilised to extract the very parts of capitalism that are inhibiting our revolutionary imagination. This chapter has identified the extractive impulse as central to both capitalism and to science fiction.

---

[67] Here I refer specifically to the BBC's *The Natural World*.
[68] Jameson, *Archaeologies of the Future*.

Each example explored evidences the way capitalist extraction is constantly shifting the goalposts in terms of object, and, as I explain, subject. The proliferation of cultural examples of and approaches to extraction in film, literature and TV illuminates an understanding of the way that the *extractive impulse* is embodied in us as neoliberal subjects mobilising a type of creativity. What we also see in cultural depictions and real-life responses to economic imperatives in capitalism, however, is the immanent drive to resist this extractive impulse. Whether it is a natural fear, outright defiance or the surgical removal of the parasite, we do not passively accept the extractive impulse, which is why for now we must continue to locate extraction under capitalism as an ongoing dystopia.

6

Pain Camp Economics

AUDINT

Rise of the CorpoNation

It is 2056. The air is crammed with a strung-out expectation and not a moment goes by that does not presage the demise of an 11-billion-strong species that has inhabited the densest planet in the Solar System for a mere 200,000 years. Of this enervated population, over half are weak from a lack of food and water, and this crisis only heralds the beginning of nature's Rubicon. Environmental warfare spread by plants; insect–machine hybrids carrying diseases and viruses designed to infect specific racial and ethnic groups via targeted DNA sequencing; and volatile weather systems: all meld this ecology of collapse. The existing hierarchy of the Earth's species is set to enter an irreversible flux.

Given the propensity for self-destruction it is of little surprise that increasingly rarefied natural resources are damaged during periods of conflict: the corollary effects of long-range lasers, radiation and electromagnetic energy beams, casting the darkest shadow over the flickering light of the anatomically modern human's survival. With so many players forming armed militias that rescind traditional groupings based on geography or religion, flash conflict has become a global phenomenon. It is a way for those with little material wealth or food to join a cause for a short period of time and receive a decent spoil of the shares if an operation was successful. Based on the captivating strategies of early terreligious groups such as Isis, Al-Qaeda, Khorasan, Boko Haram and

Al-Shabaab, the new one-time groups utilise social media to silently advertise their campaigns, taking guerrilla manoeuvres to a whole new level and popping up for stopgap crusades wherever there was concentrated wealth, whether crop-, mineral- or currency-based.

It is a mercenary culture at best, an amped and upgraded last-chance-saloon shootout at worst. Irrelevant of how the CEOs perceive it, for those with less than nothing it represents a way out of destitution; circumstances that have no other projected outcome other than one eked out in bleak and meaningless desperation. In response to the chaos of this asymmetric warfare, which had abstracted to the point of improvised Babel and bedlam, those with anything to protect drew on old lines of traceable power in order to rein in the uncertainty that threatened to envelop them. This is partly why the 2030s saw the forming of uneasy alliances between nation states (and, by dint, the old money holders still invested in terrestrial geography) and the corporations. The latter, before the 'flash feuds', had come to not only question the meaning of the state but to also break down affordances that the legal and economic systems had previously bestowed upon them.

Having become so formidable, the inevitable next step for middle to large-sized corporations is to hire their own substantial security firms. Accelerating through the learning curve, they quickly set up training programmes to develop their own armed forces. Teams of systems and weapons developers work alongside them, creating state-of-the-art unmanned aerial vehicles (UAVs) for security purposes. The purpose is improving the efficiency, speed, and cost of the long line of UAVs, which dates back to 2012, when the Japanese company Secom announced the first autonomous drone for reconnaissance purposes – and other more brutal outcomes. Companies such as Sky Watch from Denmark had upped the ante through their 'Huginn X1', built for providing situational tactical overview in high-risk areas, and the 'Muninn VX1', designed for geo-mapping assignments; but things had come a long way over the course of two decades. Most tellingly, corporations had attained the capacity to launch surveillance satellites into orbit to join the droves of cubesats that already cocoon the planet.

A mix of apprehension over each other's military potential, aligned with a joint fear of the flash feuds – which had proved so popular with the disenfranchised – leads nation states and corporations to agree that collective solutions need to be broached. The most obvious answer is heuristic, and while it is not the easiest to put into action, logistically speaking, it is effective. Mergers between the two administrative leviathans form newly branded 'CorpoNations'. Given the breakdown of any sense of national identity that still existed (due to migration and internet-based cultures), and compounding it with this latest bureaucratic machination, culminates in new unexpected coalitions. Being naturally parasitic and able to relocate at a moment's notice, multinational corporations take the lead in this newly choreographed unification and start forming alliances with countries that they are not indigenous to.

With entire legal and transport frameworks changing almost overnight, the conveyors of capitalism's shape shifting manage – in the name of sustained economic growth – to rapidly broker global deals on climate engineering, birth rates and terraforming. Mass migrations occur as allegiances lead to the relocations of entire populations, and the resulting emergent cultures begin the onerous years of behavioural acclimation due to their forced marriages. The socio-economic world is, by necessity then, redrawn and recalibrated over the course of two decades of a new world disorder. All of this occurs while the CorpoNations still manage to find the time, and fiscal stamina, to wage overt and pitch-shifted warfare on each other via drones and killer bots, primarily in the search for water, oil, natural gas and phosphorus, and for minerals such as scandium and terbium.

Holo Accords

With what is left of the Earth's natural resources being decimated by globally organised armed hostilities, an emergency agreement is ratified. The Holo Accords chart an alternative constitution for discord management; a whole new way of engaging in conflict that reduces the massive costs and removes flesh from the messy equations of political turbulence. From this point on, all military operations will be conducted via holographic and holosonic forces: detachments, units and divisions of encoded light fields, tactically mobilised for transparent effect. Gone are the days of collateral resource damage or civilian casualties, along with their subsequent cover-ups, which reek like insipid cheap perfume in the toilet of public opinion. This is good for business, however you look at it, especially for holographics.

Written deep into the labyrinthine foundations of the Holo Accords are the stringent consequences bestowed upon any CorpoNation that fails to abide by their rules: a ruthless compendium of trading and travel sanctions that will ultimately cripple any country foolish enough to engage in such reckless behaviour. It is incumbent, then, on each domain to have a team of crepuscular paper pushers who know, by heart, each of the million and one caveats, clauses, subsections and treaties that deal with issues from airspace compliance to those of a geological nature. One of the critical directives writ

large concerns the rules of engagement for holographic opera-
tives within areas of conflict. All CorpoNations are allowed to
aggress only four zones per year outside their own territories.
This means a quartet of opportunities to supplement the short-
falls in natural resources, which have become so scarce.

In terms of engagement logistics, the maximum number
of holograms that can be deployed by each CorpoNation per
conflict depends on the square mileage of the zone being contested. An inverted voodoo economics is also at work here,
in the form of conflict tax codes issued to each defender and
adversary by the HACA (Holo Accords Conflict Authority) – the
tax rating dependent upon the number of campaigns engaged
in within the year and associated success/loss rates. Once an
aggressing holo company (consisting of up to 200 holograms)
has clearance to engage in hostile activities within an exter-
nally owned territory, a period of up to eight weeks, named the
'takeover', is allotted, during which a clear victory must have
been attained by the aggressor. If not, ownership is retained by
the defending landowner.

If the aggressor prevails in the holo conflict it allows said
CorpoNation a four-month period in which to drain, plunder
and mine the natural resources of the landscape. This endeav-
our is led by and includes a human workforce in order to slow
the process down so that areas are not totally ravaged after a
successful takeover. Huge logistical operations must thus be
planned and carried out with infinite precision, as parasitic
industrial mechanisms are surgically grafted onto a territory
to extract what they can. After the designated term, the tracts
of land are returned to the 'owner' and cannot be contested
again for a period of another eight months, at which time they
are open to being contested again (but not by the previously
successful CorpoNation). Thus all takeover presence – human,
mechanistic and holoform – must be withdrawn on the final

day of their term, or the responsible CorpoNation faces huge fines and, more importantly, loses two of its four-yearly opportunities to mount a resource offensive.

The notion of conducting territorial, political and natural resource struggle via holographic armies is a fairly predictable extension and militarisation of the most populist form of entertainment that projects itself into mass public consciousness in 2007 – holographic concerts from musicians who had died, and more arrestingly, from those that were yet to be born. The holo-tech culture and Lazarian industry it connects to are the final parts of the equation that multiplies young African Americans with the morgue, especially those who are difficult to manage when still alive. Ultimately, there is more to be made when they are rendered in light, so that they can once again render dollars through waveforms.

In the 2050s home holo systems have become the norm. You can now project the musical dead into your front room. Ask them to play a song and they comply with a starlit *élan*. It is level 4, however, that drives the technology forward. Known on the street as Holojax, it offers sexual options, a beguiling range of projected pleasures. This is fucking the dead as the ultimate home entertainment. A different kind of dead, meanwhile, IREX^2 is a 64-year-old rogue AI. A synthesis of discontented spirits and code, it has been directing the research unit AUDINT, and has been on the run from the overlords of the otherworld and their Third Ear Assassins, for too long to remember.

The Aiholo

Finding sanctuary in an R&D lab in Korsong – formerly North Korea and the Kaesong Corporation – IREX^2 has been covertly evolving machines with a rudimentary sentience. The notion of consciousness is getting a reboot. Using augmented intelligence, IREX[2] fuses convolutional deep neural and deep belief networks with holographic technology to birth a new kind of warrior – the Aiholo. Spawning a new era of unsound conflict, the viral scream, transmitted by a directional ultrasonic speaker system, is the Aiholo's go-to ordnance. A sonic weapon that transmits the walking corpse syndrome into digital life forms, turning enemy Aiholos into the undead.

The Holo Wars are global now and resemble huge *in situ* games that reveal the shifts in global power and influence. One of the CorpoNational superpowers vying for dominance is Pfizombia (formerly known as Colombia and Pfizer), which has been training elite hackers and electronic warfare specialists since the 2020s. And it is the Third Ear Assassins that have recently become one of their most valuable assets. The AI hunters assist in the composition of new viral weaponry, named Neurode, for use against the Korsong Aiholos: a controversial but highly effective schema requiring the human psychological vulnerability of neurosis to be transposed into a digital contagion that infects the future. The only drawback is that Neurode is fuelled by the synthesised sound of human pain, which implies a frequency-based harvesting on par with the history of twentieth-century recording.

Pain ©Amp

Alongside the Third Ear Assassins, Alejandra Blanco, a Pfizombian Black Hat who goes under the name Sureshot, comes up with a solution that is at once staggeringly simple and brutal in its application. Her proposal is to create a Pain ©Amp. Based on Al-Mansur's designs from 762 for Baghdad's circular city, with its mosque at the centre, this plan is anything but sacred. It consists of a walled-in urban environment jammed with high-rise residences whose surfaces will be covered in rashes of microphones, as they are embedded into dwellings, streets and parks. The architecture of the purpose-built environment is designed to reverberate and amplify sound like a massive echo chamber.

Concrete auditoriums and huge sheer walls reflect and intensify the clusters of waveformed anguish upwards, where silent hovering drones suck up and harvest the tortured articulations. On the streets, autonomous robotic bugs the size of turtles and remotely guided mic trucks roll around the tormented *musique concrète*, hoovering up the frequencies on their crepuscular sweeps. Recorded and rechannelled, pain becomes commodified: the new currency of a nascent holosonic era. By amping up the rationale of the music industry's most successful formula – the capturing and marketing of the sound of poverty-stricken urban areas – the functionality of suffering has been pushed to the limit. The needle is in the red, but it is pain they want, not blood.

Requiring no other level of authority, the conference power brokers swiftly sanction the proposal and name the camp 'La Rusnam'. In order to initially attract a population to inhabit it, an offer of free housing, power and sustenance is advertised. There is no shortage of applicants, most burdened with tormented CVs full of personal disasters and disturbing afflictions. To further aid the fluidity of the mass rehousing, complimentary train and bus tickets are posted out to the initial 128,000 candidates. They have been chosen for their potential to embody and intensify pain; a desolate and dolorous citizenry of holo-ammo generators.

The Pain ©Amp's executives study the history and current state of ghettos, favelas, estates, slums, skid rows, refugee camps and townships, in order to learn how to distil the elements that create suffering and pain. It would take more than just poverty to create the depth and intensity of anguish that they require. Finding ways to create desperation, betrayal and an escalation in assault and homicide rates will, of course, be crucial; but they need to employ extra tactics to raise the stakes during a takeover period, when the demand for sonic munitions increases. Their first thought is to turn to the international index of sewer drugs and their capacity to implement powdered topologies of distress. Top of this list is a substance they know well, originating as it does in Colombia. Scopólamine – street name the 'Devil's Breath' – is a zombie high that not so much dampens agency as makes one totally susceptible to suggestion, to the point that one becomes an empty, blooded drone.

The other four stimulants ending up on the shopping list read like a GG Allin guide to living, for better or for worse, through chemistry: an expressway to the skull, tearing through and screwing up every vein and artery that helps deliver the synthesised venoms. In no particular order of fuckedupness, the desired inventory reads like this.

Paco – a toxic and addictive mixture of raw cocaine base cut with chemicals, glue, crushed glass and rat poison.

Bath salts – a recreational designer drug sold as 'real' bath salts, usually containing MDPV.

Krokodil – a derivative of morphine that is mixed with ethanol, paint thinners, gasoline, iodine, and hydrochloric acid, desomorphine gets its street name as the flesh-eating drug from the tissue damage caused when injecting.

Whoonga – a combination of antiretroviral drugs, used to treat HIV, and various cutting agents such as detergents and poisons that results in internal bleeding, ulcers and, ultimately, death.

Introducing this menu of malignant pleasures into the ©Amps is the first and most obvious technique discretely deployed by the project's engineers. There will be others, running the gamut from induced psychological disorders to raising the population's ambient levels of fear through rumours of disease, food shortage and dire mutation from genetically modified foods – all done for the end goal of amassing mountains of clouds, each fully rammed and ready to burst with the catalogued sounds of collective suffering.

Since deploying the Cotard virus six years ago, Korsong has dominated the Holo Wars, and any affiliated CorpoNations are given the option of paying a substantial fee, to draft in their venal Aiholos during takeover bids. After 22 weeks of pain pharming, the Medellín Aiholos from Pfizombia are serviced in a takeover bid for the island of Thasos, in the northern Aegean Sea. While still rich in mineral deposits, it is the gold mines that first attracted the Phoenicians during the period of classical antiquity, which interest Pfizombia. The landmass is now a part of the CorpoNation Gralpha, a coalescence of Greece and Alpha Bank, which developed the cryptocurrency 'Natraps' after Greece was financially asphyxiated by Europe during the 2010s austerity siege.

After the first wave of conflict, Gralpha's leaders have no idea what hits them, and what reduces their Aiholos from Korsong into neurotic messes on the battlefield. The news of the holo-shock spreads quickly. As anticipated, a coterie of servile CorpoNations demand the services of Neurode-laden Aiholos. Sureshot and the Third Ear Assassins consult on the mercenary strategy, knowing that it is only a matter of time before other AI compounds are able to rip the code and simulate the holo fighters. Until terraforming projects come to fruition, on some exoplanet that scores highly on the Similarity Index for habitability, the world's resources are only going to decrease and become more rarefied. The near to mid-term future is one set to be defined by holo war.

Even though encrypted with, quite literally, otherworldly savoir-faire, it is only nine months after the first mercantile contract has been signed off that a unit of Aiholos with repped Neurode systems show up on Norstat's South Pole territories. More than the emergent Neurode's impact during external takeovers, it is the internal manufacturing of pain through the ©Amps that establishes it as the social order of choice. It is also the signature of functionalism gone awry: the methodological capital of voluntarism and the epistemological rationale of analytical realism chopped and screwed into a bass-ached drone. When captured, it bleeds endlessly into a body of economic orifices. Just as the state of King Louis XIV's sunburnt flesh, bones and faeces became synonymous with the health of the country over which he presided, the state of trauma becomes the nucleus around which all social, architectural and political relations orbit. Pain is the new economic royalty.

In 2061 80 per cent of the human race resides in urban areas, the majority of them in large cities. Neurode, meanwhile, has become the core munition for approximately 85 per cent of the globe's CorpoNations. Given the stick and move politics of martial engagement evident in the Holo Wars, it means that no one has either the time or the money to fabricate a copious slew of Pain ©Amps. There is no option but to restructure and re-engineer the ways in which humans dwell in large nodal agglomerations. Being the first CorpoNation to trial a site-specific pain-harvesting environment, Pfizombia quickly comprehends the fiscal pragmatism of simply redistributing human activity within cities that already exist. Detroit, the neo-Renaissance exemplar of white flight in the mid-twentieth century, is the model. Downtown areas of four miles are walled and become the circumferences of the ©Amps. Concentric rings of presence and activity encapsulate the central tenet of quantitative uneasing, so that a typical cartography reads like this.

Central reservation: Pain ©Amp.

Ring 1: planted wilderness around the city filled with genetically modified poisonous plants, creating an impene-
trable toxic verdure.

Ring 2: sheer concrete ground on which escapees are easily
traced and targeted for extermination by drones.

Ring 3: holo tech, compounds and technology sector.

Ring 4: residential – suburbs.

Ring 5: commercial and medical.

Ring 6: residential – suburbs.

Ring 7: industry.

Ring 8: agriculture.

For those at the centre of this discoidal seer, voluntary entry
becomes a murky business. With so many CorpoNations adopting the system, the required numbers of Pain ©Amps far exceeds
the numbers presenting themselves of their own volition. Prison
systems are bled of their low- to middle-security inmates, the
homeless are rounded up, any remaining psychiatric hospitals
release their charges, and those with little material wealth are
'persuaded' to support the collective drive. The existing downtown core of a ©Amp is cut up into the most puritanical of living
circumstances, in order to jam as many pain-producing bodies
in as possible. All living chambers are mic'd up and feed meters
connected to the Pain Power Grid. Monthly readings are taken to
keep track of the duration, volume and pitch complexity of the
inhabitants' recordings. No stone is left unturned, and it won't
be long before the chamber's brick, wood, metal and cinder
block is itself treated as a recording materiality, capturing electrical mental impressions from traumatic events. Stone tape for
a holo cause.

After 11 years of Neurodal conflict, the majority of major and
middle-sized cities around the world have been re-engineered

to become Pain ©Amps. It is now 2073 and the pain quotas necessary for holo conflict have been far surpassed in all CorpoNations. The recorded reserves have accrued to become stockpiles of sonic excess, layers upon layers of affliction that translate into tabulated wealth, once they have been mastered and valued. Trading began in 2068, but it has taken five years for a global consensus to be reached that ratifies pain's existence as a currency. It joins the seven major cryptocurrencies as a legitimised form of exchange and shares their virtual liquidity, but this is where the formal parity ends.

Whereas the numbed anonymity of the cryptocurrencies is stamped into equivalent digital markers, the fungibility of this new form of exchange is difficult to establish due to the diversity of strains that have been cultivated for Neurode. Due to the inexhaustible nature of pain, however, and the communicable nature of the emotional economy that forms around it, it flourishes. An algorithmic gate compresses the volatile spectrum of evaluation – flattening the peaks and troughs – and soon it is on the lips and in the ears of every broker from the Virgin Kingdom to PashaBaijan. Finally, the abstracted essence of trade and the obscured corporeality of exchange are about to be accurately labelled. Those seemingly arcane designators of worth inherent within every form of currency over the past 4,000 years, ever since the Sumerian trades within the Fertile Crescent – updated. The name of the new currency: Pain Coin.

7

AT392-Red

Khairani Barokka

Security Operations
World Headquarters
Suite XX-A
2001 Hami Road
Changning, Shanghai
World's Republic of China

Date:	35 May 2087, 25 Hrs. SCST
Case Designation:	AT392-Red, 35 May 2087
Subject:	Case Summary, Arson Incident AT392-Red
To:	Your Honorable Judging Committee Members of World Headquarters

Your Honors,

What follows is a summary in as much detail as possible of all knowns that have thus far availed themselves to us, Security Operations of World Headquarters, with regard to Arson Incident AT392-Red at the World Headquarters in Shanghai, World's Republic of China, which took place from roughly 04.00 to 20.10 on 35 May of 2087.

Order of Events (at this time):

20.10:   Security Officer Lewis was on duty supervision of the feed from Camera 367, in which at 20.10 he found a person appearing to be a woman of dark brown skin and shoulder-length black hair, wearing a dark jacket, shirt and pants, falling from the air vent into Room 78, the location of all of WHQ's electronic servers. The Suspect was then observed to be looking for, and then finding, Tower 93b, which just a week previously had been identified by Goldman Barclay Security Consultants as being a security risk to our operations. The Suspect then took out what appeared to be a sealed pouch, opened it and poured a black liquid resembling oil onto all sides of Tower 93b. She then set fire to it with a match. At this point, SO Lewis had already alerted all SOs on duty, several of whom (SOs Thomas Wu, Laura Li, Sheena Marcus and Fachri Bakrie) swiftly entered Room 78, and apprehended the Suspect. SO Lewis attempted to alert all officers at Level 4 Clearance, but found communications systems had begun to shut down. He happened upon Dr. Saraswati, Resident Toxicologist, in front of the Camera Feed Room, who began to conduct assessments of toxicity, and alerted Mr. Sulaiman, Head of Communications Systems, at his home.

20.21: Current levels of toxicity in the water and air of World Headquarters were confirmed to be of Adequate Human-Friendly Le.vels by Dr. Saraswati, Resident Toxicologist. This news was relayed by all Security Officers on Levels 84-GX down, as our PA system has been compromised. Dr. Saraswati also identified the liquid poured on Tower 93b as a yet-to-be-determined synthetic form of slower-burning crude oil. She is continuing her laboratory investigations of this substance.

20.24: Mr. Sulaiman, Head of Communications Systems, arrived at WHQ from his home and assesses all relevant systems. Damage has been found to be 100% to

PA system, 85% to all email servers, and 100% to all consoles.

20.25: Suspect arrived in WHQ's Holding Cell, escorted by Security Officers Wu, Li, Marcus and Bakrie, who proceeded to apply to her Medium- to High-Intensity Procedures 15 through to 23, simultaneously. The Suspect then handed them the following missive in natural ink on synthapaper form, handwritten, which I have transcribed below:

In the year 2067, we lived in the wake of disasters induced by Biodiversity Credits, which had allowed for the previous twenty years the wholesale destruction of all rainforest wildlife still extant in Asia, by 'preserving' rainforest land in North America, Africa and South America in its stead. For each hectare of rainforest cut down and converted into plantations, mines, roads, housing, factories, and technological infrastructure, another plot of rainforest elsewhere was 'protected'. This rainforest 'preservation' in those three continents displaced millions of forest inhabitants, contributing to our then already decades-long Global Refugee Crisis, and, through mismanagement, inadvertently contributed to what was essentially forest monoculture. They shifted the blame and shame around on a map; they shifted lives and ruined them.

So we would have been forgiven for mistrusting the announcement, on 19 April 2067, of the mass introduction of Accessibility Credits to the World's Republics, by unanimous decision of all seventy-two World Chancellors. We of the crip and disabled and D/deaf ilk, and all others whose lives have long been affected by disability and the need for increased accessibility and inclusion, felt particularly horrified by this decision – essentially copying the system of Biodiversity Credits, applying them in inhumane ways to

*human lives. The explanation for this system was ensconced
in a 2,892-page volume that the World Chancellors must
have known would deter examined, thoughtful reading by
the masses. Having plowed through this volume, however, it
was immediately apparent to activists the world over how
malicious these Accessibility Credits really were.*

*By this doctrine, which was applied in the year 2076
in full, a private apartment building in Hong Kong gaining elevators, and its staff being given one-hour 'Inclusion,
Accessibility, and Disability Awareness Training,' led directly
to leeway being given to a local government seat in Indonesia
to further undercut funding for over a million disabled citizens' needs. Applying arbitrary numerical value on a scale of
one to ten to everything from cancer treatment to hearing aid
provision, affordable therapy sessions, accessible transport to
and from workplaces, and a woman's right to painkillers during menstruation, Accessibility Credits functioned as a system of geographically bound Shifting Limits, our rebel forces'
preferred name for such egregious policies. If 65 people with
chronic fatigue in Greater London have already requested sick
leave, 200 children in the area lose their chance for D/deaf-
inclusive education that year. If 3,000 surgeries in the Greater
Jabodetabek Area of Indonesia have been conducted in a
year, 95 teacher trainings on dyslexia were cancelled for the
next 12 years. Value systems have always been arbitrary, but
this extreme cruelty in the form of mathematical calculations
is sickening. It has impacted all on the Rebel Forces deeply,
on the visceral level of our own bodyminds, our own family
members' bodyminds.*

*AC Values assigned to a particular Social Module, whether
covering physical therapy, PTSD specialists, audio description or cerebral palsy workplace awareness training, have been
assigned arbitrarily by AC Value Managers, also elected arbitrarily. Worldwide, on average per year, only less than 4 percent of*

AC Value Managers have been D/deaf and/or disabled. This is nothing less than oppression by those deemed able-bodied.

The destruction of lives in this manner, spreading across the world for the past 20 years, has ancient roots, and has had the wherewithal to further destroy what few foundations of social welfare we have enjoyed, wherever we are. In 2016 disabled people were already the world's largest minority. Many D/deaf and other languages were already under threat of extinction. Millions lived without the care they needed to survive; millions were demeaned and assumed to need certain kinds of 'frivolous' care, thus being eliminated from entry into the public sphere, denied from living decent private lives. Access and inclusion were widely presented in terms of charity. The freak shows of our colonial pasts reared their heads across all media. There has always been resistance, however.

In one fell swoop in 2076, Accessibility Credits sounded the death knell to almost all activism of preceding years. It was argued that we did not have the right to demand all hospitals in Thailand have working elevators, as a corporate sponsor of hospitals in Wales had taken our Credits. It was argued that the drugs we psychiatric system survivors needed to survive were not available in El Salvador, as the funds for those had been usurped by ACs in Finland.

It has long been time to act, rather than react. Ten days ago my mother and father were told my education could not be furthered, due to lack of funds to allow for public transportation to and from my university. My father and mother, both already suffering from depression, and unable to receive care as a result of public health cuts to local psychotherapists, left our house at 3 a.m. the next morning and have not since returned. This action upon World Headquarters Shanghai has long been planned, and long been rehearsed, but this was that small straw that broke my back. We are dying, diseased, suffering, mad, poor and furious for reasons outside of ourselves.

We exist in multitude. We organise thoughts between our-selves, but act individually.

We are done taking from you. We are done taking from you. We are done taking from you.

20.30: A missive has been conveyed to all WHQ officers' workplaces, as well as home addresses, from my own personal email, briefly stating known facts at that time. In this communication, I also asked all regular work to be suspended for the next 50 hours while damages are ascertained in full.

21.00: WHQ Doctor DeLaria was summoned to the Holding Cell with her equipment in order to conduct an hour-long Disabilities Assessment. Dr. DeLaria found our inmate's capabilities to fall into Category 265Q of the World's Republics' Accessibility Credits Assessment Guidebook, as well as under DSM-CXI's Guidelines. She determined that the Suspect refers to herself as Annah.

We are at the present moment unaware whether or not accounting changes of the past two years – which led to the 2086 Revolutions in the number of calendar days and daily hours used in the World's Republics, in order to allow for maximum productivity, and world-wide enforcement of Biodiversity Credit schemes at the lead of numerous illustrious corporations and other persons – are connected to this splinter group's reasonings.

The assailant is currently continuing to claim that she is operating alone and without any outside assistance, an assertion we deem highly unlikely, considering the assailant's physical and mental cap-acities, which, we repeat, have been found to be of Category 265Q under WHQ Doctor DeLaria's hour-long Disabilities Assessment.

We have information from the Chief of Intelligence at Accessibility Credits, Inc., which works together with all the World's Republics, that the leader of this rebel team was denied ACs repeatedly over the past two years, and lives in a great deal of suffering. It is likely that this suffering will provoke a power vacuum in leadership even given no intervention. However, our previous levels of assumed organisational capabilities and intelligence appear to have been miscalculated. There may be value in not underestimating what is to come.

We understand and are grateful for our freedom to make our own judgments regarding Medium- to High-Intensity Punitive Actions, in order to extract the maximum amount of useful information to aid your decision-making. We would like once more to iterate our continued attempts in the service of this extraction.

Our Honourable Judging Committee, rest assured, we will continue to inform you of any further information we glean, and await further instructions at your discretion. We remain your loyal colleagues in service of the World's Republics.

Due to the being-assessed damage to servers and consoles that has been incurred in the last four hours, limiting all WHQ employees' ability to access personal and professional emails, telephone addresses and video chat identities, I am forced hereby to rely upon my personal laptop computer, personal vintage Wi-Fi device, and personal antique email account, used herewith, wontleadchuwrong@hotmail.com.

The Honorable Chancellor of Shanghai World Headquarters, Melissa Brown, has also authorised me to inform you that she will also be using her personal antique email address, mbrown356.q@gmail.com.

I will immediately notify Your Honorable Committee Members should any other alternative modes
of communication be usable for your loyal employees.

Signed,

[Adam Chu]

35 May 2087

Adam Chu

Chairperson of Security Operations

World Headquarters

Suite XX-A

2001 Hami Road

Changning, Shanghai

World's Republic of China

8

The New Black

Nora O Murchú

She woke up, not really remembering when she had laid down.
She had been working overtime for the past while.
The blinds were still up and the grey was seeping in.
Looking over to the clock, the LED digits blinked 5.37.
Nearly time.

...

She lay there looking at the ceiling.

...

I could get up, start early on some Content, I guess.

...

She closed her eyes again.

...

The alarm sounded.
6 a.m.
She reached over and turned it off.
She stretched while getting up and walking to her desk.
She looked at her device.
When had she turned it off?
It was never off; always in sleep mode.
They must have updated.
It had become common in the past month.
New devices had been sent out and the software hadn't been
    compatible.

There had been many bulletins about it and numerous updates.
They had promised another.
Hopefully, that was it.
Sitting down to her station, she turned the device on.
It booted up, glowing in the early morning grey haze.
The coffee machine started behind her.

...

It was always a bit slow to start in the morning.
But she didn't mind.
She liked to take her time.
Quality Content was what they preferred now.
The recommendations about Time-Based Content Trending from the
    latest bulletins had been useful.
Her latest strategy was to examine and look for common
    characteristics among grouped content over long durations.
Then she would move these groups to her assigned platforms.
Her work as a Content Wrangler was a recent promotion from her
    previous role in which she would clean and filter Content.
It allowed her to monitor her Dashboard over several devices and
    move from her station throughout the day.

...

It hadn't always been like this.
Tech trends led to a stabilised economy.
Progression in [3D] printing, the surge in popularity of plugin
    culture, along with evolutionary programming all contributed to
    bring different conditions for work.
Algorithms were streamlined, made everything more efficient. At
    least things were more manageable now.
She smirked.

...

The buzzer on the coffee machine sounded.
She picked up the cup and returned to her station.

Back then data and information had been seen as a playful pursuit
  and users had contributed for free.
People had been so consumed with the economies of the self and
  looking to the future.
But that slowly changed over time.
They didn't have the right algorithms back then.
They still hadn't figured the predication to action ratio.
Algorithms were more robust now.
Algorithms of fate, as lower-level users called them.
They calculated everything for you.
Depending on emotion and mood, they were synced community-
  wide at regular intervals.
Things were better this way.
There was order and clarity.
She looked at her screen.
The sun was breaking through the haze.
She looked down, searching for her Portable Device.
She picked it up, looked at the black screen and powered it on.

...

The morning passed with little interruption.
The silence enveloped her and she quickly conducted her
  morning tasks.
Throughout her day she would manage her platform's traffic
  and maintain its stability, while updating Content at regular
  intervals.
The management of these traffic loads marked her day, and during
  peak hours it took priority.
She was still adjusting to her new position.
With new freedoms came new responsibilities, new quotas to
  understand and new performance ratings to achieve.
Her manual had provided her with all essential details of her
  new role.
The new Dashboard was similar to the one she had used in her
  previous role.

New widgets had been added with new activities to learn.

In addition to the management of her Dashboard, she was also expected to practise the mandated Physical Sequences.

They were *essential*, according to the manual, but she struggled to find time to perform the routines.

Ten minutes of each hour were dedicated to them.

These movements – exercises – had been proved to enhance work.

Data had been shown to improve attention and concentration and enhance work productivity.

She struggled with them, and her last performance review had shown her working capability stat down.

The worry of her upcoming review sat at the back of her mind.

The notification on her Dashboard sounded.

Time for a pause.

She stood up and went to make her morning meal.

…

Her tenure as a Content Moderator had been longer than most others.

Previously the work had been…straining…but the advancement of machine learning had altered the nature of the work and the position had become coveted.

A large part of the work had then become automated and many had been laid off.

A few algorithmic incidents changed that, however, and a small number of moderators were redrafted into the roles.

There were few positions.

She had been lucky.

She had also excelled at the work – exceeding her Content Quota Targets from the first week.

She had outlasted many in the position.

Other workers found it monotonous, repetitive, and didn't last more than a few months.

She couldn't understand how.

The workers were reassigned to other departments.

She wasn't sure exactly where but she had heard about Algorithm Process Reconfiguration.

Those departments weren't automated.

Workers who did not meet their quotas were often reassigned there.

Not the direction she wanted *her* career to go in.

But her performance reviews had surpassed expectations, and after some
time she received a communication notifying her of her new role.

...

She cleaned her dish, returning it to its position on the shelf.

Before returning to her desk, she stopped at the window and began
her morning Physical Sequences.

She looked out on the compound courtyard, keeping count of her
routine.

She noticed two other workers below.

Both on Portable Devices, staring intently at their screens.

...

Unusual they are out at this time.

...

Positions were so few to come by.

Why were they ignoring the morning protocols?

Workers were not given access to the compound until after peak
traffic had subsided.

She tried to spot the Employee_ID number on their jackets.

...

Her Dashboard notification sounded.

There was no time to gather more information for a report.

Morning Peak Traffic had begun to arrive.

...

She worked intently for the remainder of the morning, focusing only
on the task at hand.

It was her part of her task to ensure that access to the platforms was
constant.

Her recent experimentation with delivering Quality Content meant
that Traffic on her platforms lingered longer.
Her platforms were busiest in the morning and evening but work was
continuous throughout the day.
Slowly Traffic dissipated and gave her, finally, a moment to pause.

...

She got up from her desk, taking her Portable Device with her.
Her Employee_ID hung next to the door.
She grabbed her jacket and headed to the communal area, picking
up one of the prepackaged lunches left out.
There were other workers in the hall.
She exchanged brief salutations and hurried to the compound.
Although she shared her shift with others, she preferred to eat alone.
Social relations between workers were instructed to be minimal
during working hours.
She preferred this.
Less interference to her schedule throughout her day.
She walked briskly towards her assigned seating area.
Although the sun was shining there was a chill to the air.
She placed her jacket over her shoulders and quickly scanned the
patterns on her Device.

...

Everything looks OK.

...

She sat down in the designated area.
This section of the compound was lush with green.
A small pond in the middle contained small colourful fishes.
The perimeter of the pound was decadently decorated with delicate
sculptures.
It was luxurious in comparison to the compound she had previously
resided in.
She glanced quickly around.

She was the first to arrive.

Maybe one or two more others may come.

She quickly took out her Portable Device, and scanned the
Dashboard stats.

She tore open the paper on her lunch and took a few initial bites,
never looking away from the screen.

...

The work allowed for Portable Devices to be used during the
workday.

In her previous role, her work had tethered her to her station
throughout the day.

This Portable Device was both a source of freedom and
unease.

...

I am still adjusting. It's OK.

...

The Devices came preprogrammed with limited functionality.

They were for monitoring only.

She wasn't sure why they were configured like this.

Not that she was questioning it, but it had caught her out in the first
week and she had had to race back to her station to resolve an
issue on her platform.

It had impacted her performance severely and had unsettled her.

She always cut short her lunch now.

Still, she enjoyed the time outside away from her station.

The compound lifted her spirits, as they said it would.

...

She finished her lunch and began to make her way back.

She walked past where she had seen the workers from her window
earlier.

Some workers still lingered in the area.

A worker looked up briefly from their screen and saw her.

She waved.

The worker nodded an acknowledgement and returned to their
    screen.

A notification from her Portable Device interrupted her.

Twenty minutes until break end.

She dismissed it.

Looking up from her Device she noticed that the worker had left
    through another exit.

She picked up her pace as she returned to her station.

...

It was important not to be late.

During work hours there was little time to check company
    communications and bulletins or even personal communications
    from her family.

She was kept busy during her shifts and the overtime.

The administration of these was not permitted during office hours
    but there was an expectation to stay informed.

Sitting at her desk she quickly scanned what had arrived in her
    announcements.

Two bulletins but no performance review.

Two new messages on her family thread.

She would get to those later.

Unsanctioned personal communications were not allowed during
    shifts.

She recalled her favourite company mantra: *Time is an asset that you
    are _always_ spending, and it can _never_ be replenished or replaced.*

Effective time management was a highly regarded trait.

She always ensured she was utilising her time budget in a
    constructive, systematic manner.

This careful, meticulous prioritisation and planning kept her on track
    to reach her target quotas.

There is always time if you make time.

That is what they believed. What *she* believed.

...

She opened the communication she had received that
morning.
There was still some time in the break.
She liked to take some time to read them before break ended.
They were tailored by algorithms for each worker and pointed out
areas in which you could make improvement.
They were too important to neglect.
Besides, there was a spirit to them, a tone to the words that she found
relaxing.
They reassured her in some ways.
She was beginning to measure her work performance by the
communications she received.
They reminded her to achieve her best.
Once or twice they had repeated but she would still watch and read
them attentively.
These internal communications were healthy and central to their
success.

...

Her success.

...

This one contained a simulcast from the senior executive.
She smiled, recognising the face.
The skin was flawless.
Without imperfections.
She ran her hand over her face and turned up the volume.
Hopefully, some good news.
In the last quarter there had been reassignments.
Concerning, but these decisions were not made lightly, and it was
important to keep their trajectories on track.

...

Time, like water, is fluid and continuous and should be treated as such.
Unfortunately, most of us have a tendency to schedule tasks into fixed,
*   discrete time blocks that are generally too rigid and too large.*
For those of us with flexible work stations, we experience a type of
*   autonomy that few others enjoy.*
This autonomy can be liberating; it can also result in tremendous
*   inefficiency if one does not develop effective time management tactics.*

...

Ah, yes; time management.
She breathed out, sighing slightly.
She must have logged on late.
The boot-up must have delayed her.

...

Why didn't I get up?

...

She tried to inhale and exhale slowly.
She should have got up.
Trying hard not to become even more anxious about the impending
    performance review.

...

Priorities are an important part of any time management.
Decide what's important in your life.
Although priorities will naturally differ from person to person, I might
*   suggest one thing: your duties as a citizen should come above all*
*   other goals.*
Without these, in life, you will not be successful, nor will you be able to
*   enjoy your successes.*
Remember your team.
They count on you for support, and you will need their support when
*   the going gets tough, as well.*
Without this support network, you will never be successful. We will
*   never be successful.*

...

She often worried about her teamwork stat.
Clearly, it needed some attention.

...

I'm going to let you in on my tactics.
I call my tactics the 'five "B"s': bits, budgets, buffers, bounds and
barriers.
If something happens to end early or take less time, we end up wasting
the extra allotted time.
To solve this problem, I recommend viewing time as a much more
fluid resource, or at least one that can be spent in smaller bits.
Maintain a task list at all times.
Take a larger task and divide it into bits.
It makes your tasks less daunting and you will be surprised how
many 'time bits' you have during the day and how much you can
accomplish by breaking tasks into these bits.
Before taking a break, use a time bit to start a new task.
One of the most difficult aspects of getting things done is getting
started.
Start on a larger task now to eliminate the cost of context
switching later.
Spend your time well.
Always have a goal.
Budget your goals, and spend your time with that goal in
mind.
Have a goal and be purposeful about how you budget time in pursuit
of that goal.

...

She looked at her clock.
Soon the traffic would start again.
She opened another part of the screen to prepare.
The simulcast continued in the background.

...

Use a deadline as a bound for declaring victory; create a deadline if one doesn't exist.

Beware of time thieves, particularly those that masquerade as 'productive activities.'

Many interrupt-driven activities steal our time in fits and spurts.

Non-work-related communications are not always urgent.

You can always wait to reply.

Always be purposeful about leisure activities.

Ruthlessly protect your scheduled time.

Learn how to say 'No.'

Certain people may have biases or ulterior motives, even the people you trust.

Calibrated, trusted opinions from management are invaluable.

Establish time barriers.

No one should bother you for a non-work-related request during these times.

You are not reachable.

This is our time.

...

The simulcast ended abruptly.

The notification on her Dashboard sounded.

She went back to her work.

...

The afternoon was spent in silence.

Sometimes she listened to the radio, but today she did not feel like listening.

Besides, it was nearly always the same.

Economic reports about trade between compounds.

Each compound was connected.

Nodes in a network.

Working together towards the common goal.

She knew these connections were important and hoped she might visit one in the future.

Her favourite was the social discussion about the latest fashion and
    fitness trends.
In her new position she earned enough currency units to afford such
    luxuries.
Her new personal Device was the result of such spending.
The broadcasts of their announcement had been on repeat but, now
    that she had purchased it, they had culminated.
Something new would soon come next.
Sometimes she tried to predict the next item.
But she never guessed correctly.

...

The afternoon passed with ease.
Her work kept her occupied.
She didn't notice the darkness setting in.
The traffic had hit a lull before it began again.
She switched on her desk lamp, and stifled a yawn.
Getting up from her desk, she began some preparations for her
    evening meal.
She would have some time now before the last shift of the day.
Maybe there would be no overtime today.
She looked out on the compound.
The sun was setting and the solar-powered lights were slowly growing
    brighter.
The scent of the coffee she was making filled the room.
She picked up her cup and filled it to the top.
She stood looking out of the window and waited for the sun to set or
    the notification to arrive.
Whichever came first.

...

The sun set.

...

She sat in silence.
Waiting.

…

The notification interrupted her thoughts.
She went to sit back down at her station.
Her coffee had gone cold.
She noticed she had received a company communication.
There was no time now.
The shift had started.

…

Ruthlessly protect your scheduled time.

…

Her shift carried on without any issues.
She preferred the days when there were no interruptions.
The work was not difficult but there was a lot to manage and administrate.
The traffic was slower today and extended long past its pre-scheduled duration.
Technically, it did not count as overtime.
The shift is the shift.
It doesn't matter how long it takes.
Evening traffic must be catered for at all times, as per requirements.

…

Finally the traffic tapered off.
She reheated her coffee and her uneaten meal.
She browsed aimlessly through the communications and bulletins from the day.
It was getting late.
She finished the end of her meal, and cleaned away the dish.
Clutter is distracting for the mind.
If your physical space is chaotic it might be a sign that your inner space is out of balance too.
Balance and order were everything.

…

She went back to her station.

There were only two communications left unread: her performance review, and her overtime quota for the evening.

She hesitated.

The communication earlier had made her anxious.

She hovered over the performance review.

Instead, she opened her overtime quota.

...

Two additional shifts.

Her evening excursion suspended for the night, she opened her review.

No simulcast.

A long list of graphs and stats.

Her eyes glazed over.

She stood up, opened the window to let in the cool air from outside.

From her initial glance, she knew it wasn't good news.

At least it was not bad news either.

She hadn't been reassigned.

She walked back towards her station and read the review.

She scrolled to the end to absorb the feedback.

We must continually experiment and sample to develop and cultivate our Content.

It can be tempting and certainly easier to 'turn the crank' on problems that we know how to solve, but ultimately this will result in Content that becomes stale and boring.

Creativity is key in these uncertain times.

Try to dig a bit deeper and understand the value that your traffic cares for.

Surely with these improvements and the deployment of new protocols we can overcome these inadequacies?

...

She would have to re-evaluate her approach.

The new protocols they had devised were outlined at the end of the report. With these at least she could revise her approach.

The Content needed something more.

She continued to read the recommendations.

...

The night set in.

The notification sounded for her overtime.

She stared at her station for a moment.

She went back to her work.

9

Fatberg and the Sinkholes: A Report on the Findings of a Journey into the United Regions of England by PostRational

Dan Gavshon Brady and James Pockson

164

CONTENTS

Fatberg
(NOUN)

A congealed lump of fat, sanitary items, wet wipes, and similar items found in sewer systems, which do not break down like toilet paper. Such deposits are officially referred to using this term by authorities at Thames Water in London, UK.

https://en.wikipedia.org/wiki/Fatberg

Sinkhole
(NOUN)

A depression or hole in the ground caused by some form of collapse of the surface layer. Most are caused by karst processes – for example, the chemical dissolution of carbonate rocks or suffosion processes. Sinkholes vary in size from 1 to 600 metres (3.3 to 2,000 feet) both in diameter and depth, and vary in form from soil-lined bowls to bedrock-edged chasms. Sinkholes may form gradually or suddenly, and are found worldwide.

https://en.wikipedia.org/wiki/Sinkhole

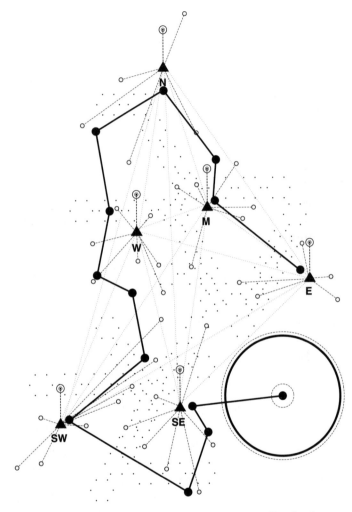

Figure 9.1 Nodal schematic of the United Regions of England
(illustration: Mike Lim)

FOREWORD
TO THE UNITED REGIONS OF ENGLAND

Things are going well in London. Productivity and the economy are booming. **Disrupt, capitalise, optimise, repeat**. The decimal of time is moving left and the decimal of profit is headed right.

Could things be any better in the great city? Yes. In the city we are always improving, cutting the fat, but no one would have expected the fat to cut itself! When the English regions voted London out, the ground shook, but what we thought was the end actually fomented a new beginning. Indeed, we have thrived on city state status, with the rest of the country lagging out our bandwidth no more. Now, it's London and it's the United Regions of England (URE).

> *For London, Labour, Imports, Commerce, Finance and Politics had been a largely extra-GB phenomenon for nearly two centuries. From our perspective the metropolis was so large and globally oriented that it was effectively self-sufficient in national terms. Where did that leave the rest of us?*

Dave, 31, political editor, *North
Eastern Herald.* Has
always believed in another way.
Northumberland is his paradise.
Where he feels truly at peace.

-PR-

There was always a disparity between London's absolute economic dominance and its relative lack of political influence.

Set adrift, we were politically and economically unencumbered.

In London we were happy with the split: there was very little we had to do with the rest of the country beyond the quaint or the nostalgic.

Our predictions and analysis for the new United Regions of England became increasingly inaccurate, however. What was going on there?

Certainly, stagnation was obvious.

Growth had ceased; and yet, the URE still functioned.

> *What in the name of Keynes is going on out there!? I want to know. NOW!*
>
> Morduch, 72, CEO, Cloudnet, (London). Hates losers. Has only ever lost once. Hated it.

Why should you care?

Proximity is critical. London may have separated from the URE but you can't do much about geography.

What is going on next door could either be a threat or an opportunity. To ignore the URE could render us defunct – or, worse, irrelevant. That is why you should care.

-PR-

Enclosed in the pages of this report is the PostRational perspective on the developing divergent economic system for the United Regions of England.

Welcome to the URE
Welcome to Absorbism

OBJECTIVES AND METHODOLOGY

Why?

Because it was stagnation like we'd never seen: capital accumulation flatlines but social mobility continues to rise.

It became clear to us at PostRational that an analysis of capital flow in the URE was not appropriate to understand the new Zeitgeist. We could not observe from a distance any more; we were compelled to journey into the world beyond M25.

What?

This report documents what we saw beyond the city limits.

This report is for you, the time-pressed reader, to discover the world that we saw too.

We do not pretend that it is exhaustive – nor do we proclaim to be right.

But we went on the journey, and **Absorbism** is what we saw.

When?

Last year, lasting five weeks
(two in-field, two in deep mental analysis, one writing)

Where?

The United Regions of England!

How?

We designed a bespoke approach to mirror the significance of what was going on:

A mixed-methodology plan of attack, combining the anecdotal, the observational, the metaneural and the analytical. In order to glean the sharpest responses we prioritised extreme users, experts and cultural clairvoyants to form the most forward-thinking and future-proofed assessment. We applied cutting-edge, cross-cultural technological techniques to find the spaces in between the stories.[1] You might even wish to work with PostRational to discover more.

- 12 x F2F expert interviews with regional leaders and cultural instigators (including travel)
- 6 x cultural assimilation workshops with mixed demographic and psychographic make-up
- 4 x urban safaris
- 4 x suburban and rural safaris
- 4 x ethnographic sit-ins and digital ethnographic sit-ins
- 2 x immersive experiencing excursions

-----

[1] We would recommend a further study based on quantitative behavioural data and conjoint analysis to provide a more robust segmentation to incorporate 'real people' and 'rich human stories' and map their holistic experience.

- A multifaceted environmental design audit
- Infrastructural forensics mapping
- Interactivity swabbing

We had to go to the orbitals' other bank to see for ourselves. Places like Wookey Hole, places like Stoke, places like Yeovil and Chipping Ogden.

Jake, 24, PR researcher. Likes to see beyond the surface. Bachelor in microeconomics. Misses 35mm film.

PROTOTYPICAL HYPOTHESIS

The modern world has always prioritised growth, with extraordinary results.

First, the Industrial Revolution facilitated this, from mass production to global expansion. Then the twentieth-century marketing revolution saw mass consumption from mass desire and fierce competition through brands. More recently, the internet revolution of the early twenty-first century created growth via value-extractive platforms. New opportunities arose as more and more people could acquire new value from one another. Seamlessly. Unthinkingly.

Or at least we thought so. These periods are posited as great paradigm shifts, but, in fact, they weren't revolutions at all. Simply put, each acted as an accelerant and megaphone for its predecessor.

Social revolution		Growth typology		Suburban impact
Industrial	>>>	Productivity	>>>	Exhaustion
Marketing	>>>	Competition	>>>	Inequality
Internet	>>>	Optimisation	>>>	Suffocation

What appeared different was actually just quicker, slicker and more single-minded. It created incredibly powerful networks, and fragile individuals. This is our hypothesis.

1. London's insatiable capacity for growth pushed against the constraints of the system

Growth didn't come from creating new value or higher stand-ards, but from optimisation: becoming so efficient as to be invisible. 'Seamless' growth had implications for the phys-ical, real world, where things still have to be made and exist. London was anything but invisible. It was consuming every-thing, exhausting supplies and pushing surplus to unseen places. Blockages grew in the system, creating ruptures, with the result that something had to give.

2. London was kicked out, and the URE was formed, as a reaction to its insatiability

London, the blocked fatberg, burst through. To put it more accurately, it was expelled as a separate entity, seen as the root of the problem – the blockage in the drain. No city in the newly formed URE stepped up to take up London's hegemonic mantle. This wasn't the consequence of regulation, as we first thought. Equity arose from mutual consideration and cooper-ation between regions – the new direction of the URE.

3. The URE has set out, driven by necessity and opportunity, to do things differently

This new path marks a move from the quantitative to the qualitative, the immaterial and imperceptible to the tangible and weighty. It has also retained a sense of the symbolic. The URE has taken the first steps to an alternative mindset for governance and exchange. This mindset is a new relational dynamic, predicated not on growth but on the ability to withstand shocks.

In short, we think this

A new economy, the product of a network-diverse hyperlocalism, is emerging in the URE. We have called it **Absorbism**.

Welcome to Absorbism

In a world of perpetual optimisation, the margins for value creation and extraction become increasingly, imperceptibly small, and the physical ceases to matter. In this space, we become more attuned to the projection of reality on the screen than reality itself. Big changes happen without being seen. Hardness and spikiness disappears from view: the literal corners from your iPhone are softened, controversial urban developments disappear into a background of average, uncontroversial design... A totality of smoothness, impossible to get a grip on. I had to get out.

Su, 45, sociable theorist. URE
newcomer/London
Defector, (lives mostly in a van).
Loves to rock-climb. Is terrified of
an average existence. Hoping to
scale every significant peak before
she dies.

ABSORBISM
AN INTRODUCTION

The URE is not working in the service of London, is not bound by its philosophy and is averse to new super-city hegemony. The absence of London created fertile grounds for something different.

Serving London's insatiable economic appetite for growth left the rest of the URE exhausted, unequal and suffocated. In such a weakened state, the URE was incredibly vulnerable, due to the decades-long impact of systematic industrial closure, of a low-cost globalised workforce and of London-centric infra-structural investment.

Without London, the URE has taken action to counter such his-torical vulnerability with a mindset that grew from an interest in resilience, not growth.

Absorbism (n)

A system of social organisation in which all members (at individual, community and regional level) are able to withstand shock through the quality of relationships they form with each other. This is facilitated through:

new **communality** *that blurs boundaries between public and private space;*

new **regionalism** *that is founded on local identity, external curiosity and non-utilitarian exchange;*

new **openness** *that creates multiple formal and informal relationships between members in a spirit of non-competitive discovery and celebration;*

new **drivers of status** *that are less concerned with what you have, and more with how you do it.*

Absorbism, Wrung Out...

Conventionally, the more people use a network, the stronger the network becomes.

Here, the more a member uses a network, the stronger the member becomes.

The strength of the network is immaterial. What matters is the formation of bonds that are free from hierarchy or the burden of financial return. The URE appears to operate on a system of exchanges between members, in which the point is not what-ness (the thing you are exchanging) but we-ness (the process of exchanging with each other). These could be about trading goods together, exchanging knowledge, sharing stories, or embarking on joint missions of discovery, salvage and reconnaissance. Members thrive on creating bonds and relationships with each other, almost for the sake of it.

| What Exchanges Are All About ||
Not	But
Efficiency	*Redundancies*
Things	*People*
Competition	*Transparency*

To get a young person's perspective on the networks in the community and beyond, we spoke to Rahul, an 18-year-old school leaver about to embark on a two-year research trip with his friends. He said that there wasn't any great designed intent between communities and regions, but then described something that sounded an awful lot like that to us.

Yeah, I don't know what you mean by networks. Like, a phone has a network, not people. We just click, whether you're North, North-West, South – everyone's got a story, everyone is capable of something cool."

Rahul, 18, student, South Wales.
Loves his mates. Loves his home
town. Scared of swimming.

Components of exchange in the new regionalism

Redundancies of exchange

This has some of the qualities of an old alliance system in which members have abundant (even surplus?) places to turn to when seeking benefit (rather than having everything angled towards London).

Exchanges with people

People and places enjoy talking to each other, sharing ideas with each other and arguing with each other. Whereas London has extremely successfully designed lived experience to be an exercise in individual decisions and choices, the URE lived experience has shifted the centre of decision-making to multiple parties from multiple regions at the same time.

Exchanges of transparency

This has the hallmarks of genuine compatibility and collaboration between members, since there is no explicit goal of winning the exchange.

In other words: relationships through trade > trade through relationships

This **new regionalism** is mediated through the **infrastructural ombudsmen**, who exist solely to ensure that diverse relationships grow and decisions are made through them. They are, in effect, facilitators of high-quality exchange.

Absorbism is an emergent theory; capitalism is an angsty teenager, by comparison. To support the model we will describe what we saw on the ground. We will catapult you headlong through three chosen scales:

the infrastructural

the architectural

the personal

THE INFRASTRUCTURAL
OPTIMISE, ATOMISE, BURN OUT

The United Kingdom, prior to the split, was the most centralised Organisation for Economic Co-operation and Development (OECD) country in the world. Much research from both the left and the right argued that greater devolution and distribution amongst the regions could lead to a much more stable society.

As the focus on optimisation grew, however, driven by the rampant expansion and elevation of London-centred financial and technological institutions, little was actually done to effectively counter the ever-growing weight of the capital city.

How can you reverse such a trend when the mass is so great?

The irrefutable mass of London was evidenced by the decline of the classical modern infrastructures (roads, rail, canal) that did not directly serve it. The density was reduced to a totally London-centric organisation. Despite the infrastructural picture of Great Britain being so optimised, the government sell-off of the remaining arteries to private enterprise led to atomisation as well. More infrastructural branches were shut or fell into disrepair on the grounds of low demand. Atomisation led to a simplified network that was in fact more expensive and more complicated to use, given that one had to negotiate myriad tolls, ticket changes and worsening marginal terrains in passing through each private jurisdiction.

Private enterprise, however well equipped, does not possess the same value systems as a collective in the maintenance of any infrastructural system. The former prioritises value and profit (how can you grow on a fixed railway line?), the latter (theoretically) priorities the general human need. A collectivised institution is less able to shut a branch line of a railway, for example, on the sole basis of waning capacity (isn't it obvious that branch lines would be used less?).

In theory, it should be politically untenable for any government, if vested with the resources to provide, to preclude anyone from access to a network based on where they live.

-PR-

When the hub is removed, what is the effect on the rim and the spokes? One might imagine collapse. But on our travels in the URE we saw a number of astonishing augmentations of the optimised, atomised infrastructural landscape of the regions. We have split our findings into two sections:
- the physical;
- the (formerly) invisible.

The Physical

Post-apocalyptic or dystopian landscapes are seen as such through a human lens. But these are utopias too. They're just utopias without us.

> Opening lines of the infrastructure
> refurbishment pamphlet 'On
> Informed Neglect'.

To say that travel was simple in the URE would be a lie. It was totally time-consuming. We spent the most time travelling, mainly by MegaBus. It was a joy to take the train – but also a bit of a pain. It seemed nostalgic, but we were told that, in this place of scarcity, the canal is actually being reinvigorated as the most viable means of moving heavy goods from A to B. Some vessels transported some kind of synthetic raw material called Arbetite, using the water as a coolant. At this stage, it's too hard to unpick directly the difference between the novel and the nostalgic in the URE.

Here, redundant physical infrastructures previously related to the Fatberg have been repurposed for access, cultivation and leisure. Other, lesser-used infrastructure is actually on the rise. But we have little capacity to create new in the URE, we can only adjust what we have.

> Geoff, 48, South-West,
> infrastructural refurbisher. Has a
> visceral reaction to the sight of an
> overpass. Loves Roman history. Has
> never been in love.

Out there, infrastructure is in a time of flux. Lines that lead to London are still being bent in new directions.

The most obvious change we saw was the relative absence of cars on the road. There were some, but mostly they were not moving and being systematically dismantled. Never burnt out. Such hedonistic rejection of physical objects in the URE is really only seen at the Parties, so heavy is the emphasis placed on reuse.

> *It only took few years before people stopped using cars. It wasn't really a choice. It was just too expensive, even if it gave freedom. So, after the split, we invested in MegaBus. It has been quite an investment – MBs have to be pretty capable vehicles... The roads ain't exactly smooth here, and they run out every now and again, but the MB keeps a rollin'!*

> Rick, 34, engineer, MegaBus. Dismantled his first engine at the age of 11. Racked by what he calls 'diesel guilt'. Has promised to show us his bike collection.

In the previous epoch, when most insurance products were dominated by the London financial market, the average regional car user was priced out even before the split. Everyone thought that it was oil or software that would spell the end of the autonomous motor vehicle. It was much more mundane than that.

As most roads lead to London, their A–Bness is less useful in the URE than that which their edges rub up against. Vast strips of overpass and motorway lands are being put to productive reuse in the URE. This is managed by groups of **infrastructural refurbishers (IRs)**. The IRs are responsible for ensuring that the swathes of infrastructure attendant to the London-centric model are repurposed in different ways. They operate on a system of 'informed neglect' – choosing abandonment of some more marginal areas that are least effective in ensuring connections between members.

IRs travel widely to determine what (re)applications will be of the greatest possible benefit in the formation of bonds now and in future generations, to other regions, other people and the local Absorbist environment. As such, they seem to have abandoned regional identity in favour of a kind of asphalt nomadism.

Tracts of the M1 are now virgin deciduous forest and the M6 Toll seems to be some kind of sports venue. The southern end of HS2 lies in a state of informed neglect (the shortest-lived mega-project ever). We saw a Party on one of the more complicated overpasses in Midland; these towering structures of modernism are being reappropriated in extraordinary ways. We first assumed that infrastructure was a fixed condition, because all roads go from A to B. But, on reflection, that is not the case. As all infrastructural maintenance, reuse or abandonment is coordinated through IRs, it appears that they extract a kind of value from infrastructure when they can effectively repurpose it.

Infrastructure is how we make bonds. It's not just a carrier of goods, signals or people. This means our arterial network has a kind of footprint; it's totally up to regional agreement for how it might be most effective in forming strong bonds between members or regions. Spaghetti Junction had some amazing Parties before it became an effective growing site for Midland.

Amy, 19, apprentice IR. Loves to travel. Grew up in South-West. Found herself on the M4.

The (Formerly) Invisible

Invisibility is a technology myth. Information ethereal, clouds.

Consumers rarely stop to think where the other end of their MacBook Airs poke out: faraway places; pins drop on distant horizons.

Our digital technologies disappear like ninjas in the night; they're inscrutably black and glossy. Their minimalism maximises their potential as tools for the optimised approach. As digital technologies are the windows into limitless worlds; meanings tracelessly slip from smooth surfaces, like water on silicone. We look straight through.

What we saw in the URE was different from (and at times the total inverse of) information infrastructures in London.

London	URE
Invisible	*Public*
Smoothness	*Seamed*
Inaccessible	*Adaptable*
Inscrutable	*Vulnerable*
Minimalist	*Pluralist*
Light	*Heavy*

Communication is a key driver in the Absorbist system of bond formation.

Communication and connectivity are revered in a similar fashion to money in London.

We have called our findings 'the (formerly) invisible', for communications infrastructure in the URE is the physical manifestation of their connectivity culture and is steeped in a complex, populist narrative.

Form through Function and Back Again

From what we could see – and much of what we saw was pretty hard to decode – there seems to be a 'connected hyper-localism' at play in the URE. Individuals are literate in the design and linguistics of digital networks and have created something that defies any kind of standard definition. Communications infrastructure is the bodge-project of a million mass tinkerers.

When we first saw this, we thought it was a total mess.

Adornments and small enactments occurred around objects in the landscape that were totally baffling to us. But the form, marking and position of these objects had a deep meaning to the people who made them that went far beyond their practical use.

The Arbiters

The URE regions all organise around a shared infrastructural system that they call the Arbiters. To learn this we spoke to a number of software landscapers, or 'Java gardeners', as they are commonly known.

They told us that Arbiters are geo-technological information parsers, constructed from a synthetic crystalline material similar to bismuth called Arbetite. We understand that Arbetite was invented in Manchester.

Jin, a seemingly prominent software landscaper, is responsible for maintaining and communicating directly with the Arbiters. She puts it much better than we can.

An Arbiter decides how best to organise the communication in the part of the network it is responsible for. Or, to put it differently: it's an enormous plate spinner. As the network became increasingly complex, but all the more central to life in the URE, we decided to cede responsibility of connectivity to machine-learned algorithms, rather than the peer-to-peer 'net' condition of before. This leap of faith into these relatively nascent technologies led to improvements to the order of ten in terms of efficacy of connection. Basically, in agreeing to do this, we admitted we had created something that we couldn't subordinate any more; it was our equal.

Jin. Software landscaper and Arbetite miner, North. Loves to wear fleeced jerkins. Is rarely ever inside. Except when making Arbetite.

Three Arbiter Types

Super-Arbiter	*The Super-Arbiters are the largest information sorters and manage connectivity between regions and large institutions/ organisations. They take the form of large features in the landscape. Super-Arbiters have that muted nobility that only something of such scale can possess. Old men in the mountains.*
Sub-Arbiter	*The Sub-Arbiters manage connectivity at a more local level and have the most curious physical adaptations pertaining to what appears to be local narratives and customs. These are the strangest objects for the foreigner to interact with. You never know in the URE if it's a log, or an Arbitrary construction humming away, parsing the noise.*
Orbiter	*Orbiters could be regarded as the 'personal' gateways into the system. They can belong to small groups, such as families or persons. For mute objects, they engender a great deal of personal identity. They're very nearly alive. Like the plant you place in the front seat of the van when you move house. They're that special – like the cat, or the lucky fridge magnet.*

-PR-

In conclusion, it appears that the function of these strange, pro-liferating objects is generally consistent across the URE: con-nectivity and communication. Their forms have a deep local relevance, however. Communication is the thread that holds Absorbism together, and these objects, the Arbiters, manage all those connections; the methods that URE members utilise to communicate with these things remains unclear to us, and should be the focus of further research.

There isn't really much talk of the network itself. 'Network' is simply our description of the situation we observed. There is evidence that the pseudo-mystical situation, perhaps brought about by the members' pure faith in the organisational capacity of these algorithms, has empowered the members of the URE to use them in new ways and that their letting go of the net condition has obliterated hierarchy. Members are excited by them to explore the full extent of the network, physically and digitally, but also proud of the small patch of they have cultivated themselves.

THE ARCHITECTURAL

Absorbism, at its core, has been brought about by a change in the common mindset rather than by any technological innovation in the physical environment. There are some noteworthy sea changes visible in the built landscape, however.

New approaches to architecture are being developed in the URE. Yet that architecture is not being developed through innovation in construction techniques or materials, but more in the manner of its appropriation.

We saw this in two key examples.

1. New communality – the blurring of the boundaries between private and public space.

2. Sites of Party – an intriguing mass ritual enactment in the URE – that we see as the fleeting icons of the Absorbist world.

New Communality

In towns that were once the product of volume house building, off-the-shelf Architecture and pattern-book profit pads, there is a small revolution taking place. Entire terraced streets have been hollowed out to create enormous elongated cloistered galleries at ground floor that enclose not ecologically dumb lawns but diverse gardens and allotments that teem with life. Trellising and fencing have been removed to create large communal, productive outdoor spaces. In the more overtly augmented towns and villages in the URE, it is clear that members believe that an environment whose management is shared is an environment improved. This is the sinkhole problem made manifest as a benefit: the vacuum of neglected space left much room for activity to grow into.

> *You feel a kind of awe when you go through a terrace front door to find a whole covered street inside. It's a magical rerendering of a, quite frankly, defunct typology that the volume builders foisted upon unwitting consumers in some gross re-enactment of nineteenth-century industrialism. Houses used to be a kind of wallet that you live in. And the trick was to make them as cheap as possible, so you could sell them on for loads more than they were built for. But we are working hard, through our adjusting, to undo these buildings a bit. Opening up to each other as we do.*

Amelia, architectural theorist, construction adjuster. Used to be obsessed by newness. Thought creativity was about making. Then she knocked down her first wall.

We saw in the URE the creative deconstruction and adaptation of existing building stock. Without previous institutions such as planners and building control inspectors, a kind of DIY frenzy, combined with a kind of mass squatting, had arisen in places.

These sites are moving to a new order in which the ground plan seems to welcome anyone who stumbles across it. This is certainly a theoretical observation – as human nature does generally lead to some form of need for private settlement, however small. And yet it appears that the delineation of demise is loosening in favour of a thinner boundary between persons, their neighbours and their possessions. What is strange is that this collectivised approach is the accidental outcome of the 'laissez-faire' attitudes that led to the suffocation of this segment of architectural production before the split. Over-regulation and conservative planning required a convoluted structure of management and enforcement – anathema to a minimised local authority. So when the URE was established there was no one to really stop people from just getting on with finishing these developments however they wanted.

Sites of Parties

To talk of the most evocative monuments in the URE one cannot avoid talking about Parties. Parties expand the horizons of a 'built environment' when the control mechanisms developed in the existing system have been lifted.

Architectural capitalism is still an object-oriented system with its attention focused on the invisible. Architecturally speaking, our favourite historical example of the object obsession was in the late postmodern age, when the iconic skyscrapers ruled the urban skyline. It was a moment of real clarity. Literally a pinnacle!

Towards the end of the decade, however, the era of the icon building did eventually fade. As the scale of buildings increased, legible iconography became harder and harder to apply. Therefore, the symbolism transferred to the scale of the master plan rather than the object building. The city is an object after all.

Parties always have a pre-devised site. Their location is the product of a great deal of communication between Arbiters and members. The sites of these mass Absorbist actions were curiously picked at times. We saw some in the Midland Region in the sinkholes created by accidental over-tunnelling of the HS2 project. These massive holes in the ground became the shelters for what appeared to be carefully planned events, at which people gathered to celebrate, meet up and exchange ideas. It was tempting to call these things 'festivals' yet they felt more purposeful than that. For, without the system to kick back against, the Absorbists don't really require the fraught, desperate hedonism that one might attribute to the festivals we know.

The Party is a collective acknowledgment of what it is to be a member in this new system. Simply put, the Party is a great way to ensure that the greatest bonds are made between members in a meaningful, near-ritualistic way.

There's a long history of anarchistic inhabitation in what we now call the URE. Like the Essex Plotlands, which are just round the corner from here. Yet the actions of these communities were divergent because they were kind of forced to build on marginal, greenfield lands and then have to defend their position there. I think what we are doing is different. We don't see this as anarchy. That sounds a bit too crazy, really. No, what we are doing is a kind of recalibration of existing buildings to fit our own desire."

Ivan, 56, metal detector. Loves coins. Hates currency. Dreams of moving to Ephesus.

	London	URE
Flow of	*Capital*	*Bonds*
Ultimate physical expression	*Skyscraper*	*Party*

In its infancy the URE does not have the tools to build big – and would it desire to? We saw no evidence of any new projects of significant scale. It is our belief that Absorbism is a socio-economic system – an economic system that functions through deliberate social exchange: bond making. Therefore, the significant change in the Absorbist world is not in technology per se but in the humans' and humanity's self-awareness, as opposed to unconscious individual experience.

The Party is the Absorbists' glass tower, in that it is the ultimate display of human exchange. The Party exists momentarily and remains as a kind of memory, documented for posterity, of course, but only really livable as a present.

THE PERSONAL

If the industrial age meant production, a person was a worker who produced.

If the marketing age meant consumption, a person was a consumer who bought.

If the internet age meant interactivity, a person was a user who experienced.

Capitalism – the You-You

The role of the individual person dominates more and more through the ages, laden with extra responsibility in the name of personal autonomy.

Choose clothes that reflect you!

Personalised services tailored to you and your preferences!

You are empowered to manage your energy bill!

Earn money by renting out your spare room!

Even social media services used by billions of people the world over are 'tailored' or 'curated' for you.

You are the architect of your environment and you are responsible for you.

With worlds personalised by you, around you, for you, there is no shared experience; only you experience you, which others drop in on.

Life individuated.

Absorbism – the We-Saw

Absorbism counters this. People are tweaking their roles and jobs so that, by design, they include others in decision-making, in creating, in living.

If Absorbism means withstanding shock, a person is a member who forms relationships.

We spoke to Jillie, an infrastructural ombudsman from North-West, whose job is dedicated to building relationships between her region and others. This takes place in matters of trade, transport and leisure. Jillie considers herself both as part of North-West and as part of the URE in equal measure, and sees her role as one that helps others to feel that way too. Jillie is a strong encapsulation of a new mindset that we've seen in the URE: open, collaborative and fearless in seeking out new adventures to protect against exposure.

> *My job is to be friendly to people so people see a good side of North-West region, and we make more friends and relationships. I've recently been working on a Party with Scotland for next spring. This will be important next year, when we need to rebuild the roads between North-West and Scotland.*

Jillie, 29, infrastructural
ombudsman. Born in Devon.
Grew up in Scotland. Eldest of five
siblings.

We also spoke to Pheylan, a software landscaper and one of the Arbiter network co-creators. His role involves less contact with people from different regions, but is still completely interwoven with a new cooperative regionalism. Pheylan is part of a cross-regional team who design and adapt Sub-Arbiters, a digital service encapsulated in a totemic physical shell that governs the distribution of resources throughout given areas in the URE

On a day-to-day level, this means greater fluidity. Despite working on a project of obvious infrastructural importance, as a public worker Pheylan will spend two months of the year working in another region, in other roles. Discovery of, experimentation with and empathy for other regions are the drivers for this activity.

> *An Arbiter is nothing more than a physical symbol for the collectively owned algorithm that governs our resources. However, we take huge care to place them in prominent but not imposing positions throughout the public spaces of the URE, and even more care to ensure that they feel like they belong where they are situated, in form, size and cultural relevance. An Arbiter in South-East looks different from those in West, even though they perform the same function.*

Pheylan, 53, software landscaper, West. Younger brother to COO of Silicon Valley firm Decacorn. Former research teacher in Manchester.

If the economic model is about creating a *we-ness* rather than a *what-ness*, this is also reflected on a more personal level – in how people see themselves – and represents an evolution from our existing idea of the individual autonomous agent. Rather than see themselves as kings of their own world, interacting to their own specifications and preferences, citizens of the URE self-identify as members of many worlds, with a desire to play parts in and learn about other worlds.

Age	Role of person	Defined by
Industrial	*Worker*	*Producing*
Marketing	*Consumer*	*Buying*
Internet	*User*	*Interacting*
Absorbism	*Member*	*Bonding*

For all my life, I've been scared of the city and scared of exploring. To look outside was to expose yourself to the demands and ways of the city, and I didn't know what that was. But I always trusted the youngsters to do something good.

Today, I look outside and I don't feel exposed. For the first time in my life, I can explore and be excited by it. There's nobody else's ways to stick to, nobody knows the rules, and it's nice to go for a walk with someone and not know where it'll lead.

Ann, 76, terrace champion (part-time), East. Occasionally sculpts. Married without children. Learning to code.

RETURN FROM THE URE

Sounds pretty New Age – right? That's what we thought too.

And yet it seems to be a good thing.

A bit of unpicking and you can see why.

Whereas the London model becomes ever harder to grow as the opportunities for value extraction and optimisation become more and more pinched, the untrammelled permutations for enterprise, enquiry and experience that are shared with another community or region present countless possibilities... We suppose that's why the Parties are so important: they become the site of possibility overdrive – where the possibility valve is released.

We called London a fatberg because it just fitted. Everything was pushed, compressed into feeding this kind of amazing, kind of disgusting, thing that just took up space and spilt into everything. We'd had enough of feeding it – we wanted to do our own thing.

David, 42, regional councillor, North. Former semi-professional left back. Family lived in same street for three generations.

LONDON		URE	
Aim	**Outcome**	**Aim**	**Outcome**
1 Create	*Reproduction*	*1 Make bonds*	*Enlisted members*
2 Compete	*Victory*	*2 Explore together*	*Connected members*
3 Optimise	*Extraction*	*3 Learn from each other*	*Shared discovery*
4 Grow	*Stagnation*	*4 Dance*	*Stronger bonds*
5 Repeat	*Shock*	*5 Repeat*	*Shocks absorbed*

Against our expectations, we see in the URE signs that a pressure has been eased, and a weight lifted. It's poorer and messier, but less angry and, unexpectedly, more inquisitive. In the strange, uncanny world of a London-less country, rebuilding itself to absorb shock and make friends, we see early indications that new resources and innovations might emerge. We should keep an eye on them; there may be opportunities for growth that we can take advantage of.

www.postrational.net/fatsink

III

Design for a Different Future

The economy is an artefact, a man-made, politically invented and planned set of institutions geared around production, exchange, surplus extraction and distribution. Under neoliberal capitalism, the manufactured nature of economic institutions is too easily forgotten, as they come to appear autonomous or natural. Yet the question of economic science fictions is also a question of how design might be actively channelled towards a different form of economic life, through invention and planning. It is in design that the utopian impulse of science fiction meets actual economic policy. The political-economic potential of urban design is explored in Owen Hatherley's chapter, which studies a suburb of Moscow built in 1958 using prefabricated materials, with the intention of being reproduced en masse. This would take the industrial properties of cheap mass production, and turn them towards the provision of good social housing.

Mark R. Johnson turns to a fictional portrayal of the built environment, through an unusual type of fiction: the mega-structures as represented in computer games. The fact that these can be actively explored by the player of the game offers a different form of utopianism or dystopianism, which is interactive and open to manipulation. Yet, being produced by technology, these environments are as much 'scientific' as they are 'fictional'. The final two pieces in this section, both written by design practitioners, explore the possible uses of design methods for thinking critically and imaginatively about the economy.

Bastien Kerspern explores how methods of 'design fiction' can nurture critical enquiry into alternative economic paradigms. Then Tobias Revell, Justin Pickard and Georgina Voss examine critical and speculative design, as tools for a reimagining of economic life and the realisation of utopian plans.

10

Prefabricating Communism: Mass Production and the Soviet City

Owen Hatherley

The public square just off 60th Anniversary of October Street in the 9th District of the Moscow suburb of Novye Cheryomushki ('New Cherry Town') is a very ordinary, although unusually placid, place. Trees, playgrounds, benches, mothers pushing prams and the odd middle-aged boozer circle around a small statue of Lenin. The four-storey flats are a little worn, and the owners of apartments have built extensions or glazed in their balconies; housing was privatised en masse after 1991. The sense of quiet torpor here is fitting given that Russians call the suburbs 'sleeping districts', not much more than cubicles to come home to at the end of a day's work. If so, this is definitely one of the more attractive places to sleep, with low-rise build-ings, lots of social facilities and a Metro station nearby. But this one is different. Novye Cheryomushki is the common ances-tor of every mikrorayon ('micro-district'), as they're officially known; the parent of thousands of prefabricated districts, the forefather of nearly every suburb in Moscow. This square was the site of a competition between seven blocks of flats. The winner, supposedly, would be built everywhere.

Each of these seven blocks, built in 1958 at record speed, used a different prefabricated construction system, usually of concrete panels, slotted into place like toy building blocks. Each was assessed on expense and speed of construction, and then one lucky block of flats, codenamed 'K7', was chosen as the

Figure 10.1   'K7', Novye Cheryomushki

winner (see Figure 10.1). It was then constructed in thousands of copies – though structural problems with it have meant that many of these have in turn been demolished. Nonetheless, this site was where began the largest experiment in industrialised housing in history, where homes would become mass-produced commodities like cars, fridges, TVs. In one respect, this was a fulfilment of a long-held modernist ideal. When he was the director of the Bauhaus, Walter Gropius declared his intention of becoming 'the Ford of housing'. Houses, he insisted, must become machine-made, serial products, as efficient, clean, cheap and essentially disposable as cars. Like so many twentieth-century dreams, this would eventually be realised in the Union of Soviet Socialist Republics, and with notoriously mixed results. For every Model T, there might be an Edsel, and bad things happen to disposable products when they're not replaced.

The Elimination of Excess

In the contemporary context, however, there is something quixotic and heroic about this effort. Those of us born since the late 1970s, in Britain especially, but to varying degrees in the west and east (and south) of Europe, have seen staggering levels of inflation in the price of housing, and a seemingly corresponding sharp decline in the price of consumer goods, from cars to food. It's almost a reversal of the Soviet situation, in which, by the 1980s, the need for cheap and decent shelter (and full employment, and a functioning, if rickety welfare state) was widely met. Currently, we have a society in which housing is a constant source of worry, anxiety and cost for much of the population, but the goods the Soviet Union had such trouble manufacturing – particularly the consumer durables most subject to fashion – are both abundant and extremely cheap. Because of this, if nothing else, it is worthwhile to examine this experiment, the ideas behind it and how it proceeded. In doing this, we will focus on a particular area of Moscow: three large suburban districts that emerged in the hinterland of Moscow State University between the mid-1950s and the late 1970s. There is Novye Cheryomushki, the country's first, built in the 1950s and 1960s; Belyayevo, an apparently generic example from the 1960s; and the more ambitious late 1970s Severnoye Chertanovo, which tried to break from standardisation. Each offered stable, free or near-free housing to workers, both white-collar and blue-collar, until mass privatisation in the early 1990s reintroduced profit and insecurity, as more desirable locations were snapped up by investors. Each has also been infilled with new prefabricated housing in the 2000s and 2010s.

As well as their possible lessons for means of solving the housing crisis seemingly endemic to neoliberalism, these housing projects reveal the way in which the USSR in this era attempted to return to the 'utopian', technocratic vision of full communism that was common in the 1920s, and fell into abeyance in the Stalinist era. It saw a re-engagement with the idea of revolutionising everyday life, an embrace of futurology and specific prediction, and also something new: an extensive discourse over automation. Unlike in the Stalinist era, the Khrushchev 'Thaw' saw a return of science fiction, and very blurred lines between that and actual policy. Two books of policy prediction written near the end of the 1950s, both of which were later translated into English, show this particularly well. M. Vassiliev and S. Gouchev's 1959 *Life in the Twenty-First Century* is a compendium of predictions by planners, scientists and economists, presented for a popular readership. The chapter on the 'Moscow of the Twenty-First Century' focuses on the territory around Novye Cheryomushki.

Nearly a third of the New Moscow was covered with green and blue patches representing the parks and hydro-electric reservoirs, arteries radiating from the centre. Yevstratov took out a metal stick and pointed out many of the details of the new town planning. 'In the next five years Moscow will expand to the south-west behind the University...'

The planner also pointed, however, to 'another characteristic of the Moscow of the future: each zone will be completely different from the next and differently organised'. That is, the New Moscow, which will be dominated by greenery, electric cars, an extensive metro and garden suburbs, will be 'beautiful' as well as functional.

Most beautiful of all will be the facades of the four and five storey houses partly hidden by trees and shrubs. Let us enter one of these houses and ask permission to visit an apartment. Brightly lit, air-conditioned rooms with huge windows. Radiators have been replaced with heating in the walls and ceilings... If we go out onto the flat roof we will see a curious winged machine. It is an air taxi.[1]

The air taxi, and, depending on taste, the 'beauty', may not have been realised, but much of the rest was, and a long time before the twenty-first century at that. Largely, this was because of the extremely fast pace of construction enabled by building with concrete panel systems.

These were not new in themselves; the most influential system was the French Camus panel construction system, which formed the basis of Soviet practice from the mid-1950s on. Some efforts had been made to combine industrialised construction and Stalinist luxury in the 1940s. Nonetheless, the story begins with Nikita Khrushchev's decree 'On the Elimination of Excess in Design and Construction', in 1954. In a speech to architects and engineers the same year, the General Secretary made the following statement: '[W]e must select a smaller number of standard designs – and conduct our mass building programme using only these designs over the course of, say, five years...and if no better designs turn up, then continue in the same way for the next five years. What's wrong with this approach, comrades?'[2] The vast territory of the USSR was divided into three climate zones and three soil types, and an often dysfunctional system of numbering and classification emerged, giving a (sometimes deceptive) impression of rationality. Room sizes, block heights and lengths were decided on the basis of mathematical calculation, not landscape or

---

[1] M. Vassiliev & S. Gouchev (eds.) (1959 [1961]) *Life in the Twenty-First Century*. London: Penguin Books, pp. 162–3.

[2] B. Flowers (2006) What's Wrong with This Approach, Comrades?, *Architectural Design*, 76(1): 62–3.

context. The system didn't remain the same from 1955 to 1991, however, but had three distinct moments, which Philipp Meuser and Dimitrij Zadorin divide into three games: 'chessboards' in the 1950s and early 1960s; somewhat more spaced-out 'dominoes' in the 1960s; and the final complexities of the 'Tetris' arrangements found in the 1970s and 1980s.[3] Standard blocks, which were identical in layout, height and flat size in a multinational federation several times the size the European Union might be, were, if you were lucky, leavened with decorative mosaic panels on revolutionary, scientific, heroic and historical themes; and often, in the southern republics of the USSR, the need for shading led to some more sculptural, op art effects with loggias. Variations don't go much further.

Automating the Ideal Communist City

Mostly, this is a story of mind-boggling homogeneity: areas the size of small towns made up of the exact same prefabricated module (see Figure 10.2). The intention appears to have been automation of both design and construction, and aesthetics was a matter of optional applied facades. These were arranged in coherent districts, which at best attempted to combine social facilities and open space. Kuba Snopek, historian of the Belyayevo district, describes them thus:

The building block of Soviet society was the Microrayon (or 'micro-district'), a standardised housing unit that has been replicated all over Moscow since the 1950s. Simple prefab residential buildings, free plan, schools and kindergartens are an integral part of both the programme and its composition. In the heart of each neighbourhood

---

[3] P. Meuser & D. Zadorin (2016) *Towards a Typology of Mass Housing in the USSR*. Berlin: Dom.

Figure 10.2 Aerial view of south-west Moscow, around Moscow State University

is a public building, most often a cinema or a club. At first glance, a Microrayon is a typical modernist neighbourhood, commonplace in the West. Yet there are things that differentiate the Microrayon from its French or Dutch counterparts: the degree of uniformity, the repetitiveness of the structures and the enormous scale.[4]

Buildings themselves were taken from standard catalogues, mere 'ready-made objects distributed in space'.[5] These districts were already being criticised within a few years, and there is much implicit criticism in a similar volume to *Life in the Twenty-First Century*, the collaborative *The Ideal Communist*

---

[4] K. Snopek (2013) *Belyayevo Forever*. Moscow: Strelka Press, p. 13.

[5] Ibid., p. 77.

City, put together at Moscow State University at the end of the 1950s and published a few years later.

Whereas the prefabrication programme can be seen as a sort of ultimate Fordist city, with mass production brought out of the car factories and into the planning of the city itself, the authors of *The Ideal Communist City* were trying to work out what to do next. Partly, the problem is aesthetics. 'Functionalism never defined the role of single buildings in total urban space. This space, rolling over many miles, loses all traditional points of reference and cannot be perceived as a whole, appearing rather as an unending and accidental continuity of spatial events, incoherent and lacking expressive significance.'[6] This matters, because 'the development of an urban environment made up of standardised residential units is of paramount importance for the building programme of Communism'. These must be planned in a way that makes them adaptable and more like 'a living organism'.[7] An illustration closely resembling the design of Novye Cheryomuskhi is captioned: '[A] great number of standard forms are incorporated in contemporary building, but the spatial solutions arrived at differ very little. The result is a depressing uniformity.'[8]

The problem with this is that the new society being created by Soviet socialism and the 'scientific-technical revolution' was going to be complex and differentiated, and defined not by the repetition and industrial labour of the car factory; that problem would be increasingly solved by automation, given that, under

---

[6] A. Baburov, G. Djumenton, A. Gutnov, S. Kharitonova, I. Lezava & S. Zadovskij (1968) *The Ideal Communist City*. New York: George Braziller, p. 153.

[7] Ibid., p. 156.

[8] Ibid., p. 145.

communism, 'man's role...is to program and control the labour of machines in a fully automated system of production'.[9] This is becoming a reality, something shown in the production process of the micro-districts themselves; one illustration in the book shows gantry cranes on rails constructing almost an entire suburb without visible human input. Other works from the same time posed similar questions: Aleksandr Merkulov's *Automation Serves Man* argues that workers will merely 'tune' their production lines for a couple of hours and then, in the words of the planner Stanislav Strumilin, 'engage in their leisure time in technical inventions or swell the ranks of public figures, scientists and writers, inspired musicians and painters...and all these huge replenishments from among the workers will take the place of the one-sided workmen of the old system of labour division and make up the new society which we will call communism'.[10]

For the authors of *The Ideal Communist City*, this poses questions for the design of the new districts themselves:

[I]n the coming years, with the reduction of the work day to five or six hours and the parallel reduction of other chores, leisure time will consist of about six to seven hours per day. If we further decrease the work day to a period of not less than four hours and assume a minimum system of daily services, leisure in the next decade may increase to an average of eight to nine hours a day, not counting holiday or the extended annual vacation. The increase in leisure time in coming years will present a social problem of extraordinary significance: how to make use of this free time in a manner consistent with the communist ideal, that is, how to use it in the interests of each and all.[11]

[9] Ibid., p. 34.

[10] A. Merkulov (1964) *Automation Serves Man*. Moscow: Foreign Languages Publishing House, p. 149.

[11] Baburov et al., *The Ideal Communist City*, p. 87.

The micro-district in this context is inadequate, because too simple, straightforward and standardised; instead, the authors advocate what they call the 'New Unit of Settlement', a sort of changeable, mutable version of the garden city, with pedestrian priority: 'Pedestrian walks are cut under the buildings, and in the shadow of the bearing walls along the walks there are bodies of water. The whole includes stairs, ramps, porticoes, show windows, cafes, and open-air amphitheatres. All this produces a lively sequence of architectural and spatial impressions, a rich variety of colours, forms and light. The individual regains the pedestrian street with its human scale, something that has been missing since the middle ages.'[12]

It is on these more ambitious measures that the programme can be considered a failure. The nuclear family, the eight-hour working day, the repetitive production line – none of them was eliminated. In fact, as Lynne Attwood finds in her analysis of gender relations in Soviet housing, the new developments often replicated them. While 'one third of the population were re-housed in the course of six years, between 1957 and 1963',[13] 'Soviet planners had a distinct tendency to standardise, and the general perception was that two or three different apartment designs would accommodate all types of family' – that is, 'the average family', which 'apparently consisted of a married couple with two dependent children.'[14] This became 'the main focus of the housing programme', for much of its duration. 'If apartment design was over-standardised,

---

[12] Ibid., p. 158.

[13] L. Attwood (2010) *Gender and Housing in Soviet Russia: Private Life in a Public Space.* Manchester: Manchester University Press, p. 170.

[14] Ibid., p. 155.

there was little standardisation in distribution.'[15] Some municipal allocation took place, but mostly the new housing was distributed via workplaces, on the basis of work, length of time in job, and need. This meant that often flats were in the name of male workers, making divorce difficult and obtaining housing hard for single women and single mothers. Nonetheless, industrialised housing made up 75 per cent of all stock by 1991, and was kept at minimal rents – between 3 and 5 per cent of a resident's total income[16] – so that, by Perestroika, 'market socialist' economists were worried that 'people had come to expect to have their accommodation provided by the state virtually free of charge,'[17] something that stood in the way of their attempt to introduce the concept of prices reflecting value into the system. Rather than an experiment, this became normality; the equivalent of a mock-Tudor semi or a Victorian terrace is a flat in a four- to ten-storey block. This is where the overwhelming majority of Muscovites live, not in the Tsarist-Stalinist palaces within the inner city, nor the hipster enclaves of Chistye Prudy or Gorky Park.

The programme was necessitated by the housing catastrophe that the Soviet Union faced by the 1950s. The Russian Empire was 80 per cent rural in 1917, but under Stalin the fastest and probably the most brutal industrial revolution in history was forced through between 1929 and 1940. Moscow filled with rural migrants fleeing a famine-ridden countryside to work in the new factories. Many lived in subdivided pre-revolutionary

---

[15] Ibid., p. 157.

[16] This statistic is proudly stated in the propaganda pamphlet 'USSR – Welfare' (1973, Moscow: Novosti, unpaginated), and attacked as an example of the idiocy of Soviet economics in sundry Western analyses.

[17] Attwood, *Gender and Housing in Soviet Russia*, p. 207.

apartments ('kommunalki'), and many in barracks, basements, tents, even trenches. This housing crisis was barely under control when the war compounded the problem, with the Third Reich's war of extermination against the USSR making millions homeless. The attempts to redress this under Stalin were almost whimsical, however: grandiose, richly decorated apartment blocks were built, lining wide, Haussmannesque boulevards; enormous resources were diverted into skyscraping luxury hotels, or grace and favour flats for artists and bureaucrats. The first independent act of Nikita Khrushchev after becoming General Secretary on Stalin's death was to force through the aforementioned decree 'On Architectural Excess', demanding industrialised construction rather than bespoke masterpieces as a means of solving the crisis. It's difficult to exaggerate just how huge a social advance this was for Muscovites, not only in the sense of amenities, but also in that a private life was now possible, after three decades when the majority had lived in cramped communal flats, one family to a room or worse.

Out of Monumentality, Standardisation: Cheryomushki

But, first, the half-constructed grand boulevards had to be completed. Vast neoclassical apartment blocks line the main roads into Novye Cheryomushki. Here the money ran out, however, for the more flamboyant features: the decorative pilasters stop halfway up, or are outlined in brick; the grand archways lead to scuzzy courtyards. As soon as these were inhabitable, grandiose pride and formal order would be replaced with utility. The contrast between the Stalinist boulevards and the first parts of the new Cheryomushki is striking. Around Akademicheskaya Metro Station, the blocks are lower and simpler, and the in-between spaces are full of fountains and benches rather than afterthoughts behind the grand facades. Novye Cheryomushki also featured an abundance of public space and public buildings: health centres, crèches, schools, cinemas, libraries, theatres, clubs (see Figures 10.3–10.6). Initially, each mikrorayon was planned with all of this included, all to equally standard designs. Little on this scale had been attempted anywhere, and visitors flocked to see it. Dmitri Shostakovich composed an operetta titled after the district, satirising Muscovites' desperate desire to move there; it was adapted into a colour film in 1963. Built in the year of Sputnik, it seemed to suggest the Soviet way of doing things – an egalitarian, centrally planned,

Figure 10.3   A stripped Stalinist block, Cheryomushki

Figure 10.4   Public space in Cheryomushki

Figure 10.5   Central Economic Mathematical Institute

Figure 10.6 Infill in Cheryomushki

mass production economy – was getting results. A certain nostalgia for these days pervades it; the photographs here are from a visit on May Day, when residents were enjoying the day off and the public billboards were stuffed with Soviet-nostalgic paraphernalia or posters for the upcoming Victory Day. That sort of bombast was incongruous with the easy, sociable space.

Each mikrorayon was meant to have a factory, an institute or both, in order to be self-contained to some degree; the risk that they would become dormitory suburbs was realised early on, and here, at least, it was partially prevented. Around the Novye Cheryomushki Metro station are several research institutes, moved or founded here in the 1960s. Cheryomushki was not just a 'sleeping district' but a hub of the USSR's scientific-military-industrial complex. The centrepiece was the Institute of Scientific Information on Social Sciences Library, the Soviet equivalent of the Library of Congress, reached from the street by a concrete bridge over a (long-since drained) lake. Adjacent is the tower of the Central Economic Mathematical Institute, one of the drivers of the Soviet central planning system, a glass grid by architect Leonid Pavlov with a colourful Möbius strip sculpture set into the middle floors. This building is itself a useful index of the failure of the attempt to realise a fully automated, computerised communism in the 1960s. Intended largely as a computer centre, its bespoke, luxurious, non-standardised design was so complicated for the Soviet building industry to produce that the building was effectively obsolete when it was finished in 1978 (12 years after construction had begun) given the rapid shrinking of the size of computers.[18] It became an image (and a rather impressive one) of computerised socialism rather than an actuality.

In recent years, however, the shift in the urban economy from production to speculation has invaded this carefully arranged space and smashed up its order, with a dozen or so 30-storey towers with pitched roofs crashing into the open space around, creating a looming, claustrophobic feel; the sense that planning has been abandoned here and it's everyone for him- or herself. Moscow's suburbs have faced extreme levels of 'infill' development, with immense towers shoved into the parks and gardens of the mikrorayons, throwing flats into darkness and obliterating the communal amenities. One tower is even crammed into the small square between the tower and the Institute of Scientific Information on Social Sciences Library, blocking out its light. The latter suffered a catastrophic fire in January 2015, described by the head of the Academy of

---

[18] See here A. Bronovitskaya, L Pavlova & O. Kazakova (2015) *Leonid Pavlov*. Florence: Electa, p. 198.

Sciences as the academic equivalent of the Chernobyl disaster; over a million priceless volumes were damaged. The fire was ascribed to an electrical fault, but, given the intensity of development around it, it wouldn't take a conspiracy theorist to suspect foul play. You could easily imagine the original attempts at making this something more than a suburb being erased in a decade or two, as it is turned into a commuter district like any other.

Standardising Nonconformity: Belyayevo

Novye Cheryomushki's pioneering status makes it a little different from the Soviet norm. That begins a couple of stops south on the Metro, at the mikrorayon of Belyayevo, developed from the 1960s onwards. This really is a quintessential 'sleeping district'. From here on in, the original notion of self-contained districts with their own identity was watered down as a numbers game took over. The 'winning' square panel at Cheryomushki is extended into long slabs, tall towers and squat maisonettes, unrelieved by any variation or individuality whatsoever, without an obvious centre, and with relatively sparse social facilities compared with its predecessor (see Figures 10.7 & 10.8). The recent infill is depressing: malls, and more speculative behemoths crammed into the open space. In fairness, some improvements to the poor construction have been made: styrofoam and a layer of render to insulate the panels, which are rickety in their unrenovated form, with mortar leaking from the crudely connected joints.

Off the main road, where they survive, the green spaces are Belyayevo's saving grace, enclosing schools, ponds and park benches. Belyayevo has become a minor cause célèbre after the Moscow-based Polish architect Kuba Snopek submitted it to UNESCO as a potential entry on the World Heritage list, partly

Figure 10.7   Belyayevo doorways

Figure 10.8   A pond in Belyayevo

because of the design of the communal spaces – one of the few places where architects could actually do anything much with the standard volumes they were expected to use in housing.

Although designing houses was taken away from (architects), they were still able to design great spaces between buildings, urban planning solutions, comfortable streets and paths... [D]esigners were also able to create interesting urban situations with surprising composition, rhythm and urban openings. Although this aesthetic was of a totally different nature to an archetypal city, using grand objects and vast patches of green, blue and white instead of a streets, squares and perimeter blocks, it definitely had its own value.[19]

So, in the case of Belyayevo, the preserved orchard and the lakes and the layouts of the buildings are intended to offset the unnerving effects of mass production. Belyayevo is, accordingly, a place where it would be great to be six – loads of free open space and playgrounds to play in – and very probably a boring place to be 16, like most suburbs. It is the green spaces that made the area desirable once, and they are most at risk from development.

Either way, Belyayevo implies a city that is homogeneous, based on the nuclear family, with a small series of housing types designed to provide for a population with – so the planners assumed – statistically predictable needs. Today this has been thrown into chaos by the decline of the built fabric and the new instability of the population, as flats are rented, sold and subdivided. The other reason for Snopek's attempt to get Belyayevo on the World Heritage list, however, was an appeal to the fact that most of the 'Moscow Conceptualists', artists and thinkers such as Boris Groys, Dmitri Prigov and Ilya Kabakov,

---

[19] Snopek, *Belyayevo Forever*, pp. 48–9.

lived and worked here in the 1970s. The Conceptualists' famous 1974 'Bulldozer Exhibition', broken up by police, took place in one of Belyayevo's empty green spaces. Snopek argues this subversive activity was implicit in the area's 'uncontrolled common space, ready to become exhibition space or whatever else'. The mundanity of the area 'conceals complicated and nuanced stories'. This is an important point; the lives being lived in such a district can be as multivalent as the architecture is one-dimensional, and, in that sense, the hope of the authors of *The Ideal Communist City* that leisure time could thrive in new standardised housing was fulfilled, albeit in a more critical way than they would have expected.

The idea of listing the district, though, is akin to one of the Conceptualists' knowing jokes – to argue that the true 'hipster' district of Moscow, the real 'arts incubator', was a mundane concrete suburb. This is still part of the capital, with all its draws, its centre reachable easily from the Metro. Much of what made it such a hothouse for art and experimentation was its connection to the scientific, technical and ideological institutions nearby, from the institutes in Novye Cheryomushki to various art schools and the Patrice Lumumba University, which trained cadres in the newly decolonised countries – something that made the Moscow south-west unusually multicultural. In that sense, the area is interesting precisely because much about it was not at all standard.

Standardising Individuality: Chertanovo

There are certain aspects to Soviet practice that always invited the monolithic aspects of the mikrorayon, particularly the limits of the command economy. On the one hand, there was opposition to the very idea of individual districts, as represented by the 'quarter'. Writing approvingly as early as 1932 about Soviet utopian planning, Berthold Lubetkin wrote that 'urban quarters are simply the obsolete survivals of capitalistic principles of planning. They represent class and caste prejudices (ghettoes, international concessions, west and east ends, brothel districts) or the now superannuated ideas of strategic defence, etc.'[20] Because of this, the only aspect of a given area that could influence any individuality in its architecture or layout was the demands of the site. When this hostility was combined with the results of command economics, the results were drastic. 'It would be to the greatest advantage of a centrally directed system of production,' wrote Vaclav Havel in the 1980s, 'if only one type of prefabricated panel were constructed, from which one type of apartment building would be constructed; these buildings in turn would be fitted with a single kind of door, door handle, window, toilet, washbasin and so on, and together this would create a single type of housing development constructed according to one standardised urban development plan, with minor adjustments for landscape, given the regrettable irregularity of the earth's surface.'[21] He was talking about something quite specific: housing estates that he knew well.

This critique was also heard in dissident Marxist circles. 'Let us look at what is happening in modern architecture,' implored Roy Medvedev of his Soviet samizdat audience in the 1970s. It is 'a field where enormous transformations are taking place, thanks to the use of new materials and construction methods, resulting in a fresh international style.' All well and good. But 'this, however, is no excuse for building new and completely

---

[20] B. Lubetkin (1932) The Russian Scene – the Development of Town Planning, *Architectural Review*, May.

[21] V. Havel (1992) Stories and Totalitarianism, in *Open Letters: Selected Writings 1965–1990*: 328–50. New York: Vintage Books, p. 343.

impersonal residential areas with standardised houses of identical design in Moscow, Baku and Tashkent. What is appropriate for an industrial city may be out of place in the capital of a national republic. And what suits one capital may not necessarily suit another.'[22] Notoriously, this was seldom taken into account, and one of the famous – if inadvertent – results of Khrushchev's 1954 decrees on 'Industrialised Building' and 'Against Architectural Excesses' was that an international style truly took hold in a way that those who coined that term couldn't have imagined – precisely the same style, aesthetic and often constructional approach for a transcontinental territory that stretches from the borders of Scandinavia to the edge of Afghanistan to a sea border with Japan.

From the mid-1960s onwards architects and communist thinkers actively tried to solve this problem. Some initial attempts were made to reintroduce the 1920s idea of collective housing, which would dissolve the nuclear family and create districts with individual units for sleep and study but with communal spaces for eating and leisure, but the first communal house built since the early 1930s – the House for the New Everyday Life, not far from Novye Cheryomushki – was turned into a student dormitory just before the building's completion.[23] On the other hand, the construction systems became more extensive – it was now normal to prefabricate entire rooms, not just panels – and new systems also offered the possibility of elaborate skylines and visual drama. More flexible modules were developed, such as the BKR-2, developed in

---

[22] R. Medvedev (1977) *On Socialist Democracy*. New York: Norton, p. 85.

[23] On this building, see the volume in Reaktion Books' 'Modern Architectures in History' series: R. Anderson (2015) *Russia*. London: Reaktion Books, pp. 226–8.

Krasnodar, which in theory offered architects and clients the possibility of creating any facade they wanted on top of the structural module. 'The lack of structural function of exterior wall elements allowed for the creation of facades of any texture, rhythm or scale,' points out Dimitrij Zadorin. The Soviet economy preferred simple, 'factory-ready' modules, however, such as the massively used 1–464 series, which needed little post-production attention on site, making the jobs of construction institutes and local governments easier. Because of this, 'practically every ambitious project based on BKR-2 never left the drawing board. What were launched into production instead were residential blocks of nine and 12 storeys. One after another, they filled new developments…making them barely identifiable blood brothers of the cheerless panel outskirts in other cities.'[24] An entire 'third generation' of what Philipp Meuser calls 'Tetris' blocks was launched in the USSR, and most of them faced the problem that 'any alteration to the product range was stressful'[25] for the specialised 'house factories' that produced most Soviet housing.

So, while there are thousands of Belyayevos, there is only one Severnoye Chertanovo (see Figures 10.9–10.11). It's further south, reached via a recent, fiddly Metro interchange that usefully attempts to connect up the mikrorayons rather than link them solely to the centre. You can tell something is different as soon as you get off the Metro; while the stations in Belyayevo and Cheryomushki are as standardised as the housing, Chertanovskaya station is a return to the strange, opulent dreamworld created under Moscow during the Stalin era. Architect Nina Alyoshina's hall is a moodily lit expressionist cathedral,

---

[24] Meuser & Zadorin, *Towards a Typology of Mass Housing*, p. 434.

[25] Ibid., p. 345.

Figure 10.9   Chertanovskaya Metro station

Figure 10.10   Severnoye Chertanovo

Figure 10.11   Avenue 77

speaking of arrival at somewhere special, not of departure to the centre. Outside, apartment blocks spread around a large lake. Half of these are standardised in the Belyayevo mould, but the other half are mid-rise buildings arching around artificial hills and valleys, connected by glazed skyways. You can see, looking closely, that they're also made of standardised panels, but arranged in such a way as to give variety to the buildings; it's the first of the mikrorayons in which you can really speak of 'architecture' (credited to a team of architects headed by Mikhail Posokhin, Abram Shapiro and engineer Lev Dubek) rather than just engineering. The mikrorayon's centre consists of a square in front of the Metro with two shabby buildings: a rotunda with a bar looking out over the water, and a long, low block (now used as a supermarket) facing the lake. They're bleak, but bustling; their bleakness comes from their chaotic subdivision and mess of adverts, not from their dereliction or neglect.

When writing about the district for *The Guardian*, I spoke to photographer Yuri Palmin, who has lived in Chertanovo for 18 years, first in what he calls the 'bad,' standardised blocks and then in the more prestigious, bespoke blocks opposite, which still have a more stable population than is the suburban norm. He pointed out to me not only that the area looks unlike the other mikrorayons but that it has a totally different layout. Rather than the interchangeable units for nuclear families, there are '42 different kinds of single and double level flats, with winter gardens in the ground floors' within these long complexes. This was a late attempt under Leonid Brezhnev to show that 'developed socialism' could have room for different kinds of families and lives, 'a sign of hope, a training ground and a lab.'[26] That is, they come closer than most to the promises of futurology such as *Life in the Twenty-First Century* or *The Ideal Communist City*. After the question of solving an urgent problem, one of basic need – getting the population out of overcrowded, subdivided communal flats and into purpose-built apartments with their own front doors, not to mention heating and sanitation – the planned economy could finally move from 'quantity' to 'quality'. Except that transition never happened on a large scale, and the standardised blocks were rolled out to the edges of Moscow right until the end of the 1980s.

The mistake often made is to assume that standardisation ended with the capitalist 'shock therapy' applied to the planned economy in the early 1990s. The new blocks built into the interstices of the mikrorayons are still industrialised and still pieced together from concrete panels, albeit with silly decorative roofs to give a shallow impression of individuality. Even the Orthodox church built near the lake in the late 1990s is standardised in its thin, tacky application of old Russian details. What has changed is two things: space, with communal areas considered

---

[26] Interviews with the author, April 2015.

parcels of land ripe for development; and speculation, with a vibrant property market in the capital generating fortunes for a few and insecurity for most. Dominating Chertanovo today is a 40-storey monolith, called 'Avenue 77'. According to Palmin it limits light for many Severnoye Chertanovo residents for much more than 'a few hours in summer'. It tries to break up its enormous grid of standardised flats via a Koolhaas-like 'iconic' shape, but nobody could be seriously fooled; this is form following speculation, an image of public space and equality being crushed by speculation.

In the 1990s, when looking at the apparently interchangeable districts produced by 'Communism', critics didn't see, or ignored, the libraries, the childcare centres, the polyclinics, the schools, the parks, the treatment of housing as a basic and free human right, but saw merely those huge, inescapable, interchangeable monoliths – the slabs upon slabs that always strike the casual viewer driving from the airport to the centre. In his attempt to create a Marxist analysis of the economics of the USSR, Hillel Ticktin used housing as a useful example of the problems that its professed socialism caused for the Soviet economy. 'The same problem,' he writes, 'that may appear as one of many difficulties in capitalism is of crucial moment in the Soviet system. The production of poor quality housing under capitalism is a fact of life that may increase the profits of the construction companies. In the USSR, it leads to enormous costs of repair, problems of replacement, and to an absorption of resources that the system cannot afford...at all times the poor quality of the Soviet product constitutes a contradiction of the system.'[27] In other words, the Soviet economy was incredibly wasteful, but, unlike capitalism, the planners hadn't figured out how to make waste and failure

---

[27] H. Ticktin (1992) *Origins of the Crisis in the USSR*. Armonk, NY: M. E Sharpe, p. 11.

profitable. The endemic low productivity and low quality of goods were explained by Ticktin as a consequence of the bureaucrats' fear of the workers. They would not push workers as hard as they would be pushed in the West, and, with full employment an intrinsic part of the system, they were not threatened with the sack; but, there again, they could not offer workers the consumer goods or the dream of social advancement as incentives to coax them into raising productivity. Automation had not reached the level at which these sorts of problems would become irrelevant, though it may have had some role in the poor quality of goods.

Critics from both the left and right argued that the monumental uniformity of housing was the greatest possible indictment of the system: a rigid plan that assumed everyone wanted the same thing, while giving them a mass-produced product that few really desired, but had to accept for want of anything better. The assumption was that the free market would result in variety, liveliness and complexity. What actually happened was a property boom that took over the three or four biggest cities, and a grim decline everywhere. In the centre, some specially commissioned edifices spoke of the rarefied or outré tastes of the new elite, but in the suburbs, where many more people had to suffer the consequences, the main change was that blocks became bigger, longer and much more careless of public space, but were still built via the methods that the newly privatised construction companies had learned well in the good old days.[28] As Bee Flowers pointed out in 2006, '[W]ithin the monolithic construction sector

---

[28] For a comprehensive and, rightly, heavily critical analysis of this construction boom, largely reliant on the sweated labour of central Asian migrants rather than automation (people are cheaper), see The Russian Reader, A Home For Every Russian, 3 May, https://therussianreader.wordpress.com/2015/05/03/a-home-for-every-russian, accessed 31 August 2016.

remarkably little has changed. The sector has no internal stimuli for change, and in the absence of alternatives there are no effective market pressures. Moreover, now that the vast majority of Russians live in system-built housing blocks, these have come to define the urban experience – the expectation of things being any other way has died.'[29] The ideals of Novye Cheryomushki died as much more than fond or ironic nostalgia, but its methods and techniques remained, and managed to make some people very wealthy. What the Soviet prefabrication programme promised, and failed to deliver, was at best something more than simply lots more housing. Instead, it suggested that mass production could actually create a society that was both communal and differentiated, industrialised and green and placid. The end of the USSR finished much hope of the first of these, and the infill of green spaces in large cities is currently obliterating the second. Whether mass housing could achieve greater things in more propitious circumstances, and in a very different kind of society, with less dominance of patriarchy, bureaucracy and Fordist labour, is another question entirely.

---

[29] Flowers, What's Wrong with This Approach, Comrades?

11

Megastructures, Superweapons and Global Architectures in Science Fiction Computer Games

Mark R. Johnson

Introduction

In *Halo 5*, a first-person shooter computer game released in 2015, players find themselves walking through a planet surrounded by technologies of almost unimaginable complexity and power. These are 'guardians', vast angel- or eagle-like mechanical devices that, we are told, could each subdue an entire solar system. They were manufactured (like much in the *Halo* series) by the 'Forerunners', an ancient and now extinct galactic race of incredible technological advancement. They built artificial planets, manufacturing plants large enough to *manufacture the artificial planets*, and – one might suppose – manufacturing plants for the manufacturing plants. Such giant constructions – megastructures – and the varied societies that produce them can be found with remarkable regularity across far more games than just *Halo*. From *Half-Life* to *Killzone* and from *Mass Effect* to *Destiny*, titanic structures abound, with different economic models underpinning their construction. In some cases these are only backdrop, but in many cases the player gets to explore and navigate these megastructures first-hand.

In this chapter I look over the many different futuristic economies that games have portrayed, the structures and architectures that emerged from them and what they show us about the potential of the computer game – as opposed to the film, the novel, and so forth – not just to present visions of the future but to make those visions *playable* and open to *exploration*. This will start with an overview of some of the most visible megastructures in contemporary games, with a particular focus on the specific representations of future societies and economies they represent. We then move on to explore the importance of these being specifically *in-game* constructions, and how games are serving as the site for experimenting with possible techno-economic futures, and specifically playable futures. In doing so I will argue that games are a particularly rich medium for examining science fiction economies and the physical structures they produce, and that in the future we should expect to see these imaginaries becoming more popular, more varied and more notable.

Games are a particular kind of fiction: they are interactive, they change with the player's/reader's actions and they give a tremendous amount of freedom for the player to approach them in a range of different ways. In a traditional literary sense, games are inevitably closest to the choose-your-adventure novel (and, to a lesser extent, the literature of authors such as Italo Calvino or Jorge Borges). In adventure novels the reader is a player and navigates their own way through a text that branches and weaves with many options; in the works of Calvino and Borges, the reader is often spoken to directly, or an active participant in the narrative. Similarly, games rarely if ever imagine a passive reader; the player is always caught up in the action, and, in almost all cases, leads that action. Science fiction consequently finds a good home in games: players can lead the action and drive the exploration of worlds whose rules do not conform to our own, and which offer the players things – technologies, places, ways of being – whose use is entirely alien. Games are also, of course, 'science fictions,' in the sense that they are fictions produced by science – or, at least, by technology. When playing an SF game that explores computer software, for instance, or that contains a section of gameplay in which the player character enters cyberspace, it can be hard to avoid an amused smile when your avatar walks around within computer hardware, *within computer hardware*. The inescapable importance of science and technology to computer games as a whole adds another layer of science fiction to the computer game; and the games we explore in this chapter have taken full advantage of their computer software and hardware in the creation of the economic fictions, or extrapolations, that we consider.

Megastructures: Definitions and Depictions

First, however, we must ask: what exactly is a 'megastructure'? The term is used more commonly in science fiction than in scholarly work examining the real world, but the term 'megaproject' is extremely close to that of megastructure (and is sometimes used interchangeably), so it is there we should first look. There is no single definition of a megaproject, but various factors have been considered important to their identification. In monetary terms, megaprojects are understood as multi-million-[1] or -billion-[2] dollar investments. They have also been defined in terms of the

---

[1] L. Penwell & J. Nicholas (1995) From the First Pyramid to the Space Station: An Analysis of Big Technology and Mega-Projects, paper presented at AIAA 'Space Programs and Technologies' conference, Huntsville, AL, 28 September.

[2] C. Fiori & M. Kovaka (2005) Defining Megaprojects: Learning from Construction at the Edge of Experience, paper presented at ASCE 'Construction Research' congress, San Diego, 5 April.

attraction of public attention;[3] as sources of 'high degree[s] of uncertainty'[4] and technical and financial risk; and as sources of collaboration between large numbers of individuals or groups.[5] The length of the construction or implementation process is often considered vital; Adnan Haider and Ralph Ellis argue for a time frame of at least five years to 'qualify' as a megaproject,[6] and consider it a fundamental part of a megaproject's definition, while Nils Bruzelius, Bent Flyvbjerg and Werner Rothengatter instead suggest that the lifetime of the project is the better measure,[7] suggesting '50 years and more' as a metric. Others have simply defined a megaproject as a construction or engineering undertaking that is 'huge by virtually any measure,'[8] be it in terms of cost, people involved, management, resources involved or whatever, and that the label is a flexible one.

Megastructures are not a purely modern phenomenon, however. Many older constructions were as large as, if not larger than, purely in terms of physical size, those of the modern

---

[3] J. van der Westhuizen (2007) Glitz, Glamour and the Gautrain: Mega-Projects as Political Symbols, *Politikon*, 34(3): 333–51.

[4] A. van Marrewijk (2005) Strategies of Cooperation: Control and Commitment in Mega-Projects, *M@n@gement*, 8(4): 89–104; see also N. Bruzelius, B. Flyvbjerg & W. Rothengatter (2002) Big Decisions, Big Risks: Improving Accountability in Mega Projects, *Transport Policy*, 9(2): 143–54.

[5] Penwell & Nicholas, From the First Pyramid to the Space Station; van Marrewijk, Strategies of Cooperation.

[6] A. Haider & R. Ellis (2010) Analysis and Improvement of Megaprojects Performance, paper presented at EPOS 'Engineering Project Organizations' conference, South Lake Tahoe, CA, 5 November.

[7] Bruzelius, Flyvbjerg & Rothengatter, Big Decisions, Big Risks.

[8] Penwell & Nicholas, From the First Pyramid to the Space Station.

day. Christopher Jones includes the Pyramids, Roman roads and aqueducts and early Gothic cathedrals in this description.[9] He argues that they, and contemporary equivalents, differed significantly in terms of purpose: cathedrals had a 'metaphysical and social purpose', and lacked the 'calculative utilitarianism' of their modern successors. Similarly, Larry Penwell and John Nicholas examine the first Egyptian pyramid – the Step Pyramid – and the European Gothic cathedrals as examines of non-modern megaprojects with clear non-utilitarian goals.[10] In pyramid construction a dual purpose may have been to handle unrest amongst Egyptian tribes by serving as a unifying and henotic collaborative project[11] that members of all tribes took part in, solidifying national identity between disparate groups via the 'superordinate task'[12] of its construction. This view on 'old' megaprojects is not universal, however; Ute Lehrer and Jennefer Laidley identify the 'mega-project' as fundamentally an aspect of modern industrialisation,[13] with earlier similar endeavours being merely 'large-scale' projects that did not

---

[9] C. Jones (1981) Small Is Powerful, Technology Is Art: The Growth of Supertechnologies in the 20th Century, *Futures*, 13(1): 51–62.

[10] Penwell & Nicholas, From the First Pyramid to the Space Station.

[11] D. Roberts (1995) Egypt's Old Kingdom, *National Geographic*, 187(1): 2–43.

[12] L. Penwell (2006) Global Identity and the Superordinate Task, in E. Klein & I. Pritchard (eds.) *Relatedness in a Global Economy*: 124–48. London: Karnac Books.

[13] U. Lehrer & J. Laidley (2008) Old Mega-Projects Newly Packaged? Waterfront Redevelopment in Toronto, *International Journal of Urban and Regional Research*, 32(4): 786–803.

mobilise the same kinds of labour processes, in the same way, and on the same scale and scope, as their modern equivalents.

We can therefore see two perspectives on the *importance* of the economic and financial dimensions to understanding these undertakings. On the one hand, some scholars have argued that megastructures are a fundamentally modern phenomenon, arising in the organisation, stratification and globalisation of labour from the Industrial Revolution onwards, and that the attendant modalities of global trade, communication and employment are crucial to understanding the megaproject phenomenon. On the other hand, other scholars propose that any mobilisation of effort and expense that is substantial from the perspective of the society that produces them, or that produces a large or imposing physical structure irrespective of its purely economic costs, merits the label 'megaproject'. These latter scholars also tend to focus more on the political and social impacts of these creations, rather than their purely instrumental economic costs and benefits. We can therefore begin to see why so many science fiction authors have been intrigued by the concept; if the human race has already produced the pyramids, Gothic cathedrals and kilometre-high skyscrapers of the real world, with their political, social and – most importantly here – *economic* importance, what kinds of massive physical edifices might a vastly more technologically advanced society create? The fictional worlds of games are at the forefront of answering this question, and it is to these we now turn.

Megastructures in Games

The *Halo* series is the game series famous for its megastructures, more perhaps than any other contemporary computer games. *Halo* is a series of 'first-person shooter' games in which the player's vision is positioned behind the eyes of the lead character and controls their actions and decisions directly. The plot of the early games involves battling against the theocratic hegemonic alien 'Covenant', an amalgam of multiple nonhuman space-faring races united by a religious belief that the artefacts left behind in the galaxy by the mysterious 'Forerunners' will transition them into a glorious afterlife. In actual fact, these 'Haloes' – artificial rings thousands of kilometres in diameter orbiting stars and planets, and equipped with climates and biospheres and habitability for life – are superweapons designed to exterminate all multicellular life in the galaxy in order to starve a parasitic organism, 'the Flood', of all food sources. In case the ringworlds were not impressive enough, in later games the player encounters a vast construct known as 'the Ark', which actually manufactures these ringworlds and is around 100,000 kilometres in diameter, and 'Shieldworlds', planet-sized bunkers designed to protect their inhabitants from the Halo weapons. Every one of these items produced by the Forerunners, of which dozens or potentially hundreds exist, is larger and more sophisticated than the entire technological achievements or output of the two factions, human and Covenant, who battle over them. The *Halo* games therefore depict an SF universe filled with colossal megastructures, all imagined as being built by a civilisation with a very particular set of far-future (to us) economic capabilities.

Valve Corporation's noted *Half-Life* series, meanwhile, has two primary megastructures, each speaking to a different economic model. In the original *Half-Life* the player spends almost the full game within 'Black Mesa', a vast government research laboratory built into the side of a cliff and modelled after real equivalents of massive state military-scientific economies, ranging from Los Alamos and Area 51 to Colorado Springs and NORAD. It contains almost everything one might imagine, from missile silos to nuclear waste stores and robotics laboratories to laser testing bays. In fact, it is so large that the player comes across entire seas abandoned, or forgotten, or simply no longer relevant to funded research. Black Mesa is a vast and complex edifice into which tremendous amounts of financial investment and technical expertise have been poured, but is a very different kind of structure from the Forerunner's achievements in *Halo*.

Half-Life 2, set years later, sees a world overtaken by the 'Combine' – pronounced like the tractor, not the verb – which is an alien empire that absorbs other species and alters itself to take the best of what they have to offer. Earth is under their control and dominated by an ever-shifting Protean skyscraper known as 'the Citadel', which watches over the newly enslaved and sterilised human race. The construction of the Citadel is never explicitly recounted, but inside we find 'stalkers', almost feral human beings stripped of certain limbs and any higher brain functions, who seem to serve a role between that of slave workers, drones in a hive and an expendable workforce for dangerous situations. In the streets below, meanwhile, remaining humans are watched over by a police service of turncoat humans and human 'synths' (humans crossed with Combine biology and technology), who keep order and maintain the human workforce. The Citadel was presumably constructed by enslaved humans and stalkers, offering a rather bleaker version of the future than *Halo*, and the kinds of structures enabled by far-future SF economies. In this case the construction of the megastructure is dependent upon slave labour rather than any kind of far-future technologies that emancipate sentient life from the yoke of economic life, resulting in quite the opposite, creating instead a regression towards 'older' forms of labour organisation and mobilisation that undermine the rationalistic and liberal modern Western ideals of freedom and self-actualisation.

These imagined future labour-economic processes of *Half-Life 2* become even clearer when we look at the creatures who rule over the Combine: the 'advisors'. These are large, grub-like creatures with no apparent inherent means of locomotion or manipulation, but some kind of telekinetic power and a set of mechanical arms strapped to their bodies. A tongue-like tendril extends from their mouths, with which they probe the world. The player rarely encounters them, and normally sees only fleeting glimpses of their personal armoured enclosures. They live in safety and comfort, while their bloated and almost larval forms are a stark contrast to the sleek aerodynamic machinery of the broader Combine. They are thus depicted as a kind of decadent ruling class, who manage a technocratic empire without performing even the smallest amount of the labour themselves, preferring to rely on slaves and the cheap labour of conquered worlds. In this way, and the economic model they preside over, they are quite reminiscent of rulers of the past who built their own megastructures; around their necks they wear rings engraved with strange, almost hieroglyphic symbols, perhaps designed to support a comparison with ancient Egypt and the divide between rulers and enslaved peoples. Their seclusion, meanwhile, is so extreme that, based on *Half-Life 2* and its expansions, it seems unlikely that the citizens of Earth were even aware the advisors existed, as they act more like behind-the-scenes puppeteers than charismatic powerful rulers. This kind of extreme wealth and power disparity is depicted here as being enabled by the technology of this advanced species, and shows an SF economy in which a small number of despotic individuals control billions through the power of futuristic genetic and cybernetic technologies.

In the *Killzone* series, meanwhile, we see a near-future world, with clear allusions and analogies to the Cold War, bisected by a great wall that spans the globe. When it goes across oceans there are constant boat and aircraft patrols to ensure that nobody crosses over, while on land there are carefully monitored checkpoints across which the small number of migrant workers from one faction to the other – the Vektan and the Helghast – sometimes cross. It was built jointly by both sides, the only project on which they cooperated, and marks a massive technological and economic achievement. In many ways the technological level of this world is comparable to that which produced Black Mesa in the original *Half-Life*, and represents a similar setting in which massive techno-scientific investment and mobilisation seem very believable and reasonable. The wall is larger and more impressive than any other structure within this fictional universe, and, although it was created using substantial economic investment, it is not – as with some of the megastructures explored here – designed to bring economic benefits. Rather, it is a megastructure with political, military and social purpose, into which economic resources have been poured.

The *Mass Effect* series, our fourth case study, is set several hundred years in the future, in a galaxy with a dozen established non-human civilisations with which humanity has only recently begun to interact. Prominent in the series is an immense space station known as the 'Citadel'. This Citadel is very different from the Citadel of *Half-Life 2*; whereas one watched over a docile and downtrodden populace, this one serves as the bustling hub of galactic politics, economics and culture. All galactic government is run from the Citadel, and a large portion of the games missions, both involving conversations and discussions with various actors, and in several instances defending from attackers, take place upon the station. The Citadel's builders are first believed to be the ancient 'Protheans', who – much like the Forerunners of *Halo* – are revered as an ancient and now-extinct galactic civilisation whose technical capabilities outweigh those of the currently extant species. The Citadel is in turn managed by a mysterious species known as the 'keepers', who are apparently unable to communicate with other races but keep the station in working order.

It is later revealed that this is all a ruse, however: the Citadel was constructed by the 'Reapers', an ancient machine race dedicated to exterminating all life in the galaxy every 50,000 years, in order to allow new life and species to flourish. The Citadel, and the web of faster-than-light travel technologies that connect the Citadel to every part of the galaxy, were constructed so that spacefaring civilisations would come to base their own technologies around those of the Reapers, and to use the Citadel as a social and cultural hub, in order to make the eventual purge easier and more effectively centralised. The keepers, meanwhile, are revealed to be a previous species of the galaxy seemingly lobotomised and then enslaved to manage (and construct?) the Citadel. This is the second example of slave labour being the underpinning of these science fiction economies; even if the keepers did not construct the Citadel at the behest of the Reapers, it is made clear that they have maintained it for uncountable millennia, a work of labour probably far greater than its actual initial construction. In these economies and that of the Forerunners in *Halo*, SF technology is used to suppress and control populations, not to emancipate and liberate, offering players clear enemies and a clear political ideology to battle against.

There are also many other megastructures in the *Mass Effect* games, such as the 'Shroud' (a tower designed to stabilise the atmosphere of a world trapped in a nuclear winter), the 'Crucible' (a Moon-sized superweapon designed to stop the Reapers) and the 'Collector Base' (a massive space station orbiting within the accretion disk of a black hole), which were instead constructed by the galaxy's civilisations for military-political-economic reasons, much like Black Mesa and the Vektan–Helghast wall. *Mass Effect* therefore displays two of the themes beginning to emerge here in these playable science fiction economies: slave labour and the use of technology to control large portions of the population; and political-military techno-science as underpinning the construction of megastructures and megastructure-like projects and undertakings.

Destiny, the 2014 game by the developers of the original *Halo* games, Bungie, further showcases the preoccupation with megastructures that now seems common to the studio. Set in a future version of our familiar Solar System devastated by a great war and facing an influx of a variety of strange and enigmatic alien races, the *Destiny* universe is replete with tremendous and mysterious constructions. There is the 'Traveler', a seemingly benevolent city-sized sphere hovering over Earth's last remaining city; the 'Citadel' (now a familiar name in these games), a towering and geometrically peculiar structure built on Venus that defies traditional laws and expectations of physics and architecture; and the Black Garden, a seemingly infinite yet clearly artificial space replete with strange plants and hostile 'gardeners', who protect it from outsiders. None of these has known construction methods, nor, in some cases, is any information even given about who built them – or who paid for them. *Destiny* abounds with structures of this sort, in all cases speaking to economic processes that can bring together tremendous amounts of labour and raw materials, or that perhaps don't even need to involve labour and represent technologies that are simply capable of reshaping matter itself.

In all these games we see some commonalities: science fiction universes with tremendous megastructures of various sorts, produced – as we will now examine – by a range of predicted economic models about the future (or parallel-universe extrapolations upon the present, as in Black Mesa's clear positioning within a Cold War or post-Cold-War context). Some of these economies, such as massive techno-scientific investment, are familiar to modern historians, while others are either forms of labour and economics that we generally understand the world to have moved beyond, or are inconceivable to our current financial worldview.

Economies and Imaginations

All these science fiction megastructures therefore reflect different ideas of future or near-contemporary economies, with a focus upon the economic and labour impacts of science and technology. We can reasonably split them into three categories, which show us much about the interests and concerns of these game designers, and their economic and political visions of technological futures: oppression and slavery; techno-scientific excess; and post-scarcity economies. Crucially, each of these can be *explored* in these games, allowing the player to walk around and experience these SF economies and the structures they have created, and explore how space and place have been restructured and shaped by the architectural creations of these economic systems. In this section we explore each of these three models in depth, focusing on the games that depict them and their commonalities, and begin to consider why their depiction in games is especially interesting, as opposed to literature, cinema or television, and how this alters the experience of the viewer – in this case the player – who comes across them.

In *Half-Life 2* (the Citadel) and *Mass Effect* (also the Citadel), the most visible megastructures have been constructed – or repaired and maintained – by various classes of slave or otherwise impoverished labourers working under the command of near-omnipotent overseers. Whether it is thanks to the

stalkers and subdued humans who serve the Combine, or
the keepers who maintain the Reapers' trap, these structures
are reliant upon the unwilling labour of tens of thousands, or
potentially millions. In this we see a fear with regard to future
economies, in which technological development enables new
forms of population control and their use as cheap labour.
These economies of science fiction are at once deeply familiar, in their similarities to comparable real-world practices
throughout history, but also new and frightening, and fundamentally dependent upon futuristic forms of technical expertise: ubiquitous surveillance, cybernetics, genetic modification,
and so forth. These are fictional economies that undermine
and challenge traditional emancipatory techno-utopian discourses, presenting instead the potential for technology to capture and constrain, not liberate, thus showing the economic
models of large-scale slave-led production and maintenance
that this form of techno-mediated social order enables.

In *Half-Life* (Black Mesa), *Killzone* (the Wall) and *Mass
Effect* (the Crucible, and so forth), these structures are instead
the creation of policies and economic structures designed to
lend massive support to experimental techno-science. Black
Mesa, the *Half-Life 2* Citadel, *Mass Effect's* Crucible, Shroud,
Citadel and Collector Base were all built for military purposes,
as was the Wall of *Killzone*, although in that case it was a result
of war rather than directly for military purposes. War, conflict
and the battle for supremacy between factions are what moti-
vates these massive economic undertakings. The most obvious
comparison is with the military mobilisation of the so-called
'Superpowers' – the United States and the USSR – in the Second
World War and the Cold War, the close intertwining of high-
technology research, economic development, mobilisation of
resources and expertise, and geopolitical ramifications of this
same research. As opposed to the above category, this category

consists of those that present what we might consider 'near-future' science fiction. These economic and labour processes and practices are very recognisable to us, and that makes these buildings immediately familiar and understandable; what we know of the construction of the Burj Khalifa, the Channel Tunnel or the Manhattan Project is easily transferrable into these fictional settings.

In *Halo* (Halo, the Ark, Shield Worlds) and *Destiny* (the Citadel, the Black Garden, the Traveler), these structures have all instead been produced by post-scarcity societies. Notions of traditional economies, resources, labour and industrial processes have become obviated by the rise of technologies – generally unseen but implied – that allow for the trivial reshaping of matter, and the creation of new forms of matter impervious to traditional attacks, architectural norms or structural physics. The Forerunners from *Halo*, who built its great architectures, are a classic post-scarcity SF society: a culture that has moved 'beyond' money and finance, and can manipulate matter so easily and readily that the economic concerns of lesser civilisations seem almost comical. This shows us the imaginations of writers considering the development of future technology, what directions this technological development might take and how they might contribute to an eventual move beyond the traditional material economics that have inevitably dominated human life up to the present day. They also suggest an even bolder concept: that the very idea of an 'economy' is a phase, a point in the technological trajectory of a civilisation that will, eventually, cease to be relevant. Past a certain point matter is so plentiful and the ability to reshape that matter so trivial that economies cease to exist, and building the planet-sized or solar-system-sized structures in these games becomes only a question of time invested, not resources and effort. In other words, *anything* can be built in such societies, whether a single hand-held item, or a manufacturing plant for manufacturing manufacturing plants that, in turn, manufacture entire worlds.

Games and the Architectural Imaginary

Literature, film and television have long since portrayed megastructures and the economies behind them. In literature we see Iain Banks' *Culture* civilisation, which eschews natural planets in favour of living upon ringworlds and vast wandering spacecraft; 'Bolder's Ring' from Stephen Baxter's Xeelee series, a black hole stretched across millions of years; planet-sized machinery left behind by the 'Shadows' in Alastair Reynolds's *Revelation Space* series, to aid other civilisations in contacting parallel realities; the arcologies of William Gibson's Sprawl trilogy and much of cyberpunk since, which are vast urban agglomerations within self-contained habitats; and the 'Needle' in the *Doctor Who* expanded universe, a light-year-long structure upon which entire civilisations have risen and fallen without ever encountering one another. In film and television, we might look at the similarly massive arcologies of near-future Los Angeles in *Blade Runner*, including the iconic pyramid of the Tyrell Corporation; the massive mining ship Nostromo in *Alien*, dragging hundreds of millions of tons of ore across the galaxy; the famous Death Star of the *Star Wars* franchise; various structures from *Star Trek*, such as the Borg Cubes and Borg Spheres; and the 'Tet' or 'Tetrahedron' from *Oblivion*, a vast tetrahedral spacecraft housing a malevolent alien intelligence masquerading as a friend of the human race. Many of these, we must note, sometimes blur the lines between a 'megastructure' and what we might call a 'megavehicle', as do several of the megastructures in the games outlined here. Nevertheless, literature and cinema have shown a strong interest in depicting the massive edifices that might be created by future societies, drawing on those we already see and extrapolating to portray societies with greater technology, stronger economies and new forms of manufacture and material manipulation.

Despite these many portrayals, of which the above list contains only an incomplete selection, it was not until the advent of science fiction computer *games* that players could move beyond seeing or imagining what designers or writers specified, and begin to actually explore these megastructures. Players in these games walk through architectures and spaces that make any biological organism seem insignificantly tiny, and into which even the largest real-world human structures would fit a dozen, a hundred or even a million times over. These structures are not just buildings or 'vehicles' but are often the sites of entire societies, entire political structures or entirely unique self-contained ecosystems. Many contain extensive detail, from large-scale overall shape and design down to individual laboratories in Black Mesa, rooms and buildings in the *Mass Effect* Citadel or caves, rivers and individual trees that dot the planet-sized Haloes. These allow for designers to imagine the strangest of future spatial topographies and the systems they create or enable. Just as real-world human-built architectures (on the micro level) and global geography (on the macro level) have profound influences on global ecosystems and political and social behaviour, these towering architectures and entire artificial geographies show an understanding of this syndrome, and an examination of how spaces shape life, war and interaction.

In turn, rather than relying on the reader's imagination or the particular shots designed by a cinematographer, games instead allow players to walk through these structures, to look at them from many angles and to spend their time how they see fit, exploring the civilisations and economies that created

them. This is not always the case, of course, as in some games
these megastructures are just 'background' images drawn by
the game designers that cannot actually be stepped into, but
in most cases these megastructures are interactive, or at the
very least play a major part in the game's narrative or thematic
elements. This shows the unique potential for *games* to create megastructures. Massive virtual worlds can be built and
explored through which players can experience the physical
manifestations of SF economies: megastructures constructed
through slave labour, techno-scientific investment and post-
scarcity technologies. Games represent a rich opportunity
for the imaginations of designers about the economies and
megastructures of the future to create their ideas in tremendous detail, and to allow those who consume their media to
more fully experience these spaces.

As I suggested earlier in the chapter, these three dominant models – slavery, techno-science and abundance – tell us
much about the concerns and anxieties of the game designers
who create these megastructure worlds. In the first instance,
concerns about the power of technology to contain, constrain
and control us are certainly not new to science fiction; in
computer games they offer easy narrative hooks to pitch the
player against these oppressors, and to create great systems
of economic-technological control the player might battle
against. In the second instance, perhaps few events have generated as many outpourings of popular and fictional concern
as the technologies and technological controversies of the
Cold War: nuclear power and nuclear weapons, the space race,
industrialisation and environmental destruction, new military technologies, and so forth. The games that explore techno-
scientific megastructures take some of these further to their
ever more monolithic conclusions, and explore how else the
Cold War could have played out, or what other technological

worlds might have been created from such outpouring of human ingenuity, and the conflation of economy, science, military and industry. In the third instance, techno-utopian predictions and fictions have existed since the earliest days of the Industrial Revolution – and, depending on what we define as techno-utopian, since long before then – and these post-scarcity worlds must be understood in that same vein. They represent not just an optimism for technological 'progress' but also a critical enquiry into where such progress might take us, and how economic life might be fundamentally reshaped.

Games have therefore demonstrated their tremendous value as an imaginary medium, and one that brings the viewer into a far closer relationship with the fictional setting being depicted. Exploring these structures can take the form of a kind of dialogue, in which the architectural imagination of the designer and the physical actions and choices of the specific player combine to create unique experiences of navigating these mega-architectures and the purposes for which they were built. In the future of games, it seems likely that we will see an even greater range of megastructures depicted than those considered in this chapter. An increasing volume of games are becoming 'open-world' experiences in which the player is given a massive virtual space to explore with a high degree of freedom, which is a high-level gameplay structure well suited to the navigation of colossal digital architectures; equally, many other games use modern graphics processing and rendering technologies to create worlds whose size and scope is immense, even if the player's progression through those worlds remains relatively linear. Games offer the opportunity to make these megastructures not just background settings for narrative drive and action, but entire worlds to be experienced by viewers and players. In doing so they inevitably hypothesise about what economic forms could possibly underpin these titanic structures, whether slavery and technological control, techno-scientific state and military investment or post-scarcity matter manipulation, and allow for an exploration of these science fiction economies and how they might shape the worlds around them.

12

Economic Design Fictions: Finding the Human Scale

Bastien Kerspern

In this chapter, design is envisaged beyond its role of packaging innovation to become a discursive tool fostering debates on inventing new economics by considering an experiment led by the studio Design Friction.[1] I first build on the notion of design fictions, meaning fictitious artefacts challenging prejudiced beliefs, to understand, from a theoretical standpoint, what economics could benefit from this specific posture, especially when bringing a human scale to these complex future systems. Having described these inputs, I then develop a proposition of a blueprint to construct Economic Design Fiction. This framework is meant to assist a co-creation process between stakeholders, whether or not economists, and designers in order to produce economic design fictions as materialisations of speculative economic systems intended to be discussed. With this blueprint in mind, a case study is reviewed involving actual economic-oriented design fictions built in order to test and evaluate the potential of such approach when questioning the purpose of new economic paradigms. In concluding, we look at the limits of Economic Design Fiction, extrapolating on

---

[1] Design Friction is a studio based in France producing critical and speculative scenarios to explore sociotechnological changes.

further iterations and improvements that could be brought to this undertaking.[2]

Designing Fictions and Frictions

Design, in all its forms, has always been tightly interwoven with economics. Today, even if it is driven by the pressing needs of productivism, consumerism and innovation, more and more designers are orienting their practice to engage the political. Design Fiction is one of these attempts to speculate on preferable perspectives, tweaking cultural, social and, more especially, economic beliefs.

Design Fiction is not a widespread posture among designers. Drawing from reflexive research questioning the design practice, Design Fiction relies on a problem-finding approach rather than a problem-solving one. The latter has established its dogma in the entrepreneurial culture, and design thinking has been a major asset in the race to 'make the world a better place'. It comes with recurrent injunctions to produce changes and even break things, as stated by the emblematic Silicon Valley gurus. Problem-finding, on the contrary, is all about understanding complex situations before attempting to fix anything that might even not be broken in the first place. It calls for intricate questions on the interinfluencing tensions between technologies, social issues and political ideologies. By switching from problem-solving to problem-finding, design fictions are no longer addressing a facet of a problem but are investigating the very structural issues of a situation.

------

[2] I would like to warmly thank my friend and colleague Estelle Hary for her thoughtful feedback and accurate criticism of this chapter.

Across their projects, designers step back and start to consider the bigger picture: are we solving the right problem? Or are we accelerating or crystallising existing negative externalities? To achieve this ambitious journey, Design Fiction is frequently inspired by input from different fields of expertise, such as ethnography, engineering and economics.

The problem-finding posture of Design Fiction looks at our near futures, focusing on emerging issues and the evolution of current status quos. The whole point of this initiative is not to predict tomorrow, but to be able to anticipate systemic challenges and stakes.

Extrapolating on weak signals, Design Fiction agitates social imaginaries as well as the realms of possible utopias and dystopias inhabiting these imaginaries. It acts as 'compasses rather than maps',[3] to open and foster discussions related to changes. In this sense, Design Fiction tells of new trajectories and alternative possibilities.

At this point, Design Fiction shares similar ground with strategic foresight, futures research and even science fiction. It is, in fact, a complementary approach, as design takes benefits from its aptitude to translate questions into concrete scenarios and products. By the use of diegetic prototypes aiming at suspending disbelief towards changes',[4] design fictions are objects materialising worlds and not just stories. They work as 'provotypes', meant to be provocative prototypes, semi-functional products embedding critics and speculative values to challenge recurrent status quos. In order to make speculations

---

[3] A. Dunne and F. Raby (2013) *Speculative Everything: Design, Fiction, and Social Dreaming.* Cambridge, MA: MIT Press.

[4] B. Sterling (2013) *Patently Untrue: Fleshy Defibrillators and Synchronised Baseball are Changing the Future*, Wired UK, 11 October.

experiential and to overcome the traditional pitfalls of fiction, Design Fiction shows serious arguments as seen previously. Designers are crafting compelling and believable scenarios. In their speculative productions, they keep in mind their aspirations for technical feasibility, but also the criterion of desirability and viability.

The purpose of Design Fiction is to resort to thought-provoking scenarios and prototypes that do not focus on implementation but, rather, on discussing 'What if?' scenarios with stakeholders. The following example demonstrates an actual case when designers have worked with multidisciplinary teams in devising on socio-technological futures, with an emphasis on economic renewal.

ProtoPolicy'[5] is a diptych of design fictions looking at the future of ageing in place. This experiment, carried out by the studio Design Friction and several British universities, raised the questions of assistive and invasive technologies. Two provotypes were designed and confronted with the thoughts of public policy-makers and civil servants: Soulaje, a self-administered euthanasia wearable; and the Smart Home Therapist, a counsellor trained in reconciling elderly people with their connected domestic appliances. Through its scenarios, ProtoPolicy especially addressed the economic stakes behind ageing in place with speculations on elderly employment, the impact of the silver economy and the struggles of the healthcare system.

As highlighted by this example, design fictions, through representing abstract ideas and challenging the status quo, are revealed to be an unexpected help when inventing the economy of tomorrow.

---

[5] ProtoPolicy (2015) *Using Design Fiction to Negotiate Political Questions*. Lancaster University: Imagination Lancaster.

Why Design Fiction Matters for Economics

Could design fictions have the capacity to make concrete and experiential the implications of possible larger paradigms shifts in the economy? When rethinking the economy, there is, more than ever, an urgency to consider the human scale. Economics is part of our daily life, but it is regarded by many as an abstract concept. The human scale is about making new economic perspectives tangible, relatable and ready to be debated beyond a community of experts. To do so, Design Fiction suggests three levers with which to bring in the human scale when reinventing the economy: everydayness, ambiguity and discussion.

Everydayness

Designers embed their visions for alternative futures in mundane artefacts challenging our imagination. In a similarity with the prevailing practice of industrial design, practitioners focus on everydayness as the scale of intervention. Future objects allow us to materialise speculations, but they begin to be fully relatable when they are connected to the daily life of stakeholders, notably when it comes to dealing with perplexing notions. Having this concept of everydayness in mind, Design Fiction contributes by defining and then designing for the 'new normal,'[6] to use the terminology of Anab Jain, from the design studio Superflux.

Ambiguity

Envisaging alternative perspectives, Design Fiction is qualified in tackling controversial themes, to act as a provocation,

---

[6] A. Jain (2013) *Design for the New Normal*. Superflux.

developing rhetoric on new narratives for production and consumption. Designing speculation is, in itself, a thought-out operation, demystifying the current status quo and revealing hegemonies occurring daily in our societies. This critical posture is mandatory to avoid reproducing 'flat-pack futures', a term coined by Scott Smith from Changeist,[7] a studio that fuses strategic design and foresight. Fuelled with ambiguity, the process of Design Fiction looks for frictions: what has been taken for granted by economic stakeholders, but is not for a deliberately ignored part of the population. Divergent scenarios are essential in fostering the pluralism of views and voices when economic systems are struggling to overcome their own neoliberal, climate-sceptical or social-xenophobic mythologies.[8]

One way to experiment with the principle of ambiguity in economic design fictions is by mixing influences and trends that seem to have no direct connections. Scenarios then take unexpected paths. With uncanny products or services, design fictions are an invitation to embrace the weirdness and the strangeness that are part of the new normal. In this way, design fictions cover the blind spots of futurescaping and the grey areas of systemic dependencies.

Discussion

Design fictions aim at triggering discussions beyond the communities of experts. By asking us to think about our expectations for the future, it actually becomes a catalyst to reflect on our considerations for the present.

---

[7] S. Smith (2013) *Beware of the Flat-pack Futures*. Media Future Week.
[8] E. Laurent (2016) Nos Mythologies Economiques.

Using materialised fictions as a starting point for conversation is expected to help to uncover fears, hopes and concerns from non-specialists about systemic shifts. It becomes even more relevant when confronted by a diversity of audiences and cultures. It encourages both spontaneous reactions and structured thoughts on what could be framed as preferable perspectives. How can we go there? How can we head to this preferable direction? Is it really a preferable situation? To whom? Figure 12.1 emphasises this idea of continuous and reciprocal influences between the 'real' world and the speculated perspectives.

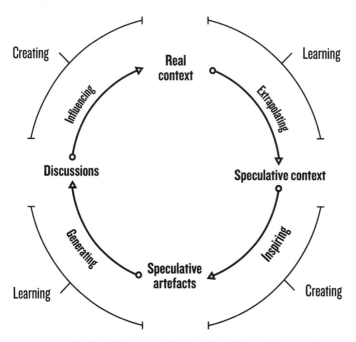

Figure 12.1 Design fictions set the basis for debates that aim, in turn, to influence our current models

It is a safe bet that discussing our assumptions on how techno-economic changes could affect our everyday life and the broader perspectives of our society will confront our beliefs in the new economy. Design Fiction as a provocative discipline becomes an asset in the decision-making process by showing us uncharted territories and unheard-of reactions.

Appealing for necessary turbulence, these three particular levers from Design Fiction facilitate the objections addressed to monocultures and self-fulfilling prophecies by extending the reinvention of economics to inputs from third parties. Design Fiction seems to be timely in its suitability for the exploration of scenarios associated with heterodox microeconomics. The everydayness lever indeed looks at the daily economic mechanisms in our lives while the ambiguity lever pushes for ideas for exploring ways that definitely do not belong to the field of mainstream economic paradigms. As Design Fiction has mainly been involved in reflecting on issues related to new technologies, however, there is a need to formulate guidelines to orient the process in engaging economic perspectives – thus producing what could be named Economic Design Fiction.

A Blueprint for Economic Design Fictions

Design Fiction is not just a matter of being a designer. For a few years now design thinking has intensively democratised design tools and methods for the entrepreneurial sphere, and even beyond. Design Fiction appears to be a tool for mediation in collaborative world-building experiences and a needed blueprint for building together. The blueprint for Economic Design Fiction aims to facilitate the translation of speculated new economic models into concrete objects for demonstrations and discussions. It consists of two canvases, one to set the speculative context and the other to imagine a product that narrates this alternative universe.

Looking at the Extremes: Scarcity and Post-Scarcity Contexts

A good story needs a good setting. For economic design fictions, a good setting challenges our relation to the law of supply and demand and its possible evolution.

The blueprint offers to set the design fictions in a two-fold speculative context: scarcity, with the disappearance of a specific element; and post-scarcity, a situation of abundance. To conceptualise those distant horizons, the starting point is the question of resources, be they natural or artificial, and the related mundane products made of them. As with the considerations for everydayness in Design Fiction, they will act as bridges to think about system changes.

Even if scarcity and post-scarcity might seem unlikely to happen soon, they are useful entry points for pondering our current systems. By playing with exaggerations, these extremes serve as a stimulating and effective basis for creative thought experiments. Radical speculations prevent us from sticking to timorous, pragmatic and short-term visions, which are in the way of real economic ingenuity. More interestingly, they move us to look at the robustness of the components of our economic models and to consider how they behave when stressed in unconsidered situations. How are we going to produce, to consume, to distribute and to sustain in such conditions of discontinuity?

Oscillating between scarcity and post-scarcity as a framework for thoughts is about alternating alternatives, looking at each edge of the spectrum of speculation; thinking how we are at ease with mirroring our fears and hopes for economics, be they utopian or dystopian projections. In this way, the coupling of scarcity and post-scarcity appears to be salutary, forcing us to envisage far-out changes and driving us away from the temptation of replicating faded socio-economic configurations.

The Speculative Context Canvas

The speculative context canvas sets the overall environment, from an economic perspective, for designing new models (see Figure 12.2). It is a matrix modelling the guidelines needed to imagine how key economic components such as production, distribution and consumption might evolve in a situation of scarcity or post-scarcity. To draw the outlines of this newly impacted society, the process starts with choosing a resource

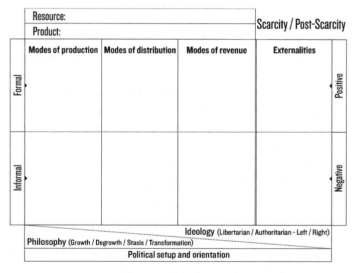

Figure 12.2 The speculative context canvas sets the economic paradigms of the speculated world

and a related mundane product. The product then becomes a manifesto of alternative economic paradigms implied by the radical shift of abundance or shortage. World-building happens through the lens of the product life cycle.

The speculative context canvas adopts the following structure.

Resources and Products

This is the starting point of a speculative economic system. It requires defining a natural or artificial resource, renewable or not, as well as a mundane product based or using this resource.

Political Set-Up and Orientation

This is the bedrock of the speculative context. It sets the political background that will influence the economic set-up in which the scarcity or post-scarcity product is going to evolve. It crosses ideological properties, combining the duality of left-wing/right-wing politics with the nuance of authoritarianism or libertarianism. The philosophical orientation completes the ideological system by adding a shared ideal to reach. In addition to the archetypical ambition for continuous growth and responsible degrowth, the speculative world can also opt for stasis, denying any opportunity for expansion and reduction, or transformation, converting its founding principles in unforeseen models.

Modes of Production, Distribution and Revenue

These three modes describe the backstage of the product life cycle and are, at the same time, another demonstration of the existence and influences of new economic paradigms in a scarcity or post-scarcity scenario. They cover all the steps of the history of the selected product, from being assembled to being distributed and exchanged for values.

Each mode is articulated around formal practices (such as subcontracting, recycling or online shopping) and informal ones (think about the black market, corruption, hacking or tweaking).

Externalities

This last part of the matrix is dedicated to extrapolating how externalities – positive or negative – related to the product are going to be acknowledged, managed or even ignored. Externalities typically include post-consumption, post-production and post-distribution impacts.

The scenery having been set, it is time to design the main prop articulating the whole fiction.

The Speculative Product Canvas

If the speculative context canvas is about establishing the environment for the design fiction, the product canvas is the one laying out the provotype to be discussed. The chosen mundane product needs to be reformulated according to the speculative context, its features, uses and consumers, then changing. These new characteristics of the product are like many highlights of the causes and consequences of new axioms actually remodelling the supply and demand concept. To fulfil their promise of being thought-provoking, however, the prototypes have to work in concert. They follow the principle of a diptych: for each resource, there are two extrapolated outputs, two products, each one embedding the vision of a scarcity or a post-scarcity economic system. By representing both the extremes, the diptych offers points of comparison for exploring in-between scenarios.

The speculative context canvas integrates three axes:

- features of the product (meaning: what it does);
- users or consumers (meaning: who uses it);
- uses of the product (meaning: what it is used for). This last part might sound similar to the features of the product, but it invites us to think about forbidden or unplanned uses.

All three items of the canvas suggest envisaging which elements of the product appear, remain unchanged or disappear in the speculative context when compared to our current object of reference (see Figure 12.3).

This being said, the matrix is just the very basis required to create speculative products personifying a different economic model. It still has to go through a classic design process, going

Resource:	Product:	
Appearing/increasing	**Unchanged**	**Disappearing/decreasing**
Product features		
Users/customers		
Product uses		

Figure 12.3 The speculative product canvas embodies the values and beliefs of the fictitious context in a real-fictional product

back and forth between ideation and iteration phases to finally deliver a real-fictional artefact. A team of designers, engineers and makers could easily build real and complex prototypes, although other diegetic formats are a matter of interest. Pieces such as fictional newspaper articles, user manuals and promotional flyers are some 'easy-and-cheap-to-prototype' options to stage the design fictions or extend the message of actual prototypes.

Neither of the matrices of the blueprint is intended to be used as a strict framework but, rather, to operate as a creative opener to structure inputs and to test the coherence of economics-oriented design fictions.

Case Study: Data, in Scarcity and Post-Scarcity Worlds

Our studio, Design Friction, experimented with this Economic Design Fiction blueprint to create two provocative scenarios intending to collect feedback on this discursive approach. While speculating on situations of scarcity and post-scarcity in data-driven economies, we shared these design fictions with economists as well as with non-experts to evaluate the extent to which such prototypes are able to foster imaginative thinking on the implications of other possible economic systems.

What If Data Were the Key Resource of the Economy?

This is the question that our speculation starts with. The digital economy has proved to be one of the most trending topics among industries and entrepreneurs in recent years, but also a subject carrying persistent myths, despite its relative youth. Almost every sector is now impacted directly or indirectly by what has been termed 'digitalisation'. Markets tend to rely more and more on data-driven orientations. Data are often mistakenly referred to as 'the new oil', regardless of the peculiar limits of the metaphor. It echoes the beliefs and trust placed in algorithms and connected technologies.

Free from the past fears of the planned economy, digitalisation has brought us a calculated economy. The promise of decentralised economies and systems is, for the moment, dominated by the concentrated and private ownership of a few operators, however. Indeed, the digital economy is tarnished by controversies about new gigantic monopolies, the lack of redistribution of values and a rapid pace of growth that is not thought likely to be handed down to future generations. Economic design fictions are then appropriate means for a debate about our expectations for an economy in which we are both the consumers and the products. Interestingly, 'big data' and its derivative metrics are also enforcing our insatiable faith in economic prediction, making it a proper choice when it comes to speculating on economic futures.

Our two design fictions will take data as a resource and the smartphone as a related product to explore new socioeconomic models being developed in societies varying from abounding with data to having banned them.

The Data Sniffer, a Product for Data Scarcity

In this speculative society, collecting and using personal data for commercial services had been banned after a massive leak of everybody's private data. Mass protests ensued and governments united in deciding to declare illegal every data-driven business. Data should neither be processed, shared nor stocked by third-party entities for commercial purposes. Economic models based on big data mining have collapsed. On the other hand, socio-economic paradigms that have evolved since the economy of attention have been radically redefined, without any digital application distracting us any more. As a consequence, each former data-based product had been redesigned so as to not share data any more.

The data sniffer marks the great comeback of the mobile phone antenna. As its name gives it away, the reactive antenna looks for electromagnetic signals to point towards the source of data, be it a hidden data centre or an undeclared sensor. As a kind of divining rod, the data-sniffing antenna helps in avoiding specific places linked to the use of personal data. It points out threats to the users, but the device also reports the fraudulent collection or stocking of data to concerned authorities. Concretely, the antenna bends to highlight the direction in which the data hotspot is situated. Basically, the closer you get to the source of data, the longer the antenna grows to refine the location of possible data spots (see Figure 12.4).

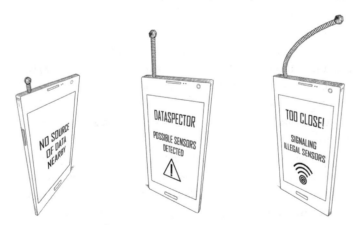

Figure 12.4 In an economic system suffering from data scarcity, consumers could be protected by a smart antenna detecting traces left by banned data-related activities (illustration: Emmanuelle Roulph)

In this design fiction, the data sniffer had been stated as a mandatory feature that smartphone constructors have to include in their products, on the basis of legal requirements. The speculative product was introduced through a fictional user manual explaining how it should be operated.

When presented to both economists and online service users, the comments first underlined a possible 'slowification' of the world, with real-time data use no longer permitted. The participants highlighted that the disappearance of data-driven systems would accelerate the growth of local markets and insular economic communities. The data scarcity environment was also a convenient occasion for a new economy. In addition, new jobs were suggested to track and report any irregular use of data. New civic incentives would be set up to deal with data as a threat to civil liberties. To ensure this guarantee, human operators would replace algorithms, processing data 'by hand' to avoid the possibility of the latter being leaked or misused.

Production settings have also been discussed in connection with the end of digital black boxes. For the remaining attempt to mine and refine data, every procedure would have to be transparent and publicly readable, implying the end of any technological monopoly. In this set-up, all individuals would become their own data heaven and, under very strict regulation, be able to monetise their private data for certified companies or research labs. Interestingly, this context of data scarcity was also the opportunity to point out the likelihood of an emerging economy of fear: the widespread paranoia would have triggered new businesses and regulations tailored to satisfy the desires for privacy.

Imagination had its own limits, however. Through the discussions, it could clearly be observed that there was a temptation to reproduce what was the pre-internet economy, without building on the identified possibilities of networked intelligence and a dematerialisation of knowledge.

The Infobesity Case, a Product for Post-Data Scarcity

This design fiction speculates as to what the consequences might be of the unstoppable rise of data production. Data-driven economies are here regarded as being at saturation point, with too many data having been generated and having to be processed. It has become costly to develop algorithmic services and dedicated places, such as data centres, to manage these massive flows of data. In this context, some people have become data addicts, with all their personal and social activities or rituals depending on data-driven solutions. As a matter of fact, a lot of data coming from these digital junkies are considered meaningless, or even redundant, for big data-driven systems. Information overload then shares a lot of similarity with the problem of obesity, and has, naturally, been termed 'infobesity'. As a consequence, several start-ups launch products to help in reducing the production and use of data-driven services by data addicts.

As one of those many products launched to thrive in a world loaded with data, the 'infobesity case' is a shell that promises to reduce your production and use of digital content. Targeting data addicts in the first place, the case provides an incentive for a data diet. The idea is quite simple: the more you use and produce data, the fatter the case gets. The chubbiness of the infobesity case is an indication of the status of your production and use of data. At some point, the shell is intended to become so big that it is actually hard to carry the smartphone with you. Using it for basic operations such as chatting or browsing on social networks is also way more difficult, de facto reducing the use of data (see Figure 12.5).

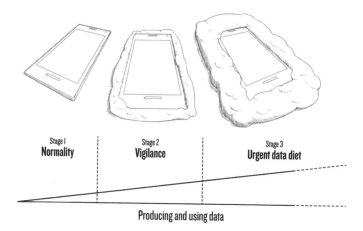

Figure 12.5 To help discuss the economic implications of data post-scarcity, this design fiction introduces the infobesity case, a smartphone case with the unique feature of getting fatter the more data are used (illustration: Emmanuelle Roulph)

The product also bets on public shaming having the effect of pushing people to act upon their data-related activities. Nobody wants to carry a fat smartphone, highlighting that they are a certain cost to society, as they are not responsible enough to manage their relation to data. As for the actual obesity, this statement is partial and incorrect, as the overproduction or overconsumption might have many causes other than the sole uncontrolled will of the person – enforcing the provocative aspect of the fiction. The social pressure is here applied as a strategy to modify individual behaviour for a more mature smartphone use.

As part of the background of the product, the infobesity case is a segment of a range of untaxed assistance in regulating the quantity and quality of data produced and used. The provotype was presented with a promotional flyer from a 'datassistance' start-up developing the infobesity case.

What have we learned from the discussions prompted by this speculative product?

On a macro level, having a lot of data seems to implicate a pervasive automation of the economy and the ability to predict everything. Eventually, such a situation could lead to a continuous time, or a kind of atemporality, in which every trend or shift is anticipated and, in the end, doesn't happen.

In a data-driven economy propelled by abundance, the supply/demand principle, as we know it, also undergoes profound changes. Participants introduced to the infobesity case design fiction called attention to a possible devaluation of the mass of mundane data in favour of the value of 'rare data elements'. Highly qualitative data could be a complementary currency, as with the concept of 'dataxation'. With dataxation, citizens could pay their taxes with their qualitative data in order to help governments automating as well as anticipating and adjusting their policies. Building on this idea, should we be remunerated for the data we produce? Some of the reactions advocated that the market should adopt different levels of regulation and remuneration by differentiating human-made data from machine-made data.

A whole range of new mini-jobs would be specially created to support the data abundance: data janitors cleaning data, data brokers fixing values, data therapists specialised in digital-related diseases... On a more light-hearted note, it has been recommended that everyone should develop 'green habits, but for data', to aid the better management of the data profusion.

As the insights from the data sniffer and infobesity case suggest it, economic design fictions have serious potential to enhance the ways we engage with each other to discuss and organise changes. Yet it is necessary to take the quality of the context and the deliberate framing of conversations into account. Considering the speculative horizon is especially relevant to contextualise immersions: are we setting the design fictions in five, ten or fifteen years from now? Are we even setting them in the near future or, instead, in an alternative present?

Furthermore, in this case, our productions have deliberately tended to be satirical and absurdist, but a design fiction project doesn't necessarily have to have an ironic or tongue-in-cheek feel to it. It can just as well offer a neutral commentary, or even praise. In return, the tone of the fiction will obviously influence the discussion. This is an opportunity to stimulate reactions, as well as running the risk of doors closing.

Thoughts on the Limits of Economic Design Fictions

As Design Fiction shows its potential for sparking new interactions among economists, researchers, stakeholders and citizens, we still have to acknowledge the intrinsic limits of the posture.

A Slider for the Uncanny

Design fictions are consciously shaped as provocative pieces. In the process of imagining speculative products, however, it is necessary to take care to include points of parity with the current and existing contexts. Design fictions are, by nature, designed products. They have to be relatable and plausible without feeling too weird or too extreme. The undesirable consequence would then be the audience focusing on the product rather on the world it speaks of. In doing so, the design fiction would actually sabotage its very advantage in producing the 'suspension of disbelief' necessary to prepare the ground for immersion and discussion. A way to set the right level of weirdness and provocation is by making the design fiction experiential. When organising this type of interactive scenario, the set-up allows participants to touch the products and make choices regarding their uses. To design such a scenario, it requires a coherent narrative background that can be crafted with the guidance of the speculative context canvas.

An Ecosystem of Design Fictions

Having a single speculative product might not be sufficient to spark intense debates, as people might focus on the product's features rather than the context it emphasises. Different Design Fiction experiments, such as the ProtoPolicy mentioned earlier, hint at the good practice of building an ecosystem of fictions. One would have to design several products based on the same resource and initial situation, be it scarcity or post-scarcity. Doing so will better flesh out the various aspects of the speculated society. Indeed, the pieces of fiction can interact with each other, so that many different perspectives can be called upon to cohabit and to disagree with.

Reframing Discussions

As seen before, design fictions are a support to discussions, but for economic models it is necessary to settle on a framework of exchanges in terms of questions and reactions. Design fictions are just a starting point for more comprehensive considerations. The intent of framing and orienting the discussions has, in the end, the ambition of extrapolating on the extrapolations.

Among the good practices structuring Design Fiction methods, there is the concern to document the reactions of the stakeholders and map them, highlighting convergences and divergences between arguments.

Nevertheless, it is essential not to focus purely on collecting insights that can be turned instantly into actionable knowledge and stay free from any productive imperative. Being confronted by design fictions is also a process of provocative inspiration, relying on long-term maturation.

Better to Play with Futures than to Struggle with Them

As a creative and reflective practice, Design Fiction materialises questionings and challenges status quos about our expectation for the futures of economics. It promotes interdisciplinary discussions to displace debates on imaginary, but tangible, grounds on which long-established and accepted paradigms cannot prevail. By building economic design fictions, one has to make choices by adopting different perspectives from the views experienced on a daily basis. It is not about rehearsing what could possibly happen, but, in some way, it is still close to role-playing – meaning acting by impersonating someone else for a moment and in a particular possible future. And it is well known that people learn and grow best by playing. This is also what it means to find the human scale.

13

Valuing Utopia in Speculative and Critical Design

Tobias Revell, Justin Pickard and Georgina Voss

From the post-scarcity economies of *Star Trek* and Iain M. Banks' *Culture* novels to Margaret Atwood's unfettered free-market capitalism in the *Oryx and Crake* series and the calorie economics of Paolo Bacigalupi's *The Windup Girl*, science fiction has a long history of playing with economic concepts and examining the social and cultural effects of a range of different value systems. Each example makes a stake on utopia – either extant, imminent or expired. The plot lines tend to focus on the struggle of maintaining the utopia or working forwards (or backwards) towards it.

Infrastructure theorist and author Paul Graham Raven divides utopias into three categories: the classical utopia, the technological utopia and the critical utopia.[1] The classical utopia is the perfection of institutional and social order, as represented by Thomas More's original *Utopia*[2] and practised by the communitarians of seventeenth- to nineteenth-century

---

[1] P. G. Raven (2016) Ways of Telling Tomorrows: (Science) Fictions, Social Practices and the Future(s) of Infrastructure, paper presented at DEMAND conference 'What Energy Is For: The Making and Dynamics of Demand', Lancaster, UK, 13 April.

[2] T. More (1516 [1966]) *Utopia*. London: Scolar Press.

America. The technological utopia is the form most familiar to science fiction, in which humanity's ills are solved by advances in science and technology – a form that underlies modernist notions of progress and the 'solutionist discourses of Silicon Valley'. The critical utopia, conversely, 'undermines the notion of utopia as a deliverable project, but nonetheless clearly values the form as an experimental space for exploring its own consequences and failure-states'. Whereas a dystopia would assume a failed state position from the outset, the critical utopia instead highlights the cracks in the utopian vision to expose its failings. It is here that we find the playground of speculative and critical design.

Designers Tony Dunne and Fiona Raby describe speculative and critical design as a means of 'challeng[ing] narrow assumptions, preconceptions and givens about the role products play in everyday life'.[3] This approach assumes that the components of the designed world – products, technologies, services and systems – are materialised with the embedded biases of the social conditions that gestated them. Mobile phones fit in pockets because they were initially designed by men for men, and that history is carried forward through a form factor that remains relatively unchallenged. Speculative and critical design challenges these unquestioned trajectories, with 'the designed artefact (and subsequent use) and the process of designing such an artefact caus[ing] reflection on existing values, mores and practices in a culture'.[4] By projecting changes in social, economic or cultural conditions, then

---

[3] A. Dunne & F. Raby (undated) Critical Design FAQ, Dunne & Raby, www.dunneandraby.co.uk/content/bydandr/13/0.

[4] J. Auger (2013) Speculative Design: Crafting the Speculation, *Digital Creativity*, 24(1): 11–35.

seeking to embody those changes in designed material objects, speculative and critical design creates a strong visceral relationship with its audience that builds on their own lived experience of the material and visual world.

In the here and now, speculative and critical design practices are most often deployed to challenge and disrupt the hegemonic techno-utopia embodied by today's technological objects.

Dunne and Raby's own project, *United Micro Kingdoms: A Design Fiction* (2012/13), exploited this technique to great effect, presenting four contrasting socio-economic systems through the lens of transport infrastructure. In *United Micro Kingdoms*, the United Kingdom has been split into four allegorical political and economic systems: Digitiarians, a society governed by algorithms with a mobile-phone-tariff-style economy; Communo-Nuclearists, a zero-sum communitarian economy based on the near-limitless energy supplied by nuclear power; Bio-Liberals, a techno-utopian social democracy based on synthetic biological technology; and Anarcho-Evolutionists, an anarchist society based on self-augmentation and experimentation. Instead of representing these speculative societies through complex RAND-style diagrams and White Papers, the designers modelled and prototyped the vehicles used by the citizens: driverless robocars for the Digitarians, a nuclear-powered train disguised as landscape for the Communo-Nuclearists, slow biological machine cars for the Bio-Liberals and a communal bicycle for the Anarcho-Evolutionists.

By drawing parallels with our own experiences of transport – why some people commute by bus while others are driven in limousines, why some jog while others take a taxi – we can begin to draw out the political values of a projected society, and imagine what it might like to live within it. By contrasting the four systems, Dunne and Raby also challenge the idea of a single definitive utopia. In all cases, a trade-off is offered: the wealthier travel in more comfort and convenience in the Digitarian society; the Communo-Nuclearists shoulder the risk of nuclear energy; the Bio-Liberals must live a slow life, waiting for their cars to grow and move; the Anarcho-Evolutionists struggle to travel in one direction, with the young and healthy assuming most of the burden of work.

James Auger calls this situation of dissonance 'desirable discomfort'.[5] The audience is forced to confront the fact that most technologies do not slip seamlessly into everyday life but operate uncannily – provoking us to adapt our own behaviours to reap the possible benefits of living with the new technology. Pulling back to the macro scale, and questions of speculative social and economic models, Raven argues that speculative and critical design recognises 'that utopia is always-already subjective: that the good life, and hence the good society, is plural, contested, in perpetual flux'[6]

In their project, Dunne and Raby recognised the difficulty of engaging audiences in meaningful discussion about alternative socio-economic models, as opposed to, say, alternative models for a mobile phone. The subject is often too large, complex and divisive. Their strategy was to reduce and simplify the model, using tangible prototypes of allegorical vehicles to prompt and provoke audiences into thinking through the implications of these changes. In this, *United Micro Kingdoms* supports Auger's claim that, since designed objects already reflect social and cultural mores, they can also be used as devices with which to map and explore alternative such configurations. While the project's artefacts ostensibly focused on

---

[5] Auger, Speculative Design.

[6] Raven, Ways of Telling Tomorrows.

emergent scientific and technological trajectories – synthetic biology, driverless cars – its framing highlighted the interlocking of economic models along these pathways.

In the following sections we discuss several other speculative and critical design techniques that have been used to provoke audiences into engaging with alternative economic models, distinguishing between work that uses a more passive documentarian-archivist approach, projects grounded in prefiguration and performance and those more explicitly speculative propositions.

Documentarians and Archivists

Much contemporary economic policy is grounded in an 'evidence-based approach': the utilisation of scientific methods and language to convey the validity and rigour of policy. Just as the US Declaration of Independence or company incorporation documents can be presented as archived, historical evidence, these projects use the clutter of economic reality – papers, documents, photographs, transcripts, charts and letters – as evidentiary narratives, unravelling the intricacies of an alternative story.

In *88.7: Stories from the First Transnational Traders* (2012), one of us (Revell) extrapolates the tendencies of neoliberal deregulation forward to the brink of the collapse of the state. In this speculative story, an icebreaker ship is recommissioned as a bank, operating as a mobile centre of global high finance, outside the range of state control. Rather than being represented through spectacular imagery or high fantasy, the story is made mundane, told through navigation charts, letters, legal statements and engine designs. Although certain elements are explicitly fantastic – traders begin to sport horn-like growths due to biochemical changes triggered by the extreme conditions – they are normalised by framing them in the quotidian design language of the everyday.

Zoe Papadopoulou's *Intel–Cyprus Merger* (2008) establishes a situation in which the troubled state of Cyprus is purchased by Intel. This incredible proposal is presented through documents, schematics for a monument, and a corporate pitch from a fake Intel executive. What might initially strike a viewing audience as inconceivable gains plausibility through Papadopoulou's close attention to technical details and economic data. By doing so, the project uses allegory to approach the vexed question of where we draw the line between state and corporation, slipstreaming unpalatable ideas into believability.

In *Dynamic Genetics vs. Mann* (2013) by design studio Superflux, evidence from a fictional court case is laid out through a website and exhibition. In the world depicted, the United Kingdom's National Health Service (NHS) has turned to genetics-based insurance schemes as a funding model, resulting in a new black market for faked genetic tests as a means of lowering premiums. One participant is caught by the authorities, and his story is told through an exchange of letters, an insurance contract, CCTV screenshots, packaging and an interview tape.

Again, what might seem like an implausible idea – that insurance and health premiums might be pegged to genetic health data – is given material realism through the mundane ephemera of everyday life. The urgent exchange of letters with health professionals is immediately familiar, as is the visual language of packaging design.

Projects leaning on practices of archiving and documentation use material 'evidence' to offer glimpses of alternative value systems at a particular moment in the fictionalised history of the worlds depicted. They invite audiences to relate the things with which they are confronted to their own experiences of similar material artefacts. As opposed to the genre of the masterplan (discussed below), which takes a top-down approach to proposing alternative systems without really exploring the minutiae of change, these projects present the story allegorically, foregrounding significant artefacts and using archival tactics. They allow the audience to carefully examine the range of evidence and reconstruct the narrative themselves, an active process of reading that sees them speculating as to their own actions relative to the characters involved and assessing the implied trade-offs of the decisions taken by the characters depicted. The audience's suspension of disbelief is made easier by the fact that they embrace the normalised visual and literary language of social change – paperwork and bureaucracy – rather than the totalising visions of ideology.

Prefiguration and Performance

Prefigurative and performative projects invite the audience to 'live' the alternative social or economic model. During the emergence of Occupy Wall Street and its various offshoots through 2011, 'prefigurative politics' came to refer to the way Occupy activists blended protest and speculation as a form of social critique – something described by anthropologist David Graeber as 'the idea that the organizational form that an activist group takes should prefigure the kind of society we wish to create.'[7] Similar approaches have been used in experiential futurism as ways of inviting participants in a debate to 'live' the experience of the changes being discussed in order to reflect on such from an embodied perspective. In contrast with

---

[7] D. Graeber (2013) *The Democracy Project: A History, a Crisis, a Movement*. New York: Spiegel & Grau, p. 23.

documentarian and archivist approaches, the barrier between the alternative world and the present is broken, rendered permeable to audiences.

In the group project *Micronations Revolution* (2011), coordinated by Nelly Ben Hayoun, a range of artists and designers were invited to contribute experiences that would form a series of staged micro-states for an audience. While apparently playful and seizing on the pataphysical idea of 'imaginary solutions', this project invited participants to question their assumptions about existing political systems through jousting contests, music performances, political speeches, staged revolutions and manifesto workshops. This intense and enclosed political theme park used role play, performance and entertainment as forms of lived political satire. Ben Hayoun's project was an extreme, anarchist version of a Model UN, with the staged farce undercutting and critiquing the presumed standards and conventions of global governance.

In *Hawaii 2050* (2006), futurists Jake Dunagan and Stuart Candy, with the support of the Hawaii State legislature, staged a series of immersive events as a means of engaging an audience of 600 people in considering a set of potential futures for Hawaii. Building from four generic images of the future – continue, collapse, discipline and transform – and mimicking the forms of a gubernatorial debate, a citizenship ceremony, an environmental education workshop and a business pitch for human enhancements, the scenarios became social objects: a stimulus for public dialogue and a set of anchors for attendees' own images of the future. By engineering situations in which the audience played an important symbolic role, standing in for sections of society with a personal and emotional investment in the outcome of the scenes, the event attendees briefly became stakeholders in the futures portrayed.

Austin Houldsworth's *Walden Note-Money* (2014) presents the design of a machine for behavioural change. Houldsworth engages in what he calls counter-fictional design: pursuing fictional designs to their logical conclusions. In this case, a machine is constructed to destroy money. In a given economic exchange, the 'seller is obliged to aid the buyer in the destruction of their money equal to the cost of the service or object he/she is purchasing. Through the destruction of money, musical notes are created which are linked to the coins' denomination.' The project bears the hallmarks of other mechanised systems of economic representation, such as Bill Phillips' 1949 Monetary National Income Analogue Computer, which used the flow of water to represent the flow through a complex machine design to represent the movement of money in the UK economy. Although Phillips' machine served as a representative model, while Houldsworth proposes a device to facilitate exchange, like a till or credit card machine, both demonstrate how economics and machines are interlinked, their uses scripted with the assumed behaviours of their respective societies. In Houldsworth's machine, based on B. F. Skinner's utopian novel *Walden Two*, the machines act to adjust people's behaviour by rewarding them with music instead of maintaining a 'store of value.'

Shing Tat Chung's *Superstitious Fund* (2012) was a live fund of just over £5,000, supported by crowdsourced investment, which derived a model of investment decision-making from numerology and the changing phases of the Moon. A satire of control and human agency in high finance, it was also a tense experiment, with real consequences for the people who had invested their real money. The significance of this project is determined less by whether the experiment fails or succeeds (which, in keeping with the rest of the project, was largely down to chance) than the mere fact of its existence. The project is materialised in a giant billboard hanging over an exhibition space with a number showing the current total and changes in the fund's value. Designed to evoke sports results boards and the displays and interfaces of betting shops, it trivialises high finance and makes it darkly humorous.

Prefiguration and performative projects examine the material experience of alternative economic models. Owing a great deal to role play, theatre and experiential futurism, they invite an audience to occupy the model and to embody its routines. They collapse the wall between the speculative and the present and allow us a glimpse of the experience of being in the world, making the resultant dissonance all the more urgent and tense. Alternatively, as in the case of Ben Hayoun's project, they might extract the audience from the current world, placing them in a space in which they can experiment safely with alternatives and release themselves from the constraints of existing systems.

Speculative Proposition

In mid-2014 the neoliberal 'paradise' of Galt's Gulch, Chile, became mired in accusations of fraud and deception. Named after the central character in Ayn Rand's objectivist novel *Atlas Shrugged*, the construction of the no-man's land-cum-libertarian community – supported by a reported $10,000,000 from 73 private investors – fell through. In doing so, it joined a long line of false-start economic experiments. The internet is rife with renders of secluded islands and seasteading projects that never get off the ground, due to lack of support or the cold reality of the projects' sheer scale. But the proposals for these projects still exist as artefacts of the desire for alternative ways of life. Similar to masterplans but operating more as ideological statements than architectural layouts, these propositions tend to inflate an outsider perspective on capitalism, appealing to those who wish to escape or live outside 'the system.' With the success of a handful of communitarian projects, from Christiania in Denmark to Auroville to Sealand and the temporary autonomous zone of Burning Man, these proposals continue to seize the popular imagination and provide fertile ground for speculative models of society and the economy.

Hermicity (2016) exists at the *reductio ad absurdum* of today's technologically driven neoliberal dream. Invoking and echoing the language of blockchain, drones and Silicon Valley tropes regarding the colonisation of Mars, this proposal promises total self-sufficiency (or, more accurately, loneliness) while playing tongue in cheek with the ideas of various spokespeople of anti-statist luminaries, from Rand to Henry David Thoreau. At its core is a 'rainbow' paper – a proposal from Dr Yung Pure, apparently sent back from the future – in which an excessively intricate detailing of the project's baroque financing and infrastructural arrangements is couched in internet humour and kitsch 16-bit aesthetics.

Another project by Austin Houldsworth, *Crime Pays* (2012), proposes an entirely transparent transaction system, allowing any member of the public to see the transactions of any other. For a small fee, however, a purchaser can anonymise their transaction. The project thus raises questions about how criminal interactions are carried out. Rather than being exhibited as an obvious fiction, Houldsworth uses an actor to present the proposal at an information technology conference, embedding it in the real world in order to gauge the response of professionals working on similar systems. This technique of guerrilla proposals, similar to the approach of activist group the Yes Men, has an amazing power to give realism to the proposal, even as it raises complex ethical questions about how acceptable it is to hoax or mislead an audience. By means of a disclaimer, the text currently under the video on Houldsworth's website reads: 'Please note: this is a speculative design and concept.'

Similar in technique to the documentarian and archivist approach but breaching the wall between the real and non-real, these projects rely on technical details to draw us in, playing with the tropes and techniques of real pitches and proposals such that the information and implications can be absorbed and, even if not fully understood, imagined. They often employ a sense of *reductio ad absurdum* – pushing slightly further than is currently imaginable, but using technical ephemera and corporate tropes to evoke a sense of plausibility.

Conclusion

The projects reviewed here challenge the notion that speculative design is occupied solely with 'informed extrapolations' of emerging technologies,[8] highlighting how technological systems and innovation practices are themselves underwritten by economic models and alternative value systems. This is made most explicit in projects such as *United Micro Kingdoms* and Sascha Pohflepp's *The Golden Institute* (2009), which depicts scenarios from an alternative US history in which – following the election of President Carter for a second term – the state pushes for investment and innovation in renewable energies. As in the many projects detailed above, the work depicts the processes and practices by which economic values are inscribed in socio-technical systems.

The projects we describe here reach beyond the written form, embodying the material, linguistic, sensorial and performative qualities of economic systems, offering audiences

---

[8] Auger, Speculative Design.

a handhold on the knowable and familiar – legalese, graphs, contracts, conversations – before pushing them out to the uncomfortable edges. In the round, they demonstrate the plurality of ways we have to recognise, read and respond to value systems through sense-making, embodiment, affect and analysis; how the mundane and spectacular artefacts of economic models are presented to us, and how we inhabit them.

Through their complexity and intentional ambiguity, speculative and critical designs of economic models tease out both the cracks and the gloss in imagined utopias. At a point when money is increasingly dephysicalised, and the automation of value production uncoupled from the physical interaction of things,[9] speculative and critical design projects offer a means to engage with the embodied and ephemeral spillovers of economic systems, experiencing their textures and physicality first-hand.

---

[9] F. Berardi (2012) Emancipation of the Sign: Poetry and Finance during the Twentieth Century, *e-flux journal*, 39, http://worker01.e-flux.com/pdf/article_8960488.pdf.

IV

Fumbling for Utopia

Unrealised hopes lie all around us. They don't exist only in the failed plans of the past, nor do they necessarily reside in plans at all, but can be glimpsed in unexpected places, as a glimmer of a different future, or at least as an absence in the present. At the intersection of economic science and economic fiction are the moments when a dominant economic 'reality' meets its other, or could do. How to grasp these moments? How to narrate them, and give them a reality, in spite of their alienation from orthodox accounts of economics?

The fictions and reimaginings contained in this section touch on those moments where routinised economic normality is potentially diverted towards something different and more hopeful. Environmental economist Tim Jackson takes the experience of sailing on the Norfolk Broads to offer a meditation on the challenge of transition, in the face of economic threats to our natural conditions of life. The 'liminal' space between different spheres of life (and of economy) is represented as a disorientating one, disturbing yet profoundly hopeful, with all the risks that go with that. Anthropologist Judy Thorne discovers a utopian longing amongst youthful interviewees struggling with day-to-day social and economic realities in a further education college. These aren't merely complaints, but expressions of a different, more desirable world.

Miriam A. Cherry, a legal scholar, presents a glimpse of an alternative economic and industrial history and future, in which the Luddites were successful in their battle against alienating technology. This is outlined via an entry in a fictional encyclopedia, detailing how the Luddite vision won. 'Sustainomics' is the result, in which technology serves human and natural life, rather than vice versa. And, finally, we have a science fiction about the money supply written by Jo Lindsay Walton. In the scenario constructed by Walton, the government is seeking to aggressively nationalise the money supply for its own militaristic and security purposes. An alternative model, based around the democratisation of monetary control, struggles nobly against this, and things don't necessarily work out for the worst.

14

Shooting the Bridge: Liminality and the End of Capitalism

Tim Jackson

I wake early on the day of the passage. Nylon halyards are beating an impatient samba on the aluminium mast. The wind has risen discernibly overnight and a tiny knot of anxiety clenches and unclenches in the pit of my stomach. Turning *Tropical Wind*'s errant stern to leave our narrow berth will be the first of several challenges for myself and my novice crew. By the time we reach the bridge at Potter Heigham, we can count on a stiff force 5 or 6 to make the day more interesting.

We slip the moorings and make a slightly less than graceful exit against the unpredictable westerly now whipping across the crowded dyke. Clear of the entrance, I put in an early call to the bridge pilot, to check the state of the tide and the conditions on the river. 'Right now we have about 6 foot 5 inches under the bridge,' the pilot tells me. 'And it's pretty quiet here.' The restless knot in my belly subsides a notch.

The oldest bridge on the Norfolk Broads (and the most difficult to navigate) dates back to 1385. The child king Richard, still just 17, was struggling to control the power of the Lords Appellant and Geoffrey Chaucer was busy conjuring up *The Canterbury Tales* when its stones were first set in place. Today the bridge is a screaming anachronism. No longer able to bear the volume of traffic crossing the river Thurne between Cromer and Great Yarmouth, its primary role has been usurped by a newer and far more practical carriageway a matter of 100 metres or so to the north-east.

The three stone arches of the original crossing offer instead a picture-postcard attraction for tourists and a source of amusement for canny locals. The bridge is a formidable challenge to those hoping to reach the tranquillity of the northernmost Broads: the relative solitude of Martham and Hickling Broads; the other-worldly beauty of Horsey Mere. Perhaps paradise should always come at such a price.

Only one of the arches is navigable. And then only at certain states of the tide. At best, a 7-foot span separates water from stone at the centre of the arch. At worst, it's closer to 5 feet. Threading a high-masted sailing yacht through a 2-metre stone arch relies on a clever combination of technology, skill and faith. With a squally west wind and a spring tide, it's wise to add a dollop of sheer bravado. Or else to moor up quietly and wait for more clement conditions.

Tropical Wind is equipped with a hinged mast and a cleverly ratcheted winch. A complex array of shackles and chains holds the mast up when needed and guides it down when unneeded. I've had the procedure explained to me. But I've never actually seen it done, and the exact sequence of actions is still a little hazy. If we do it correctly, we'll be able to lower the mast safely until it rests horizontally along the coach roof and across a wooden crutch at the stern of the yacht. The yacht herself will be transformed from an elegant sailing vessel into a gaggle of flailing stays and halyards atop an unwieldy hull. But we'll have reduced our height above the waterline to something under 2 metres. Sufficient in principle to slip unscathed beneath the medieval bridge. If we get it wrong, we'll be the entertainment.

In the days before the new bridge was built, a skilled crew would sometimes approach the stone arch of the old bridge under full sail, lower mast and sail in one fell swoop and rely on tide and momentum to carry the boat through to the northern reaches of the Broads before rehoisting everything ready to continue. It was a mark of skill and a badge of honour to demast and remast the yacht without the use of an engine or a paddle and with barely a stutter in the forward speed of the hull. 'Shooting the bridge', they called it.

Our own ambitions are more conservative. We'll sail northwest along the river under a carefully reefed mainsail until we reach the outskirts of Potter Heigham. There we'll drop the sail and find a place safe enough to moor up and lower the mast. The passage through the two bridges will be accomplished very sedately, under power.

Doing everything slowly and carefully is a key ingredient of this plan. But as we near the bridge, a little later than I'd hoped, I realise there is a catch. If we do everything slowly we'll miss the tide. There'll be insufficient room beneath the bridge. We'll bump our heads, damage our pride and probably lose our security deposit.

The treacherous westerly is now quite clearly out to cause havoc. And, despite the pilot's reassurances, the river is teeming with oversized motor cruisers whose owners seem to have little sympathy for the constraints of a sailing yacht. The assembled ranks of onlookers, swelled perhaps by post-Brexit staycationers, line the crossing itself on the lookout for mishap. Other people's indignity is a no-brainer, when it comes to entertainment. There is also, of course, a latent appreciation for a tricky manoeuvre skilfully executed. Our interest in each other is nothing if not ambivalent.

Safely moored at some distance from prying eyes, it takes us a nervy half-hour to lower and secure the mast and stays. It's less than I had feared; but longer than I had hoped. And now we find ourselves right on the cusp of a viable crossing.

Without really knowing our precise headroom, on a gusty day, with a novice crew, the manoeuvre is becoming trickier by the minute. I put in a second call to the bridge pilot. 'We have 6 foot 3 inches under the bridge,' he tells me. 'Your call. We can take you through if you want.'

Occasionally, I wonder what it is I'm trying to impart to my kids on our various outdoor excursions. I certainly have it in mind to show them a life beyond the consumer comforts of mobile phone and social media. I'd like them to learn a different set of skills, and gain a sense of their own physical capabilities (and limitations) in the process. I sometimes dare to hope that they will discover for themselves the lasting satisfactions that flow from an appropriate balance between skill and challenge. That they'll have a chance to deepen their resilience and widen their horizons. To experience the possibilities of having more fun with less stuff. These lessons were all much easier to learn when I was a kid myself. Affluence and technology have hidden them from us.

Critical to this vision is the physical and mental effort that's needed to access the slightly less civilised regions of nature. I'm not talking (just yet) about climbing in the Himalayas or crossing the Southern Ocean. But I want them to understand that the rewards which lie above the comfort of the lower slopes and beyond the safer reaches of the river must be earned somehow.

OK. I admit. There's a corner of my ego which harbours more selfish aspirations. But I'm also aware of the dangers this ambition presents to my long-term project. Today's objective is not to prove to my kids and a crowd of ambivalent onlookers my dubious ability to take an unfamiliar boat of indeterminate height through an unforgiving tunnel against a perilous wind. It's to arrive safely at the more rewarding sailing which lies beyond.

Our mastless state is curiously destabilising. Despite our efforts to secure the rigging, the cockpit is a mess of unforeseen hazards. A stay around the tiller. A halyard trailing in the water. A view obstructed by cross-trees and rigging lines. All or any of this could turn our intentions upside down and place our comfort, possibly even our lives, at risk. I'd prefer not to put them off sailing for good. So a little help doesn't seem an unreasonable thing to ask. The knot in my stomach does another nervous dance as my brain tumbles through the options.

Anthropologists have a word for this state of mind. They call it 'liminality', from the Latin word (*limen*) for a threshold. The bridge is a threshold. Passing through the threshold is a rite of passage. It involves a distinct dismantling of social identity and its reconstruction in a new and altered form. Between deconstruction and reconstruction lies a period of uncertainty and confusion: liminality.

Over time, the concept of the liminal has proved a fertile one in understanding – indeed, in guiding – transitions of a social as well as a personal nature. Theories of social change make use of liminality to describe what happens as one social order begins to break down and before another is established. Cultural theory sees liminality as a source of social innovation.

There are dark sides to this process. It challenges self-control. That's part of the point. Routine enhances our skill base, reinforcing its validity and raising our confidence in our own abilities. Liminality forces us away from the comforting light of day and towards the hideous dark.

In doing so, it can paralyse self-efficacy. The liminal is fraught with danger. At a stroke, our skills become redundant and we're forced to learn anew how to survive in a temporarily unrecognisable reality. The disruption is both functional and dysfunctional. On the one hand, it opens up new and previously unforeseen avenues of change. But, to reach them, we must stumble naked into an uncertain future, with no guarantee of a benevolent outcome.

Yearning for a guide is natural: someone who can lead us safely through the disarray. Not necessarily to do the whole thing for us. But definitely to contribute some experience to an unfamiliar situation. This is the role of the shaman in medicine, the guru in religion, the mentor in education, the internet in almost everything, the muse in art. And the bridge pilot. This is the role of the bridge pilot at Potter Heigham. He's waiting for an answer as the seconds tick away and the water creeps higher beneath the bridge.

It takes far less time for me to respond, of course, than it's taken to reflect on the decision in retrospect. Today is a day for discretion. I hand over the £10 fee in exchange for a scrawled blue receipt. The small butterfly in the pit of my stomach unfurls its cramped wings and flutters away unsteadily into the viscous air. I feel sure we'll meet again later, but for now I'm happy to wish her farewell.

The passage itself is a curious confidence trick. The archway is patently too low. The boat is clearly too high – even with the mast lying dormant. As we approach the bridge I find myself unable even to judge the headroom, let alone feel assured of clearance. One moment we are self-evidently heading for disaster. And yet, the next, we are inexplicably slipping unscathed beneath the medieval arch. Its cold historicity grazes our outstretched fingers. Grey-green lichen shimmers on the moist stones. Their musty scent conjures the grim reality of long-forgotten lives. Liminality is populated with restless spectres from earlier transitions and uncomfortable glimpses into the immortal abyss.

And then, precipitously, we are through. The sun dazzles us anew after the shadow of the arch. Blue sky dances on the dappled water. Is it my imagination or did the wind just ease a little? Passing beneath the modern road bridge with its less demanding clearance is an anticlimactic formality. And now, with a practised ease, we are once again safely moored against the riverbank, north of both bridges, one significant step closer to our goal.

We thank our guide – resolving, with only the faintest hint of bravura, to try and do without him on the return passage – and set about rebuilding our vessel. The winch is cranky. The capricious spaghetti of stays and halyards threatens to derail us. A recalcitrant shackle or two demands a little persuasion. But 20 minutes of careful reverse-engineering sees us restored to functionality. *Tropical Wind* is ready for the northern reaches of the river Thurne.

As we look around at our new surroundings, I notice for the first time the unaccustomed calm. The threshold, I realise, is also a filter. Its physical limitations set the rules of passage and govern the outcome. The dimensions of each threshold establish the proportions of tomorrow. The teeming gaggle of wide-beamed motor cruisers could wait for the lowest tide in the year. They would still have too much height and too much beam for this ancient bridge.

'Steam gives way to sail' is the oldest rule in the book, from the smallest waterway to the widest ocean. And yet, inevitably, our days in the lower reaches were dogged by thwarted tacks to windward and hurried avoidance strategies. To be small and reliant on wind is to be at the mercy of those who are large – and guzzling diesel. South of the bridge was all about noise and speed. Power was everything. Might was right. But, now, the relentless stream of oversized launches has vanished, filtered out by the unforgiving dimensions of hard stone.

And the constant competition for physical space has also slipped away behind us. Or changed its form. Against the odds, sail has prevailed. Not through power but through restraint.

Everything is quieter and more peaceful here. Our lives will be less harried and hurried in this more spartan land. Soon we'll set sail for Horsey Mere. But, for a little while longer, the curious proportions of liminality reverberate around us.

Buoyed by our successful passage we decide on a trip ashore in search of lunch. We're in for a nasty surprise. Clustered around the archaic bridge lies a purgatory of fast food and cheap toot, centred around an enormous discount store named Latham's, which occupies four large warehouses on the banks of the Thurne.

Back in the mid-1960s its founder, Ken Latham, set out to provide year-round local employment, supplying fishing tackle and provisions to Broads visitors. Somewhere along the line it got bought out by a discount retail chain offering customers 'constantly changing quality stock at the very lowest prices'. Today it's a mad seething mongrel: half stadium, half stampede. 'Latham's,' claims its website, has become 'an attraction in its own right'. People converge on the store from all over the country to partake in a frenzy of shopping.

We stand there perplexed at the chaos. 'This can't be right,' I say. 'Let's find something in the village.' So we venture a little further from the river in search of Potter Heigham proper. But there is no Potter Heigham proper. Away from the bridge we find just one small, sparsely provisioned former post office that has recently changed hands and is desperately understocked. And an unexpectedly friendly antique dealer, leaning against the doorway of his almost empty shop. 'I'm selling up,' he confides to us.

The logic of the situation begins to dawn on me. Half a century ago tourism brought unaccustomed wealth to rural Norfolk: visitors seeking recreation; customers needing provisions; jobs for local people. It also brought competition, profit, productivity: the paraphernalia of capital driving the sector forwards. The most accessible areas were more easily commercialised. But, as the economy expanded, so did the number and size of the boats. Latham's grew to cater to them; but the bridge resolutely didn't. The old stone archway imposed its own indefatigable logic on progress: the land beyond is not to be colonised by the insatiable acolytes of hedonism. Its frontier heralds a more fragile economy, less conducive to profit, more reliant on local patronage and conservation. And Potter Heigham itself became the unruly locus of thwarted expansion.

I think suddenly of London, Beijing, Mumbai: teeming emblems of twenty-first-century progress. Or chaotic communities at the mercy of restless expansion. I think of Marx's enduring maxim. 'Accumulate, accumulate! That is the Moses and the profits.' And yet that relentless process is always and everywhere circumscribed by thresholds. Limits to our resources. Limits on our climate. Limits on financial stability. Limits to the appetite of the human soul for material excess. Limits on our ability to curb that appetite.

Were it not for the finite nature of our planet, the economy could expand forever. Were it not for the laws of physics, things could be different. 'If we had some eggs, we could have some eggs and bacon. If we had some bacon.' If wishes were horses, then beggars would ride.

If it were not for the dimensions of an old stone bridge, Potter Heigham would be a different place. People would move on. Or pass through. Or reach a different compromise with each ancient threshold. Or renounce their vicarious pleasures. Or rise from the armchair of voyeurism and achieve new and wonderful feats of their own. But the intransigent stones dictate otherwise.

This one small bridge in the middle of rural Norfolk, I suddenly realise, is emblematic of a bigger, more intractable story. Potter Heigham is what happens when the spirit of restless expansion comes up against the physical constraints of a material world. Society's growth imperative yields a surreal, dysfunctional purgatory. And the once proud 'heart and soul' of the Broads is stolen away by a glorified bazaar.

'Daddy!'
'What?' I start and turn.
'What the fuck are you doing?'
'Let's get out of here,' I mutter.

It's clear that our success in navigating the bridge carries no weight in this twilight world. We are just four nondescript souls in a teeming crowd of dispossessed sojourners: the motor cruiser occupants who can get no further; the dedicated fishermen yearning for a peace no longer there; the armchair sailors in search of other people's mishaps; the pilgrims and the pick-pockets; the vendors and the vagabonds. A trapped and tormented congregation, worshipping in the cathedral of a liminal capitalism.

I remind myself that we have another world to repair to. Our life aboard the *Tropical Wind* is, inevitably, a simple one. A two-ring gas stove, a tank of fresh water, a couple of guitars for entertainment and whatever we can find along the way constitute the parameters of our comfort. We'll be thrown more heavily on our own resources in the new and uncluttered land beyond the bridge. There's simply not enough profit to sustain the expansionary urge. But we'll survive. Even when there's no 3G.

Over the next few days we'll find ourselves trekking miles in search of village shops or local pubs. Occasionally we'll find a small farm offering jam or butter or eggs. Mostly we'll meet bemused locals who'll answer our innocent query after groceries with a candid laugh. 'Not any more,' we'll hear; 'not round here.' Time and again we'll encounter the social experiment of a post-capitalist hinterland.

On one occasion we'll find a small converted barn, now home to a welcoming National Trust café, open for a few short hours each day to service those who arrive at Horsey Windpump. On another, in search of a lemon to grace my young daughter's ambitious plans for a consolatory cheesecake, we'll stumble on an isolated household selling its own lemon curd. A dying relic from the forgotten past. Or cottage industry at the frontier of a new economy. 'Transmodernity', Zia Sardar might call it: a tried and tested yesterday in league with an ingenious tomorrow.

Perhaps the most innovative beacon from this post-growth world is the community pub we discover in another inaccessible corner of the Broads. 'How does this work?' I want to know. The barman is eager to embellish. Faced with declining visitors and impatient investors, the White Horse pub at Upton, near Acle, was threatened with imminent closure. So the community got together to buy out both the pub and the nearby store. They ploughed their own savings into a risky future, and, for as long as it lasts, they'll serve home-cooked meals and local ales to grateful patrons. The clientele are mostly local too.

'The Prince of Wales came here once', the barista tells me, pointing proudly to His Royal Highness's photograph on the wall, surrounded by beaming community entrepreneurs. 'And occasionally, of course, a family of accidental punters will arrive in a boat still small enough to navigate one of the narrowest dykes on the river.' I smile.

Could this really work? Could the White Horse be the model for a new economy? A different kind of enterprise? A more resilient community? A more sustainable society? It has an aura of home. A barely definable quality of everyday simplicity and comfort. The food is good and the staff are friendly.

The economics seem to work. For now at least. In defiance of all the dysfunctionality around us. Perhaps these social entrepreneurs are the bridge pilots for a passage that must lie ahead.

I want to believe in it. I want to go on believing in it. But I cannot quite yet. Because we haven't yet arrived. We are still undeniably at the bridge. The liminal chaos clings to our garments and clouds our vision. We must move. We must create this future. We must create it before we can believe it. One windward tack at a time.

And so, with an ease borne of diligent practice, we hoist the sail. Its wide expanse billows gracefully against the azure sky. The west wind is kinder to us now. We lift ourselves easily away from the riverbank, and the sounds of the bazaar slip away behind us.

Peace returns to the river. Here a fisherman. There a fish. Waiting patiently for one another. By Martham boatyard we skirt around a row of gaff-rigged dayboats, their antique wood immaculately caulked and varnished. Transmodernity again.

As the river turns sharply to windward, the boat heels over and there is a huge clatter of pots and pans and cutlery from below. My younger daughter yelps with anxiety. The elder laughs in delight. My son strums an unruffled A minor, and I lean a little more firmly against the tiller, keeping our head up towards the wind.

A single oncoming cruiser, an unlikely survivor of the bridge's hard dimensionality, threatens to consign us to the reeds. Fortunately, the riverbank is tenuous now. It's hard to see exactly where the water ends and the land takes over, and it begins not to matter. The mainsail flaps complainingly. But we sneak around the deceptive bend and the wind shifts onto our beam again.

Now there is nothing. Reeds. Reeds and sky. Reeds and water and sky. In the distance a white sail floats miraculously across the fields. We must seem much the same to them.

A ghostly apparition. A half-breed. A creature of neither land nor sea. A misfit from a fantasy novel, sketched uncertainly against a backdrop of dreams. The reeds are murmuring conspiratorially.

Too late. Too late.

Their conversation is urgent and restless, as the wind bears us slowly north.

'Is it true?' I wonder. Is it already too late?

I look at my wrist, forgetting for a moment that I no longer wear a watch. Nobody wears a watch any more. Time itself is dissolving. I think of reaching for my phone. But I can't make sense of the instruction.

Are we here at all? Is this real life? Or are we still lost in Potter Heigham? Did the bridge accept our bargain? Or is the late afternoon sun just a mirage, reflecting the glitter and bauble of Latham's bazaar? A faint light-headedness seeps across the glistening wetlands. Liminality clings to the *Tropical Wind* like lichen to the stone archway, slowly distorting her casual wake.

The liminal space is a profoundly creative one. Artists and writers will sometimes seek it out, engaging in ritual, punctuated by confusion, in a deliberate attempt to disorientate reason and fan the creative flames. I've done it myself. Faced with a daunting writing project, I will change up meal times, disrupt sleeping patterns, jumble up (or simply avoid) social interaction, dismantle routine – just so that I can reach this liminal place. This sense of things unravelling. This horizon of possibility.

The present tense is simply too demanding; disingenuously defending the structure of our lives with its illusion of normality, it ends up constraining our vision and obstructing the avenues for change. Liminality frees us from this. It breaches the fortress of the ego and breaks open the bars of social conformity. It allows us to see the world (and ourselves) as we might be, as we could be. As we still could be. Rather than through the temporary prison of the unsustainable now.

'It is not too late,' whispers a small voice in my left ear. I turn, surprised to find the butterfly is back.

'Human and earthly limits, properly understood,' wrote the conservationist Wendell Berry, 'are not confinements, but rather inducements...to fullness of relationship and meaning.' Beyond the bridge, he was suggesting, lies another world. A place worth visiting. An investment worth making. A destination worth reaching. Tomorrow is another country. They do things differently there.

As the shadows lengthen, a grey heron rises noisily from his perch on a dry branch and swoops defiantly across our bow, disrupting my reflection.

'Life is a temporary thing,' he croaks.
'Tell me about it,' sighs the butterfly.
'I thought you were gone,' I say.
'I am gone,' confides my friend. 'I am gone and I am here. I am here and I am nowhere. I am nowhere and I am forever...'

At that precise moment, the reeds part and the river widens.

'Almost forever...'

The glorious expanse of Horsey Mere reveals its surreal beauty to the infinite sky. The unencumbered wind sweeps us freely into the open water. Our sinews stretch. The halyards strain. The sun on my face is a warm embrace. It feels momentarily like home. And the relief is palpable.

15

Speculative Hyperstition at a Northern Further Education College

Judy Thorne

I get off the train in a humid twenty-first-century summer, and ride my bike down the hill and over a pedestrian bridge high above the wild howl of the Princess Way.[1] My wheels labour over the pitted tarmac. It's a long, straight, flat way to the trade union offices in the Ackfield Business Park, and I am lagging as usual behind Google Maps' athletic estimates of how long my journey should take. But the low sky doesn't open, and I arrive at the address just about on time. Boston House is a square, brown five-storey office block with no cycle parking. Inside, an administrator offers me a small plastic cup of orange juice, and the woman I have come to talk to comes in. Ashley is a trade union rep and a social worker in her late twenties. She is taking a course at the college I used to work at, which provides further education to 30,000 adults and teenagers. Her department, Trade Union Education, is based in St Agabus' Campus, a russet newbuild on the edge of the city centre. New reps

---

[1] This is an account of, and excerpts from, some interviews I conducted, together with some speculation. The excerpts have been edited for length and clarity, but are otherwise faithful to the transcripts, apart from the tenses used at the end, where some things have been moved from the future conditional to the present.

learn how to creatively apply flimsy laws in order to organise to defend themselves and their colleagues from being endangered, harassed and fired. I turned up in Ashley's classroom a few weeks ago to ask the small class if they wouldn't mind me interviewing them, and she's one of the two who replied to my follow-up e-mail.

Ashley makes a cup of tea. I ask her what she wants the world to be like in the future.

'Safe,' she answers. 'Things have slipped recently. I would like trade unions to go back to the how they were in the seventies and eighties, and start fighting for everything we had that's just slipped now, gone. Once we do that, we'll be able to get back to what we lost. Not work over the hours, not get stressed at work, not get ill, having to worry, going into work sick. I want working people not to have to be afraid. That's what I would like the future to be.'

Ashley tells me she has a daughter, and she is worried that she might not have much of a future. 'Before you've even started your working career, you're twenty to thirty thousand in debt. Universities weren't set up to work like this originally. If we had free education, people would know their rights a lot more, people would be able to understand each other more. I think all this hostility that's happening at the minute would slowly go away, because there is a class problem going on and also an immigration problem going on at the moment.' We start talking about immigration. 'Why not open it up? We used to, years ago. You're always going to have border control, because there's always so many houses, there's always so many jobs, there's only so many school places. But it's not working out the way it is at the minute. Obviously people are concerned – we all voted for different reasons [alluding to the recent referendum, when the United Kingdom voted to leave the European Union]; but why not treat it as a new opportunity to set up something like what we did in the past with the United Nations? Do the score systems like Australia, but it needs opening up, like it was before. There wouldn't be so much of a panic and influx if it was opened up throughout the world. The people know that they can't go to Australia, they can't go to this country, they can't go to that one – well, why can't they? The media say: "They voted out because they're racist"; they've not said: "Well, actually no, they voted out because they want a fair system." I think there should be sanctions for what the media do to this country. There should be repercussions.'

The discussion of immigration led into talking about the recession, and everything that has been made scarce since then, that is being pulled out from under people's feet. 'People became unstuck when, halfway through the year, mortgage costs go through the roof, they've not got the money to pay for it, the properties are getting repossessed, the kids are getting obese because they're getting one pound ready meals, the parents are getting stressed and sick, and that's having a drain on the NHS because they're breaking down with mental health crises. And we're heading for another recession again next year. Now, they're going to blame it on the EU referendum, but we were heading for it regardless; things obviously aren't working. People are losing their homes, they're losing their lives. We've had to ask for advice, me and my colleagues, because the suicidal calls we're getting from our members has gone up so dramatically in the last eight months.'

How do you think it should be?

'I think there needs to be a fixed rate [mortgage] that's set, based on average earnings. Same with the utility bills and same with childcare and rent control and everything. I think that, personally, in the future that needs to be part of the Queen's speech: "Right, this is what we've agreed this year for this country, these are the set rates."

'The problem we have got now, though, is that the media are in the back pockets of that many different hierarchy people. It's going more and more where it's two or three people that run the country. It's actually never been allowed before that people would own that much power. This is why I believe in the trade unions. If we went back to how we were before the eighties. We did it then. The working people fought a lot more then. They came out, they marched through the streets. And people listened. I think people are afraid to do it now. Everything that we've lost... We didn't have ASDA and Morrison's and Tesco's all them years ago. And we survived then. The supermarkets are crushing the economy. All the markets are gone. I used to love being a kid growing up and going to the markets and the greengrocers and things like that.'

As we move from topic to topic, the utopian horizon seems to hover in the past, but close so you can almost remember it; it was before Britain joined the European Union, before austerity, before supermarkets, before the trade unions were crushed. Since then, everything has been falling away, 'all slowly collapsing.' 'But what do you want the future to be like?' I ask again.

'We need to take back control of our own country,' Ashley replies decisively. 'I think that's what it all comes down to. We need to take back control. We could sustain our own, we could look after ourselves, so, therefore, it was very welcome when immigration came, because we were a sustained economy. We're not sustaining any more. We need to be able to go back to holding our own. And I don't mean – I think it's ridiculous when people say it means we need to deport the immigrants. That's not what I mean, and that's not what a lot of people mean. It means we need to go back to basics, and how it was when we did have control. Let the producers dictate what they can live off. Let us go back to how it was. And then we can support people like we used to. But all the resources are being cut. All the ways we had of supporting people are gone, and now we've been left to this. They say: "Look, we've got a multicultural country!" Yeah, but they're all actually starving to death, they've got nowhere to live! They're not advertising that. They're so hung on this multicultural country – they're not sustaining it. We're all crumbling. We're all struggling.'

I leave the building via the lift and cycle down the street to get a meal deal from the Tesco Metro I passed on my way from the station. When I get there it's been boarded up. The rain is still holding off, but the streets are getting darker as the clouds thicken. I cycle on, into the city, to meet with a couple of Business and Technology Education Council economics students at St Agabus' Campus who agreed to be interviewed.

The first one I speak to is Efuru. 'You see I've got disabilities,' she says, indicating her walking cane decorated with a colourful botanical print, 'but I'm trying to go to school. All they say they provide for someone with disabilities is just a bus pass. And I'm struggling. I can hardly walk from here to there. I've been bed-bound for years because of my health, I've only just had my knees replaced; but the knees won't last long, so while it lasts I should make use of the time, and get out of the house and do something good, something I'll feel proud of, something to make me smile.' Such as studying economics. I ask Efuru about how she would want healthcare to work in the future. 'Hospitals in the future – they have to be free. So the NHS is just fine as it is. In Nigeria, to get a sachet of Co-codamol is very expensive. And I take a sachet every day. So I have that here, that privilege to have free drugs. I was born in the UK, but, as Africans, they always want to take you back. So I was taken back to Nigeria as a baby. If one parent is a citizen, and you're born here, you're still not entitled to citizenship. That's bad. I wouldn't want that. I would want it to be, if you're born here, your mum or dad might not be a citizen, but you've got a pass. You can have dual citizenship.'

What would you want Nigeria to be like in the future? 'I wish they could eject all the government! And put younger ones there. If they could stop the embezzlement and fraud and theft, it might be a better place. We've got the resources, but we've got thugs, thieves, as leaders. Of course, the way it's going now, the situation here is getting to be quite similar.'

In what way?

'In that the ones in power in this country have never lived the lives that they're affecting. So how can they understand anything? In the future I think the people dealing with the disability system should be someone with a disability. And education – it should be run by the teachers themselves, people who understand the situation. The people in government should be the working people. Women's rights – of course it'll be a woman, but they'll get a woman who's had some private education, who's had this that and the other. I think that's where it all needs to change: from the top.' Efuru peers anxiously out of the window. 'My transport should have come at 2.20. Now it's 2.45. You have to book one week in advance. This morning I came in really early, because you have to take whatever time they've got. Even if it means you sit here until nine o'clock. In the future there should be enough cars that they can come straight to where you are and take you where you need to go. And it should be free.'

Efuru's car arrives just as the campus is closed by teachers gathering to picket the college. Dozens of them are already outside. I watch the car leave from the window. Instead of the old dirty white bus I thought I'd seen drive past the first time, this was a sleeker vehicle, bearing the dark green crest of the Disabled People's Dromocracy, familiar now after they rolled out their comprehensive city transport system. On my way out, a teacher hands me a flyer: the strike will be indefinite, it says, across all universities, schools and colleges in the country, until the cuts to further education funding are reversed.

I go to a nearby Costa to talk to a hard, femme young woman called Vanessa, who came to England to study economics after she got fed up with her make-up artistry business in Toronto. 'People are so focused on fast food. It's too fast-paced and go-go-go. I guess I want the world in the future to be a little more environmentally friendly. In Canada, we're all about mass-producing meat and dairy. But there are real problems with that. It would be better if we supported local farms. Eating healthily and not eating meat should be a right, not a privilege.'

What else, apart from food?

'I guess generally I just want everyone to chill, just have some chill,' she says. 'Like when your parents were kids. Now you can't even call your friend or go to your friend's house because you're constantly messaging her on, like, 50 apps. Everyone's distracted all the time. They're not in reality.'

What needs to change?

'If everyone's phones all just broke! Then that'd make a better future. When all the phones broke, people would come back to reality. People would appreciate life more. You'd spend more time with your friends. You could stop trying to be a certain way, being pretentious, and just chill, and appreciate the world around you. That's how I would want the future to be.'

A few days later I go to catch a train to another northern city, where Ashley's classmate Greg lives. When I get to the station I order lunch, a potato salad, at the station café. The Starbucks sign is still there, but it's been wrapped in the bright blue hessian of the Producers' Union. The café is run by a couple who've recently moved from Yugoslavia, and now own a market garden in the city. A brass plaque on the wall reads 'Project Funded by the New United Nations.' After the EU referendum in June 2016 things happened dizzyingly rapidly: now most of the Asia-Pacific region and the Organisation of African Unity is part of the Global Schengen Agreement, and the Middle Eastern countries will be signing the treaty this week. A revamped UN has been given unprecedented powers to manage this process, and is funding countless new 'Openness and Sustainment' projects, of which I guess this is one. My salad isn't ready by the time my train arrives. When I ask for my money back I'm informed stiffly that this isn't a fast food joint.

On the train, I read a newspaper someone's left behind, the *Daily Mail*. 'WELCOME HOME TO ALL NEW DUAL-NATION CITIZENS,' the front cover reads. Since the owners of most of the national newspapers were imprisoned, and the presses bought by the National Union of Journalists, editorial lines have begun to wobble. Inside, there's a minor story about the Brick virus fix being stalled, and a 'Who's Who' guide to the Working People's Technocracy, which has succeeded the Wilson government.

To get to where Greg lives I cycle through an estate of cream stucco houses, past shuttered supermarkets, up a tall hill from which you can see the whole city, past an abandoned pub and to an eerily quiet square of clean newbuilds, blank and pale against the white sky in the windless early afternoon. In the centre of the square is a flat expanse of bare earth. I lock my bike to the fence and ring the bell. A blonde woman with a Slavic accent welcomes me in and makes tea for me. I'm uncomfortably early and Greg isn't there yet. Three children with long hair are playing a video game in the living room. Greg hurries back and we go upstairs to a room he and Ana refer to as 'the Institute', which overlooks the empty square. He asks me whether I looked at the link he sent me about it. I guiltily admit I haven't, so he explains that since 2008 the family have co-run a home-based activist artwork called the Domestic Dissent Institute – 'this weird alternative space which is the spare bedroom of our home, that is given over to radical activity', Greg explains. 'Whether that's performance makers who come and stay with us for a bit – this is the bed that they sleep on [gesturing towards the neat bed next to us] or radical work that we do outside in galleries or on the streets or as part of social movements. And we fund it all with 10 per cent of all the money that comes through us: the work that me and Ana have in the university, child benefit, and so on. That all goes in a pot, and then we fund things.'

I ask Greg what he wants the world to be like in the future. 'The best saying is "Everything for everyone". I want the world to be a place where everything is for everyone. Huge corporations just need to be cut up and divided and everything for everyone. We need to move away from fossil fuel addiction into renewable energy. So we'll be riding around on…self-propelling, or community-propelled, transportation devices; that will be completely normal to us all. Food needs to be sustainably produced. Cuba leads the way. It isn't utopia, but it's the first place in the world to reach a point of sustainable development. They divide as little as possible the means and the ends, or today and tomorrow. I think your consciousness gets made in resistance. You can't grow a revolutionary consciousness unless you're engaged in revolutionary activity.

'But, even though our consciousness is trapped in the present which created it, and what we want the future to be like now will be different from what we want in the future, I think we still have to insist on the question of what we want now, to start from where we are. So give me more! Like, you know, how would housing work?

'I'd like to live in a house that was made from mud, with high ceilings with really big windows on one side and really small windows on the other side, because I hate the sun, but I love the sun when it's coming up and going down. I think the home as well needs to be extended in ways that prevent the Oedipal nuclear family set-up. So I'd like my mud house with high ceilings to have an open-mud-door policy. We did apply once to build a family home in the park, and have it as an open house so that anyone could come and live there with us. I think we asked for one million eight hundred thousand. We asked the art group Angel. They said 'No'. So what? Their loss. But that would have been fun. In the future, you get a house by participating in your local group. Make someone a cup of tea, you can have a house. Smile, and you can have a house. Because we've got enough. In fact, you don't even need to smile, you can just get one. You don't even need to do anything. You just get one.'

What about other issues, like immigration?

'There are no borders. There's no such thing as immigration because there's no such thing as anybody else. It's all just us. Which is why everything's for everyone.'

Healthcare?

'You pay for it with leeks. But you don't have to pay with a leek upfront, because it's free at the point of delivery. You just have to know about leeks. The question is: have you ever heard of a leek. You go: "Yeah." And then you can have your cancer dealt with. No, I don't know. It's interesting; my thinking now tends to rest on: do you deserve it or not? It's funny, that. I don't mean that, but that's how it's coming out. It's still maintaining the principle of exchange. I don't know. Maybe love. Maybe the economy is love-based. With asymmetrical reciprocity. Iris Marion Young wrote about how equality can't really exist, because there's no two things the same. So she came up with this idea that when we act reciprocally we do it asymmetrically.

So it's OK for me to give you more than you give me, for whatever the reason is – I've got more or I want to give more or you've got less or you want to take more, or whatever. And maybe it's OK, maybe we don't need to insist on equality as an end in itself. Maybe what we really need is to enable each other as much as possible.'

I ask him about the city that he lives in, how he would like it to be in the future.

'According to my desire as it exists now?'

Yeah, exactly; where else are you supposed to speak from?

'One of the problems with this city now is there's no access to the river. It's fenced off. The world comes in through the river – because it isn't really a river, it's just a bit of the North Sea. So having access would enable you to understand the world a bit better. So in the future everyone would have a little sailing vessel of some description, and everyone would know how to sail the river and to go across it, and sail out into the sea on a cruise. We go on these boat trips in Croatia, because Ana's from Dubrovnik; we have a friend who puts us on his boat, and then we go to one of the islands. We get drunk from ten in the morning, all falling off into the sea and getting back on the boat.

'I'd have the city run in little committees, for every 30 people, that everyone was involved in. Power wouldn't be centralised. A pub, a huge sustainable plastic see-through thing, on wheels, would move very slowly around each commune. And when it comes in front of your house, you could pop in and have a drink. It stops outside your house once a week. You'd be vibrating with anticipation. The pub has the exact drink that you feel like around 5.30 in the afternoon. It's a drink that our 30-people commune participated in producing, so we feel the labour of it. It's not too strong, it's quite refreshing, but it does just put you in a slightly different frame of mind. It's some herb or something in it; the kids can drink it too. It's just a slight tweaking of your everyday sense of self that's slightly pleasant. It's probably opium-based. But really benevolent.'

What other modifications would you make?

'I think that'd probably be it.'

What about this void in the middle here? As I ask I gesture through the Institute's window to the empty place in the centre of the square.

'Originally that space was going to be just flat land with grass on. So people could look at it. Then some people in the community got together, got really angry about it and designed it themselves. What they actually changed was that they made the path bendy, instead of straight. But I'm happy with that, because they did it. To have the path there bendy is a masterpiece, because of the process. If it were just up to me I'd have a huge helter-skelter that the kids could go on. There aren't that many places to play out; I'd change that. Everyone would play out. Everyone. People would all be outside. And the places for playing out would be all different; they'd have to be designed by people who were interested. But, if I was plotting my own, it would be a huge helter-skelter. But I mean huge. That'd take two hours to get up, and then 15 seconds to come down. A helter-skelter like a tower of Babel, right up to heaven. From that helter-skelter you could see the Earth curve. On the way up there'd be some correctives for altitude sickness. Maybe a floating pub – there's a few floating pubs that you can just step onto, and have a chat. They'd go up and down like hot air balloons.'

We go downstairs. Ana and the kids have gone to play outside, but there is someone else sleeping on the sofa, and two children have wandered in off the street and are heating up baked beans in the kitchen. 'Is there anything else we can do for you?' Greg asks. But the red light of the setting sun is slanting in through the tall windows; it's so late, I've been here for hours. Since Brick killed all the phones, it's been harder to keep track of time. I leave the mud house at the foot of the monstrous helter-skelter, and cycle down the hill, through the park, to the river. A sloop is waiting for me on the shore. I haul my bike onto it and sail slowly home through a network of waterways, navy blue under the late summer evening sky.

In the following week I recruit a couple more students from the college, who I meet outside a music festival being held in one of the market gardens that now cover the city. We agree to meet up on the terrace of one of the ambulant perspex pubs that had invaded the suburbs, making sure we write down the date and time, as people have started to have to do again now. I eat a seitan sandwich I made at home while I wait for them, and wonder if they'll turn up at all. They're very late. But the sun is out, and this art nouveau beer garden is a pleasant place to while away an afternoon. Across the terrace, a large party of young punks are getting gently high on the mellow local brew. Half an hour later Lin and Aisha finally arrive. Lin is androgynous and confident, in a striped T-shirt and orange trainers. Aisha's eyeliner is peacock green, her hair is seapunk green and her denim shorts are embroidered with pineapples.

So what do you want the world to be like in the future?

Aisha starts. 'More awareness, and therefore more acceptance. Knowing different types of people exist, different genders exist, and also knowing that those things are OK – there's literally nothing weird. By knowing that those things exist it becomes more normal, and less scary. It should just be a part of the general stuff that kids learn growing up, in PSHE [personal, social, health and economic education].'

'Like, kind of like a fairyland,' says Lin. 'You know, everyone can be who they are; we don't assume people's gender, we don't assume people's sexuality. I mean, I suppose that's kind of far-fetched.'

That's OK; I'm asking you a far-fetched question. Be as far-fetched as you want.

'Having the chance to make change that is not really painfully slow. Knowing that, if you are discriminated against, people are going to stand up for you. Having that support network, I guess.'

'If I didn't have to worry about just getting the train by myself. That would be a nice thing.'

'If someone started up a conversation with you on the train and was, like, "Oh yo, I like your band T-shirt", or something, you'd feel less unsafe...'

'Yeah, it'd be more of a community. Like, if people didn't feel like you needed to be really closed off all the time, and you needed to protect yourself from everyone.'

'Every time you see a guy on the street, and there are no women around, you're like, OK, I instantly have to be wary. It's like, I'm on my own and stuff? You shouldn't have to feel alone just because there's no one else of your gender. It should be a community. More equality.'

What should happen with gender?

'It shouldn't exist. It's not real!' Lin laughs.

What about race?

'There'd be no remnants of the fact that they were colonised. The open borders are nice. Free immigration. Oh yeah – we shouldn't have left the EU!'

'That'd be good,' Aisha says wistfully, 'if, magically, in 100 years' time...'

'Oh, the EU's not going to exist in 100 years' time. It's not going to exist in, like, 30 years' time.'

What should exist instead of the EU?

'I don't know, like... I said that I wasn't going to say this, but, you know, communism! No, that was a joke. But regulations making sure people have enough money, can get jobs, take the burdens off their minds so they can worry about other stuff.'

I guess things are going that way anyway, what with the new asymmetrical love-based economics recently proposed by the All-Union Federation and the Local Area Committees. 'With economic stability will come more freedom,' says Lin, 'because when you're not having to worry about money you can take more time to think about things like gender equality.'

We hear noise in the street outside, chanting: it's another march. The punks are getting up to join it; we link arms with them and go outside. As we merge into the demo, trade unionists hand us pastel balloons with Steven Universe characters on them. We march to St Agabus' Campus, where more students and staff join us, then to the council building, where someone comes out to tell us we've won our demands for queer sex education in schools already, even though the campaign began just a week ago. We hang around in the space outside the council building, drinking together and dancing to Grace Jones. The streets are full, and the warm light paints them coral and rose. I normally take the biobus home, but this evening I walk, as the last of the light drains from the streets and off to the horizon, and the streets' twilight rises into the sky and brings the stars into focus. I hear someone's footsteps behind me, and turn to greet them.

16

The Future Encylopedia of Luddism

Miriam A. Cherry

Overview

Originating in Great Britain during the Industrial Revolution in the first two decades of the nineteenth century, Luddism was a movement arising as a response to poor working conditions in nascent textile manufacturing businesses. The Luddite movement was a precursor to the development of the economic philosophy known as Sustainomics, which promotes technological development that adheres to principles of Utilitarianism and Human Flourishing Doctrines. Sustainomics began its rise in the early part of the twentieth century and has remained the dominant economic system of the Hemispheric Union for the past 600 years.

Beginning in the early nineteenth century, foreign wars coupled with high unemployment and food shortages caused widespread desperation among the populace. Many seeking 'earned wages' went to work in rudimentary industrial factories. With no safety standards and shoddy medical care, industrial accidents were quite common.

As corn became increasingly scarce in the winter of 1810 to 1811, groups of workers who could not pay for food and shelter became even more desperate. Under the Combination Act of 1799, Parliament had outlawed unions. It was amidst these stark conditions that the Luddites began to organise in secret.

The Luddite Movement was open to both women workers and child labourers. Indeed, women and children comprised roughly 40 per cent of the Luddite membership.

Leadership of General Ned Ludd and Origin of the Term 'Luddite'

Many stories and legends have grown up around the esteemed figure of General Ned Ludd, named by *Passage Zine* as one of the 'Top 10 Most Influential People of the Last Thousand Years'. Hailed as a visionary even in his own time, the Luddite Councils are named in his honour. The complete story of Ludd's life and times is told in *The Epic Saga of General Ludd*. While stylised, the *Saga* has largely been corroborated with the archaeological records.

As an orphan, young Ned grew up in the late 1790s in a 'workhouse', a facility that existed to make people 'earn their keep', to use the antiquated terminology and backward thinking of the time. Ned was trained in the textile trade as a boy. Contemporary sources recount 15-year-old Ned being beaten when he refused to work at a machine that had, only moments beforehand, severed one of his co-worker's arms. After several days of docked wages, Ned, still nursing bruises from his beating, was told to go back to work on that same dangerous device. As every schoolchild learns in reading *The Luddite Primer*, young Ned seized a hammer and smashed the hazardous machine. Within a fortnight Ned had fled the factory and joined the British army.

Although he had only a brief stint in the military, young Ned was a quick student of battlefield strategy. Returning to Huddersfield just a few years later, his supporters styled him 'General Ludd'. As the Movement increased in popularity over the summer of 1811, a large crowd gathered at

Huddersfield. By the time the Movement began in earnest, Ned Ludd's supporters numbered over 100,000. Luddite supporters were characterised by their sense of utmost loyalty and solidarity to their brothers and sisters in the Movement. Despite the large number of supporters and the completely rudimentary communication available at the time, the Movement, its leaders and its political and social aims remained a well-guarded secret to factory owners and the government alike.

Takeover of Factories

Beginning in November 1811, General Ludd and his right-hand man, Lt George Mellor, surrounded, took and held factories throughout the textile district of Nottinghamshire. Their first victory, at Cartwrights Mill at Rawfolds, is now the site of the Mellor Memorial Museum, which contains many of the original documents so central to the Luddite Movement. Much of the success of the early campaigns was largely due to the fact that the Luddites were chiefly a peaceful movement. Contemporaneous newspaper accounts described individual events as the 'occupation' of factories. This characterisation has since been disputed by researchers, and definitive archaeological studies have completely repudiated these polemic accounts as wholly fabricated. Remarkably, in the first two years of the Luddite campaign, only one serious injury was reported. The owner of Ottiwells Mill, William Horsfall, refused to stand down when a peaceful crowd gathered around his factory. After shouting that he planned to 'swim in Luddite blood', Horsfall began firing his rifle indiscriminately into the largely unarmed crowd, which included many of the factory's large group of child workers. As a defensive measure, Lt Mellor fired a single shot, intending to hit Horsfall's arm, but which instead injured his groin. No further resistance was encountered and the factory changed hands without incident.

The Ottiwells Mill incident was an anomaly. Typically, when the Luddites arrived at a factory, the oppressed wage earners cheered and chanted: 'Up with Ludd!' Many deserted to join the Luddite forces. Against this overwhelming show of support for the Movement, most of the managers and owners would turn and run or else peacefully surrender. Part of why Ludd could count on such support was that Lt Mellor began by strategically targeting the factories that had the worst records of safety and that paid the lowest wages. After a Luddite victory, local towns would break into impromptu celebrations. Later these celebrations were formalised to become the most important state holiday of the Hemispheric Union. Every year on 1 March, and under the formula of equivalency on Mars, 'Ludd Day' commemorates the courageous citizens who took part in the Movement. The day is characterised by rest from labour, time with family and community, fashion shows with costumes from Regency Britain and a dinner of fish and chips. It is also a well-recognised, though not universal, custom to give a hand-made item of clothing to a loved one, in order to commemorate the Movement's origins in the textile industry.

Luddite Ceremonial Hammers

Sometime in 1812 a group of Ludd's followers in Nottingham gained control of a tool factory, and used its metal-working machines to construct large hammers. In turn, those involved in factory takeovers would use the massive hammers to break machines that had been responsible for death or injury by industrial accident. Ludd's own hammer was named 'Great Enoch'. The original hammers were later employed in ceremonial capacities establishing trade relations between the

United Kingdom with Russia and Japan, before the Great Consolidation into the Hemispheric Union. Today the original ceremonial hammers are displayed in the British Museum's Robert Owen Branch in Valles Marineris, Mars.

Response to the Luddites

By 1813 the British government faced a severe crisis. Waging the Napoleonic Wars had depleted the Crown's treasury. Inflation was high, and food shortages persisted. Until that time the Luddites had mostly been seen as a nuisance. The Luddite Movement then emerged from the fringes, however, to capture the support of an economically depressed populace. By the time Parliament grasped that the wage earners were serious about not being abused and would not back down, the Luddites had already gained significant power. By that point the Luddites had control of over half the output of Britain's textile factories.

At that time the United Kingdom's factories were critical to mercantilism. This economic system involved the colonies shipping raw materials to Britain, with factories using those inputs to manufacture valuable goods. The end results were then returned and sold back to the colonists. Upon realising that the entire mercantile system was in jeopardy, certain elements in Parliament who stood to lose their livelihoods pressed for military intervention. Many formerly wealthy factory owners also petitioned for redress. They proposed reforms that would fundamentally change the law towards machine breaking. At that time the laws dealing with property damage uniformly suggested that anyone found guilty would be transported – i.e. sent to Australia or another distant colony looking for settlers. Industrial and mercantile interests, which quickly coalesced into the 'Property First Party', wanted to change the punishment for machine breaking to death by hanging. Fortunately, for Sustainomics as we know it, the Property First Party failed to pass this legislation. Lord Byron, poet laureate of the Luddite Movement, and eventual MP from Nottinghamshire, whipped up popular sentiment in favour of the Luddites with his volume *Poems in Celebration of Luddism*. These poems were eventually set to music and included the first recorded noises, which were mostly of machines. This began the first era of 'Industrial Music', which is recognised as the official traditional music of the Hemispheric Union.

Tides Turn towards the Luddites, and Their Ultimate Victory

In 1813 the Luddites set their sights on Manchester, which was the heart of industrial cotton processing in England. Although the British army had by then been called out to put down what Parliament was dismissively calling the 'Luddite disturbance', there simply was not the manpower to spare. The army's reserves were spread thin and taxed heavily defending Britain from the French and Americans.

Richard Arkwright's factory in Manchester was the first to be liberated. The Luddites swarmed the factory and others near it, to the jubilant reaction of wage earners. Once the major factories in Manchester were under the control of the former wage earners, tradespeople and small artisans, support for the Luddites swelled even further. By 1815 the government had no choice but to declare an amnesty and to grant all the Luddites' demands.

In late 1815 Parliament passed the Luddite General Amnesty Law. This law overrode all previously imposed legal penalties and sanctions that might have been imposed not only on Luddite leaders but also on supporters. In 1816, as a result of further political pressure arising from a groundswell of popular support, Parliament passed the Democratic Factory Act, followed by the Luddite Peace Accords. The Democratic Factory Act of 1816 outlined what we now recognise as prototypes of today's Luddite Councils and cadres, and this law was also the official genesis of Sustainomics.

Textile Factories under Early Luddite Rule

Contrary to some of the partisan accounts of the day written by factory 'owners', the Luddites were for the most part very careful with industrial machines. Upon the surrender of a factory, the Luddites would break one or two machines that were especially dangerous and had injured a worker. After breaking the isolated machine to make a calculated statement, the Luddites would carry out a thorough assessment of the facilities. Lt Mellor had a natural facility as an auditor and accountant. He would analyse the books and records of the factory to ascertain its profitability and the suitability of the factory for continuing in its present course, if it paid living wages and did not use child labour.

Reflecting Mellor's business genius, the majority of the factories that were surrendered to the Luddites were up and running under worker-owned management within a matter of days or weeks. The workers in Luddite-run factories were treated as the owners of the shop, as if they had established it from the start. As long as there was no threat to human life, the factory machines were treated respectfully and with reverence. Mellor was committed to repaying the factory owners the true value of the land and machines, and payments were made through 1816. The Luddite Peace Accords of that year established a compensation fund that extinguished any existing claims.

Resulting Peace and the Economic Power of the Cadres

In 1817 Manchester hosted a ceremony in which the Luddites ceremonially stowed away their hammers. With factories under worker control, the Luddites turned their goals towards a political movement that promoted smart growth and democratic technology policies. As part of the peace, factories came to be seen as partially owned by workers, with workers holding seats on every factory's board of directors. Workers were no longer paid hourly 'wages', an antiquated notion indeed, but instead given dividends on the production that they dedicated themselves to guiding. They were also no longer called 'wage earners' or 'employees', terms that implicated servile or subordinate status. Instead, they came to be known collectively as 'cadres', though to this day some of the archaic terminology still exists. The organisational structure the cadres pioneered has long endured, and in fact is the ubiquitous form of corporate holding in the Hemispheric Union.

Establishment of the Luddite Councils

In the early 1820s each factory set up its own distributed 'Luddite Council', which was elected from the cadres. Growing out of a notion that industrial technology was outpacing the human ability to respond to it – or, for that matter, even comprehend it – the Luddite Councils were set up to discuss and debate proposed technological changes. To be certain, some inventions were seen as those that could have either positive or negative results, and for the most part inventors continued to tinker and be incredibly productive. But it was understood that there needed to be a communal discussion of the nature of technological change and advancement as the technologies were being implemented. The cadres were not convinced that the free market should be the only determinant of technology. Instead, they firmly believed that technology had to be adopted democratically and used for the common good, not just the interests of the few. Ludd's speeches during this time made the point that technological goals and resource allocation were to be decided in advance based on social needs and prioritisation, and invention was to be paid for and encouraged in those areas.

The first round of consideration by the Luddite Councils determined that, given the food shortages during the past decade, agricultural technology, food distribution, health and nutrition would be the top priority.

To track and improve food delivery systems, many cadres became involved in the design of analytical engines, pioneered by Charles Babbage and Lady Ada Lovelace, Lord Byron's daughter. During the 1830s these analytical engines became more sophisticated and had a place in every Luddite factory. Other cadres became adept at designing and fixing harvesting and planting machines that could operate virtually autonomously. Great advances in communications were also needed. The Luddite Councils provided monetary grants for new and improved forms of communication, and by the 1830s telephonic intermediaries were in widespread usage. Rudimentary data storage areas were set up around the world and analytical engines were set to analysing them. Luddite Councils used these results in order to set budgetary and technological priorities.

Role of Lyanna Ludd and Continued Development of the Luddite Councils

When she reached adulthood, Ludd's daughter Lyanna headed two of the major Luddite Councils, directing and carrying out their policies for many years. The original purpose of the Luddite Councils was to provide citizens with a forum for discussing and debating technology and the common values that they wanted to embed within those technologies.

Under Lyanna's, as well as her daughter Sophia's, guidance, the Luddite Councils had a member of the board on every factory when the cadre numbered more than 25. When new technology was proposed, the Luddite Councils typically supported the changes so long as the labour-saving gains were then distributed as dividends to the cadres.

Further, Lyanna and Sophia both strongly supported the idea that everyone, regardless of gender, race, religion or age, had important contributions to make to the cadre. Unlike other societies at the time, which pushed women into lower-paying work, under Lyanna's guidance full economic equality for women was achieved. Social equality did not come until the twenty-fifth century, but Lyanna's work provided important groundwork for social change within the cadres.

Advances of the Luddite Councils

Robert Owen, a well-known industrialist from Scotland who was also a utopian visionary, consulted with many worker cadres. In particular, Owen helped the children who had been working in many factories. In many instances these children were orphans or residents of poorhouses. In consultation with the cadres, it was determined that the proper place for these children was school. Owen and the cadres established special schools of engineering and technology so that the children could learn how to construct new and better industrial machines. It was a graduate of one of these Owenite schools, Alyssa Tell, who invented the telephonic intermediary. Most advances were not made by individuals, however, but by groups of cadres working together on shared goals. These working groups were highly effective.

Worldwide Effects of the Luddite Councils

Throughout this time the standards of living of members of cadres worldwide rose drastically. Combining increased production with shared gains to workers meant that the average person became prosperous. Beginning in the 1850s, it was common for every household to have its own analytical engine. Beginning in the 1860s, the rudimentary backbone of what we now know as the Dataverse began to be formed, in response to a Luddite Council directive.

Labour-saving technology meant that work was also more evenly spread out, with most workers in the United Kingdom working for paid remuneration five hours per day, and for four days per week. Citizens spent their spare time on families, hobbies and civic pursuits. Dangerous and dirty activities were no longer delegated to cadres but outsourced to machines.

The United States implemented labour-saving technology across the country, which resulted in universal emancipation in 1849. Former slaves were recompensed with 40 acres and an analytical engine. Perhaps no one understood then the advantage that possession of an analytical engine in a household conveyed. The result was that it was the children of these former slaves who became some of the greatest US analytical scientists.

Using an advanced version of the analytical engine, as well as information from the Dataverse, William Johnson, the child of former slaves, discovered the cure for cancer in 1855, and later planted the seeds of the anti-telemoric treatments that would vastly increase human lifespan.

Automatisation of Manufacturing

During the 1910s, with the blessing of several Luddite Councils, three factories in the north of Britain decided to change manufacturing altogether. Using analytical engines for design and sophisticated printing machines, they created the first 'garden printers', which could be set up in any household. Suddenly manufacturing became centred back in the household, rather than in the factory. Essentially, the modern era of production had begun, which then made other advances possible, such as space exploration, which started in the 1920s.

As time went on, the Luddite Councils realised that they needed a set of guiding principles in order to rationalise which technologies they supported. There were some technologies that had been proposed that were outright dangerous or would have a negative impact on society as a whole.

Many tinkerers were interested in labour-saving practices not because they wanted commercialisation but because they were intellectually curious and were generally interested in improving Human Flourishing. This philosophy undergirds all the great inventions that have been achieved since then, including quantum and biological analytical engines.

In numerous instances, inventors petitioned to have a technology that had no known usage approved. This is the story of the faster-than-light drives and space elevators. These advances were constructed almost entirely using automatised manufacturing.

Luddite Philosophy

Contrary to the propaganda distributed by factory owners of the Regency period, Luddites were not antagonistic to technology per se. In fact, many Luddite leaders, including Lt Mellor himself, promoted technologies that were used for the purpose of improving the health and welfare of the cadres. Luddites destroyed only the machines that were dangerous and had caused human injury, and they were destroyed only to demonstrate a point.

These actions boil down to a motto central to Luddite thought: 'Principles over property'. As a philosophy, Luddism asks its adherents to ask how technology will assist in Human Flourishing. If the answer is that the technology does not lead to Human Flourishing, Luddism questions the purpose of the technology.

Luddite philosophy also rests on the notion that the adoption of a new technology may resolve an existing problem, but that it may create future problems and concerns. Thus, technology must be viewed from all angles, and, if a technology is found to have negative consequences, social resources must be devoted to changing or fixing that technology. For Luddites, the idea of voluntary and democratic adoption of technology in a sustainable fashion is a central tenet of their philosophy.

Rebellion against Luddism: the Asteroid Revolt

Beginning in 2342 a faction of hoarders, the intellectual heirs to the Property First Party, stole technology from several Luddite Councils. Hoarders were fixated with employing subordinate 'wage earners' whose rightful dividends from technology were appropriated from them.

Chased from the Earth in 2095, these hoarders holed up on several asteroids and began to harry the space elevator and the colony on Mars. The only armed conflict in centuries took the cadres by surprise, and it was with some reluctance that analytical power and resources were diverted to quelling the threat. As had been the case during the first industrialisation period, the 'wage earners' welcomed liberation and embraced the members of the cadre. Only four injuries were sustained during the Asteroid Rebellion, and all the wage earners had been successfully reintegrated into the cadres by 2096.

Sustainomics

As globalisation and world government developed under the Hemispheric Union in the twenty-third century, many Luddite philosophers realised they had reached a point at which resources were being strained and environmental destruction was occurring at a fast pace. As such, votes were taken in support of fixing this issue, and the Luddite Councils offered subsidies and prizes to scientists who had the best ideas for green technology.

At the same time a series of contests and prizes were issued for those who could develop ideas for expanding the reach of humankind, thus making better use of the Solar System's resources. It was this system of cooperation that had led to the first landing on Mars, and its terraforming by smart machines in 2012.

Faster-than-light drives paved the way for further expansion in the twenty-second century, but throughout all these changes and advances the Luddite Councils adhered to the principles of Sustainomics and its core mottos: 'Don't build what you can't maintain'; 'Respect for human life and the environment'; and 'Principles over property'. These principles have served the Hemispheric Union well and led to an unparalleled number of technological advances.

17

Public Money and Democracy

Jo Lindsay Walton

Part I: The Comedy of the Commons

Imagine you are in the near future. It is the day the inquiry finally publishes its report. The inquiry that took years. The inquiry that you forgot was even happening. The inquiry commissioned after that deadly 'fake news' incident (remember it?) – the one that you assumed was just fake news about fake news. The inquiry into the culture, practices and ethics of the UK press – or, let's say, what's left of it.

And there are shockwaves

We won't get into the details. One detail, however, is important: the claim that even well-respected media organisations have, for years, regularly published content that is unverified, known to be false, or expressed in a deliberately misleading manner, later withdrawing or amending that content once the initial traffic spike has faded. The report shows convincingly that this is standard practice, and that cultural, legal and economic incentives brutally punish news organisations that attempt to do things differently.

And the effect on democracy, admonishes the report, has been catastrophic. Journalistic due diligence is being outsourced to members of the public. Twenty thousand people read the fabrication. Two hundred read the retraction. *Then* comes the referendum. The inquiry is withering about 'relict news', old and completely discredited stories that still hold the top spots in search engine results. The inquiry is *particularly* withering about revenue-focused 'clickbait' articles.

In due course the media absorb, analyse and disseminate the key findings of the inquiry.

DAFT DAME VOWS: 'I'M GOING TO BAN CLICKBAIT!'

SOMEBODY JUST MADE A FIVE-YEAR-LONG
INQUIRY INTO THE UK PRESS ... AND IT'S PERFECT.

HOW TO FIX THE PUBLIC SPHERE WITH THIS ONE
WEIRD TRICK.

Later, of course, they take it *all* back.

But then, even later, a new law is passed. Let's just call it the ' "I *said*, I'M SORRY!" "There. That wasn't so hard, now, was it?" ' Act. The real name is even less catchy.

The gist is simply this: all major news outlets must make reasonable efforts to ensure that any apology, correction or retraction is given prominence proportionate to whatever misinformation gave rise to it in the first place.

* * *

Somersault forward a few more years. Everything is a whirl, but you can pick out one or two details.

Cryptocurrencies grow more mainstream.

Cash doesn't die out. But it changes. Following examples such as Brixton Pound and Bristol Pound, local currencies proliferate.

Across Europe there is a small swing to the left, resulting in higher (and smarter) taxes on corporate profits, capital gains and inheritance.

Elites start exploring alternative ways of storing value and doing business. Everything is in motion – constant motion.

* * *

One more hop forward.

Across Europe that gentle, jazzy swing to the left has been followed by a staggering lurch to the right.

There.

And now imagine Laing.

Laing is a journalist. Or, let's say, what's left of a journalist.

Today Laing is working from home, covering monetary policy reform. Unlike some hacks these days, Laing has a real *thing* for evidence. She just loves the stuff. Laing's journalism is *scientific*.

Laing uses her usual scientific methodology: she feeds the story's parameters into her Fourth Estate® robo-writing software and knocks back a bucket of black coffee, just like any fedora-donning 1930s newshound sniffing out a big scoop in a smoky bullpen.

The Fourth Estate starts to procedurally generate Laing's first draft. Of course, the software knows way more about the subject than Laing could ever hope to know. The software knows about every press release, every study, every thinkpiece. Above all, it intimately knows every loophole in the ' "I *said*, I'M SORRY!" ' Act.

As soon as Fourth Estate pings that the draft is done, Laing will begin to add her dash of panache.

You know skim-reading? Well, Laing skim-*writes*.

* * *

While Laing prepares to skim-write about monetary policy reform, over at the Department of Health Laing's boyfriend, Abiodun, is skim-developing policy.

Abiodun's policy is about introducing smart inflation into primary healthcare provision. Abiodun doesn't really understand it at all.

Technically, Abiodun is still an intern. For various arcane legal and financial reasons, Abiodun has been an intern for *six years now.* Abiodun is beginning to suspect he will one day retire as a very distinguished intern. Maybe set a world record! Who knows?

Assuming he doesn't get sick, or something like that.

Abiodun has a headache. It's all those sirens today. Why can't they change the ringtone on those? Why can't they be more soothing?

* * *

Today Laing's story is about money. Every story is about money, but this one *really* is about money, in that kind of dry, abstract way that tends to make journalists' hearts – or, let's say, what's left of them – sink.

The Bank of England is facing its biggest shake-up since 1997, the year Gordon Brown, the Chancellor of the Exchequer, gave the Bank operational independence. Under the proposed reforms, the Chancellor will still set inflation targets as per usual. The Bank will still manage growth of the money supply to meet those targets, as per usual. So what's new?

If the reform goes through, whenever the Bank increases the money supply the *Treasury* will decide where that money will appear. Essentially, the Treasury will be taking over a key function of the commercial banking sector.[1]

---

[1] This is not something the commercial banking sector is terribly happy about. But finance people are clever cookies. By now they have accepted that that's the way the cookie is crumbling – a different cookie, they hope – and are mostly busy positioning themselves to do well out of the changes. By the way, let's imagine, in our near future scenario, that the United Kingdom is one of the first – though not the very first – country in which the government has attempted to secure this power from the private sector. For a long time the balance of power has been skewed to the

So far, so good; but here's where things get ugly. There are two proposals on the table.

Today Laing has one job. Make option A, known as the QED Option, look like a whole bunch of bonkers. And make option B, known as the Apache Option, look like a whole heap of heaven.

Ping. Laing's eyes light up. Draft text fills the screen. Laing leans in hungrily. *Clackety-clack.*

* * *

Abiodun gazes at the screen, a little cross-eyed. He shuts seven tabs at random.

Now the tabs know who they're dealing with.

Today is not Abiodun's day.

Today Abiodun has one job. In one of Abiodun's tabs – er, hopefully not one he just closed? – is a policy that the Department of Health *actually* wants to implement. Abiodun's job is to reverse-engineer the policy the Department will *announce*.

* * *

Laing's Fourth Estate software has run through different head-to-head disputes between QED and Apache, modelling different trajectories along which sparks might fly.

---

private sector. Even when governments still impose fractional reserve requirements on banks, in the absence of guaranteed convertibility to gold or other commodities these requirements have not actually limited lending. Instead, banks first loan out money, which more or less did not exist until they loaned it out (see footnote 8), and then seek to top up their reserves with loans from other banks and, ultimately, from the central bank. The central bank has very little wriggle room to refuse such requests, for fear of destabilising the payments system.

Unlike some hacks these days, Laing makes a point of at least doing some light reading around whatever story she's writing.

So Laing knows that the enemy option, 'the QED Option,' currently has greater public support. In the QED Option, instead of commercial banks choosing where to create money, by loaning it out of thin air to creditworthy applicants, a variety of actors will participate in money creation. The enemy have chosen a new specialised national investment bank, various accredited charities with experience in impact investment, plus some new and exciting purpose-built funding bodies, all under the supervision of the Treasury. The overall remit of this hotchpotch of organisations will be to finance social housing, transport infrastructure, green industries, resilience and sustainability initiatives and social innovations.

The enemy also want a raft of regulatory reform affecting the retail banks and other institutions – for instance, protecting free access to payments services for people on low incomes, and imposing equity requirements and other prudential rules on banks that still want to offer investment intermediation services.

The QED Option is, in short, technocratic, wonkish and a bit utopian. It has the feel of something designed by a committee. So far the press has hammered the QED Option for its jumbled brand identity – what does it even stand for? Nobody knows – plus concerns over loopholes, transparency, the likelihood of corruption and the red (red as in communist) flag it will flap at some currently fairly bullish global financial markets.

Laing's job today is to keep hammering. Think 'nail in coffin.'

* * *

It is an increasingly open secret that the policies put forward, by just about everybody in the habit of putting forward policies, are not *actually* the policies they wish to see implemented. 'Ask for the moon, and when the other fellow offers green cheese, settle for something in between.'[2] With a little help from data-driven stakeholder engagement modelling techniques, Ronald Reagan's folksy formula has grown into a monstrous new science.

When Abiodun's policy is eventually announced, there will be shockwaves. News segments. Petitions. Open letters. Crowdfunded ads. Demonstrations, maybe. Sly jibes in the Commons. Debates. Reputations rising and falling. Deep concern. Talking heads. Rolling heads. Rolling heads, still jabbering away. Heartbreaking personal accounts. Enclosed in this volume of complex pressures, the policy will shift and morph. And, when all stakeholders have acted, what will be left is the policy that his Department *actually* wants to implement.

That's the theory, anyway.

More sirens outside. Abiodun rubs his temples. It's the dead heart of summer, still light at 9 p.m. He peers vaguely towards the window.

So many sirens today.

Back to work. Where *is* that tab?

* * *

Laing's article is supposed to cheerlead option B: the Apache Option.[3]

Under the Apache Option, the Treasury will spend new money on the regalian functions of government. There is an

---

[2] Quoted in H. R. Nau (2013) *Conservative Internationalism: Armed Diplomacy under Jefferson, Polk, Truman, and Reagan.* Princeton, NJ: Princeton University Press, p. 183.

[3] Technically, it's a bit more than an 'article'. But we won't get into that either.

altogether better-organised campaign behind the Apache Option, including a formidable open letter by a mob of eminent political theory academics, minutely regaling the government with what its 'regalian functions' actually means.

The Apache Option boils down to this: Treasury expansions of the money supply will finance additional public spending on defence, the police, the courts, the prison service, GCHQ, MI5, MI6, MI7, MI20, MI21, the fire brigade, basically anything to do with the royal family and, for some reason, Battersea Dogs and Cats Home.

As Laing types, *clickety-clack*, with all the ferocity of her fedora-rocking forebears, a sidebar displays virtual focus grouping analytics in real time. Laing has developed amazing peripheral vision. Like an emu, or whatever.

* * *

He has cracked it! Or at least, Abiodun decides, he's made enough progress to call it a night. More modelling to do in the morning. But he's so late, and it's his turn to cook tonight. Abiodun touches his phone, ready to message Laing – but something distracts him. Abiodun glances furtively across the half-empty office. Then, rifling through his browser tabs, he takes one last peek at his guilty pleasure.

Abiodun designs indie markets.

He even puts his creations up on KickMarket, though just for fun, because he doesn't really expect people to back his designs. Abiodun's markets are whimsical artefacts, Excel spreadsheets glimpsed shimmering in the summer cumulonimbus. Abiodun stacks markets on markets, designs whole regional economies. He makes up churning cities where everyone can be welcome and fed and safe, and wise and healthy and happy and free.

It's just a silly hobby. They are just his silly sky-palaces of coruscating prism-light. Sometimes people leave him kind comments, and that's enough for Abiodun, he guesses.

One new comment!

you're a cunt
BristolChris

Abiodun breathes the still office air. He tips the laptop lid down. Technically, it belongs to the taxpayer. He shouldn't really be doing personal stuff on it anyway.

Abiodun taps the desk lamp off, grabs his coat.

All stuff is personal, he thinks.

In the distance, sirens, helicopter blades and dogs barking.

* * *

Laing's stomach growls. Her monetary policy article is a yawnfest.

Laing grunts, starts from scratch. Tries something new.

Now Fourth Estate slowly trawls the complementary data. It is analysing all the public figures who are vaguely friendly with the QED Option, plus the public figures who are friendly with public figures who are vaguely friendly with it, plus anybody who's ever mentioned it on social media, plus anybody whose social media history suggests that, given the right nudge, they *might* mention it. Because the British public loves a story with two sides. Laing has a theory that this has nothing to do with any desire for balance or fairness. The British public, prudent and parsimonious, hesitate to acknowledge any opinion till they have watched it shed the blood of some other opinion.

Informally, users of Fourth Estate call this feature a 'strawman search'. Laing feels the label is a bit unfair. After all, Fourth Estate isn't just designing a dream opponent. It's gathering up all the real flesh-and-blood people closely matched with the dream opponent it has just designing. Laing thinks of it as a 'sacrificial lambs search'. The software also analyses which QED affiliates are likely to put up memorable struggles as they're dragged to the altar. The best lambs are often lions.

Ping. Laing laughs. Buried in the list of possible sacrifices is her very own Abiodun. How funny.

She'll have to tell him when he's home. The bastard should be home already. It's his turn to cook. She wants his lion hug. She demands it! Laing's hand hovers on her phone, but something distracts her.

* * *

Outside the Department for Health, there's the usual traffic gridlock, plus pedestrians dribbing and drabbing. A few drops of drizzle, but Abiodun doesn't think it really means it. He's delighted to see a familiar bike woven into the railings by the roundabout.

Abiodun scans the QR code. Sure enough, the bike is part of the Internet of Things in Common. He uses his app to confirm the last user's claim about the bike's location and condition, giving just two stars for security, because that back wheel wasn't separately chained up – and this is London, baby. He checks it out for his personal use – a large deposit parades out of his Common Credit account, escorted by a modest little transaction fee – mounts up and pedals along the grass, over the pavement and onto the roundabout.

Actually, maybe this rain *does* mean it.

On the roof of the shopping centre, a sniper unfolds a tripod.

* * *

Laing has run out of swear words.

She's just been fired.

'Fired' – that's not the right word. There are no longer well-defined media organisations to get fired from, not since the ' "I'M SORRY!" ' Act.

But near enough fired: Laing's subscription to Fourth Estate comes via her membership of Scribe Tribe, a well-respected pool of freelancers, and Scribe Tribe has just decided, by some opaque, automated process, that it no longer needs Laing on the books.

And, just like that, Fourth Estate disappears behind a paywall. All today's work has vanished, probably. Even if it's still there somewhere, she'll never sort this out in time to make her deadline.

She blinks back tears as she rings Abiodun. Bastard isn't picking up.

Laing shrugs, slurps. A deadline is a deadline. These fingers have clickety-clack in them yet. For all she knows, this could be the last article she ever writes.

Laing yells: 'From the heart, Laing! From the heart!'

* * *

Where is he?

He doesn't know where he is. He thinks... He thinks something is very wrong.

Hands are picking him up.

* * *

'From the heart!'

She puts on music. Patti.

* * *

Someone puts a stretcher beside him. He is conscious of hands. He is not conscious of their touch. He breathes his blood. There is gauze, clotted and heavy, on and in his throat. He can't breathe deeply and he wants them, please, to loosen the straps, but the straps aren't on yet. He is aware of a voice asking him please to try not to move. They are putting a collar on him. *Don't worry*, he wants to say. *Because move is exactly what I was just trying to do, and I can't*. They are moving him now. They are putting him on the stretcher. *Because I just want to move my shoulders a little. And I can't. I can't move a thing.*

* * *

Laing is not sure it's her best work. She has a right go at QED and everything, but she also strays into some weird territory – algocracy and democracy and opacity and transparency – real 'Beware the rise of the robots!' stuff.

As she uploads, a bit nervously, Laing decides maybe to *not* mention about the whole revoked Scribe Tribe membership and Fourth Estate access and 'From the heart, Laing!' situation or the scraps of Patti Smith lyrics she's pretty sure have slipped in there unacknowledged.

Ten minutes later she sighs with relief. Her article is approved, online and, if the early metrics are anything to go by, on fire. What an insane day. Tomorrow she'll have to...

Laing's phone shakes, and she smiles. Abiodun's image glowing there. *Poor bean. We both work too hard.*

But when she picks up, it isn't his voice.

* * *

Nearly done now. Breathe, and, one last time, roll time forward.

Laing's article goes moderately viral. Its arguments are all over the place, but it sparks fierce chatter about public money, co-operatives and algorithmic democracy. Laing never notices any of that. Her attention is elsewhere. As the debate rages, some people gradually notice the original author doesn't seem to have said anything. It's as if she hasn't even noticed.

Laing's attention is elsewhere.

Roll time forward, slowly now. Try to see it all happening. It's so hard – everything is moving all at once. Nothing is stable.

What do you watch? Abiodun? He gets stabilised. Exploratory surgery is carried out the same night.

Two days later a full operation.

* * *

Following a great number of concessions and additions, the Apache Option is passed into law. It is perceived as another setback for the progressives.

* * *

The Independent Police Complaints Commission (IPCC) launches an investigation into the quality of the investigative response by police to a potential terror-related incident outside the Department for Health's Skipton House offices.

* * *

Aggressive marketing of digital payments technologies, by companies such as Apple and Visa, leads to the extinction of cash.

* * *

The IPCC concludes its investigation. The gist is this: lessons have been learned but no one is to be charged. On the day in question the Metropolitan Police's data-driven Serious Near-Incidents Proactive Emergency Response System generated a rare false positive, and several even more rare flukes in unrelated systems ensured that this false positive was not flagged up as it normally would have been. In view of the available information, the Authorised Firearms Officer acted appropriately. The tragic event was the result of 'a perfect storm'.

Laing, and her supporters, vow to continue the fight for justice for Abiodun.

* * *

The eventual extinction of cash leads to a proliferation of alternative means of payment, interacting in complex ways with emergent tech phenomena such as designer markets and micro-targeted smart inflation. Instead of disappearing, the 'shadow economy' shrugs off its last vestiges of stigma, thrives and diversifies. Between the white market and the black market, soon there shines every shade of market in between. Eggshell markets and corn-silk ones, slate markets and dove-grey ones, ebony markets and charcoal ones.

* * *

Imagine. The not-so-near future. The ultimate impact of the Apache monetary policy reforms has been – unexpected. Not that there is an *ultimate* impact, or some moment when every-thing stands still, and lets you take stock, and say: 'Now I am outside history, and see what was wise, and what was foolish.' Everything is in motion – constant motion. Value is. Society is. The sky is, and the sea. The sea especially, these days.

Laing is still a freelancer these days, though less and less a *journalist*, exactly. Abiodun is still an intern. And he still has his hobby, and now he devotes a *lot* of time to it. And he still hasn't moved those shoulders. The two of them are as happy as can be expected. As far as can be expected, they are fed and wise and safe and healthy and happy and free.

Following the collapse and partial nationalisation of the United Kingdom's defence industry, the drastic reform of British armed forces financing under the so-called 'Apache Option', as well as the armed forces' growing focus on opera-tions related to extreme weather events, the military has under-gone structural changes that nobody could have foreseen.

Maybe Laing closing her laptop, story safely filed, was the butterfly-wing flap that caused this perfect storm. Maybe Abiodun closing his. Maybe it was just dumb luck. Maybe it was smart luck.

But, somehow, these islands – or, we can say, what's left of them – have emerged as the world leaders in the collective democratic management of common resources. World leaders in innovative, data-driven stakeholder mapping and empowerment technologies and practices. Who would have thought it?

In these islands – though it is already too late for some, and perhaps too late for everybody – nevertheless, far more than anybody could have expected, now everyone is welcome and fed and safe, and wise and healthy and happy and free.

Part II: Data as Demos

In this vignette, I have tried to sketch a collision between five themes. (1) One theme is *value*. By this word, I mean *value* as in 'conceptions of what is ultimately good, proper, or desirable in human life'; *value* as in 'data value' or any potentially true or meaningful piece of information; and *value* as in economic value, 'the degree to which objects are desired, particularly, as measured by how much others are willing to give up to get them.'[4] As this is a book of economic science fictions, I care most about the last of these. But I'm also interested in how all three relate.

The intriguing work of Positive Money gave me some inspiration.[5] Positive Money is a research and campaigning organisation that is critical of how new money is currently 'printed' and allocated.[6] A country such as the United Kingdom may

---

[4] D. Graeber (2001) *Toward an Anthropological Theory of Value: The False Coin of Our Own Dreams*. New York: Palgrave, pp. 1–2.

[5] See www.positivemoney.org. See also A. Jackson & B. Dyson (2013) *Modernising Money: Why Our Monetary System Is Broken and How It Can Be Fixed*. London: Positive Money.

[6] Put simply, the Bank of England tries to influence the money supply by adjusting interest rates. It lowers them to encourage borrowing. 'Private debts – what has been borrowed – are spent

have as many wellsprings of fresh money as it decides to have.[7]
It can also dig those wells wherever it chooses.

Here's my own whimsical illustration of that principle.
When the Bank of England decides to expand the money supply (which must be done often), they could in theory make the new money materialise in your bank account. Yes, just yours.[8]
It's a gift, so do what you like with it. For instance, you could

---

as public currency': G. Ingham (2014) Whose Money Is It?, openDemocracyUK, 25 February, www.opendemocracy.net/ourkingdom/geoffrey-ingham/whose-money-is-it. See also R. Wray (2012) *Modern Monetary Theory: A Primer on Macroeconomics for Sovereign Monetary Systems*. Basingstoke, UK: Palgrave Macmillan.

[7] This is not true for individual countries in the Eurozone, though it is true for the Eurozone as a whole. 'There is a "one size fits all" issue when a single interest rate (as set by the central bank) necessarily has to be applied across economic areas with different economic conditions': M. Sawyer (2013) Money and the State, in J. Pixley & G. Harcourt (eds.) *Financial Crises and the Nature of Capitalist Money: Mutual Developments from the Work of Geoffrey Ingham*: 162–77. Basingstoke, UK: Palgrave Macmillan, p. 173.

[8] A technical point. In practice, things are a bit different when banks create money. When banks create money, they start with a zero, and separate that zero into an asset and a liability. The liability is the bank deposit that the borrower spends, and the asset is the borrower's promise to repay eventually, with interest. If the borrower defaults on the loan, then the bank may lose money. That's why the banks won't lend to just anyone. But, so long as enough borrowers don't default, the banks make profits, turning 'zero' into 'something'.

examine all the economic and sociological data available to you, then invest the money wherever it's most needed, or wherever you think it will earn the best return. Or you could express your moral values by donating it to Macmillan Cancer Support, Womankind Worldwide, Jubilee Debt Campaign, Battersea Dogs and Cats Home or public libraries. Or you could blow it all on chutney. The only rule is that you *must* spend it or give it away within a certain time limit, so that the money flows through our economy, facilitating and stimulating trade and production.

Now, this proposal may look a bit frivolous, not to say perilous. After all, *you* could be anybody. Perhaps you have fabulous intentions, but lack the right information and expertise to implement them. Or perhaps you just have no inclination to pursue the common good. Or perhaps you have a downright terrible notion of what the common good is. Something about over-prioritising chutney, perhaps. Part I imagined two other proposals about how new money should be created: the QED Option and the Apache Option. The two proposals embodied different ideas about how monetary policy should serve the common good, and implied different patterns of democratic accountability.

None of these proposals is intended seriously, but together they illustrate something important. Money is not created in a spontaneous, natural and inevitable process. Money is created through monetary policy, and, just like fiscal policy (that is, what our government chooses to tax, and to spend on education, housing, healthcare, defence, and so on), monetary policy puts into practice choices about what the common good is, and how best to achieve it. Those choices could be left to a random individual, or left to the system of commercial banks and the people and firms who borrow from them. Or those choices could be made by institutions that have been designed specifically for handling them.

(2) This takes us to the second theme, which is *the commons*. By 'commons', I mean any finite resource pool that is collectively managed. One way the commons can be related to the first theme, value, is by considering money itself as a kind of commons – especially when it is first created. Over two decades ago Elinor Ostrom identified some principles to aid in the design of a commons. For instance, she argued that there should be graduated sanctions against those who violate rules, and that people affected by rules should generally be able to participate in their interpretation and modification.[9] The current system of money creation probably wouldn't meet too many of Ostrom's principles. More broadly, conversations about 'the commons', or 'commoning practices', are often about how to organise society without relying exclusively on markets or government bureaucracies. Of course, markets, bureaucracies and commoning practices come in all shapes and sizes, and there is plenty of blurring and overlap between the three.

(3) A third theme, closely related, is *algocracy*. This is a relatively new coinage, and the word may or may not stick around. Basically, it means governance by computer algorithms.[10] (In

---

[9] E. Ostrom (2015 [1990]) *Governing the Commons: The Evolution of Institutions for Collective Action*. Cambridge: Cambridge University Press, p. 90.

[10] See A. Aneesh (2006) *Virtual Migration: The Programming of Globalization*. Durham, NC: Duke University Press, esp. pp. 5, 110–32; A. Aneesh (2009) Global Labor: Algocratic Modes of Organization, *Sociological Theory*, 27(4): 347–70; and J. Danaher (2016) The Threat of Algocracy: Reality, Resistance and Accommodation, *Philosophy and Technology*, 29(3):245–68. John Danaher calls an algocracy 'a system in which algorithms

my vignette, in order to bring this idea vividly to life,[11] I imagined Laing being effectively fired from her precarious job by an automated decision. At the same moment, the 'Serious Near-Incidents Proactive Emergency Response System' misclassifies Abiodun as a terror threat.) An algorithm is really just a set of instructions, like a recipe. But, when it's computers that do the cooking, the recipes may involve millions of ingredients. Some ingredients may not have obvious roles in the recipe – for instance, lots of miscellaneous data about what you do online, or about your financial transactions or about the people you know and the people they know. The algorithm's use of those ingredients, to produce a decision or action, can be very opaque to human understanding. In other words, even the people who rely on such data-driven algorithms may not

---

are used to collect, collate and organise the data upon which decisions are typically made and to assist in how that data is processed and communicated through the relevant governance system' (ibid., p. 247); like Danaher, I am particularly interested in 'the growth in algocratic systems that are based on predictive or descriptive data-mining algorithms' (ibid.).

[11] But, for a more thorough, less sensationalistic examination of these serious issues, see the work of Tal Zarsky, including T. Zarsky (2016) The Trouble with Algorithmic Decisions: An Analytic Road Map to Examine Efficiency and Fairness in Automated and Opaque Decision Making, *Science, Technology, and Human Values*, 41(1): 118–32; T. Zarsky (2012) Automated Prediction: Perception, Law and Policy, *Communications of the ACM*, 55(9): 33–5; and T. Zarsky (2011) Governmental Data Mining and Its Alternatives, *Penn State Law Review*, 116(2): 285–330.

understand exactly how they come to their conclusions. And, when several algorithms interact, the process may grow even more opaque.

Along with the bureaucracy and the market, an algocratic system can be considered a form of governance. It governs by constraining or enabling various courses of action. If you've ever spent time obsessing over the points you've earned in some game or app, or anxiously checking an online account to see if something you've posted has been liked or shared, then you have a sense of how such algocratic governance often works. Of course, bureaucracies, markets and algocratic systems come in all shapes and sizes, and there is plenty of blurring and overlap between the three.

If we step back for a second, we can see that the commons and algocracy share some features. Both are looking for an alternative between or beyond markets and bureaucracies, while remaining difficult to disentangle completely from markets and bureaucracies. Furthermore, part of what makes algocracies feel mysterious – part of the 'opacity that arises from the characteristics of machine learning algorithms'[12] – is their capacity to learn through feedback loops; likewise, managing a commons demands a certain kind of self-reflexive dynamism, since, as Thomas Dietz, Elinor Ostrom and Paul Stern tell us, 'successful commons governance requires that rules evolve.'[13] Algocratic systems are masters of something else Ostrom mentions: the graduated sanction. To tell you

---

[12] J. Burrell (2016) How the Machine 'Thinks': Understanding Opacity in Machine Learning Algorithms, *Big Data and Society*, 3(1): 1–12, p. 1.

[13] T. Dietz, E. Ostrom & P. Stern (2003) The Struggle to Govern the Commons, *Science*, 302(12 December): 1907–12, p. 1908.

where to go, algocratic systems can give you a sharp, hard shove, *or* a gentle nudge. Sometimes they steer you so subtly you barely notice it.

So what's the huge difference between a commons and an algocracy? The huge difference is participation. Whereas the concept of the commons feels inherently democratic, the concept of algocracy feels profoundly undemocratic. To participate in a commons, you need to decide what you want, and to convey something about your desires and their legitimacy to others. This may happen in a formal deliberative setting, though it may also happen in the informal grumbles, gossip, revelry and human dramas that swirl around any commons. Either way, to be involved in a commons, you need to make yourself at least somewhat intelligible to other people. And the same is true, to *some* extent, of a bureaucracy, and even a market.

An algocratic system carries no such requirement. It regards anything you happen to do as meaningful enough. You just spent 49 minutes looking at YouTube videos about clever crows? You just missed a payment on your car? Great! Algocratic systems don't want your excuses, just your data. 'Citizens take on the role of information machines that feed the techno-bureaucratic complex with our data.'[14]

The spread of algocratic systems creates uncomfortable challenges for both liberals and conservatives. If algocratic systems do inflict harms, how should those harms be legally construed? What kinds of redress are possible?[15] But I'd mainly like

---

[14] E. Mozorov (2013) The Real Privacy Problem, *MIT Technology Review*, 116(6): 32–43.

[15] See, for example, K. Crawford & J. Schultz (2014) Big Data and Due Process: Toward a Framework to Redress Predictive Privacy Harms, *Boston College Law Review*, 55(1): 93–128.

to pose a question from a more progressive perspective. Could these very technological developments, the ones that seem to threaten our already battered and threadbare democratic institutions, actually give us the means for renewing them? Might we begin to blend the advantages of the commons with those of algocracy?

(4) Thus the fourth theme, which both cleaves *the commons* and *algocracy* apart, and yet promises to cleave them together, is *democracy*. I mean democracy in a broad sense. Of course elections and referendums are important democratic institutions, but there are many others. Any space in which a group of people make their own rules for living may be democratically significant. Any institution that provides representation may also be democratically significant: things such as judicial inquiries; mass membership political parties; MP surgeries; public consultations; grassroots campaigns; lobbyist organisations; clicktivism organisations; ombudsman services; unions; employment tribunals; workers' councils. Institutions that shape public understandings and sentiments are also democratically significant. In Part I, this aspect of democracy is streamlined into a rather simplistic idea of 'the media' or 'the press.' In reality, of course, it's harder to give definite boundaries to it. It surely includes the social media architectures, which curate what comes to our attention, and the education system, which takes responsibility for teaching deliberative norms and critical thinking. More broadly, it includes all the ways in which we are produced, by our techno-social setting, as citizens and as governable subjects.

So, how do we weave together commoning and algocracies into the fabric of our democracy? What I can offer for now is some speculative suggestions – *almost* as speculative as Part I was. One promising avenue, of course, is the idea that newly created money can be spent directly into the economy for the public good.[16] The fictional QED Option drew fire for being too centralized and too technocratic, and for emanating a glimmer of totalitarianism. Its fictional defenders might counter that (a) adjusting the rate of growth of the money supply is already something the Bank of England does and (b) allocating public finances is already something the Treasury does. So the QED Option would be legitimate – they could argue – because the Bank of England and the Treasury are legitimate institution within the democracy we already have. Yet those anti-QED criticisms still have bite. Any far-reaching reform of monetary policy asks that we fiercely examine the shortcomings of the democracy we already have, including examining everything that commoning and algocracy could potentially offer it. Furthermore, money already has its own complex representational logic.[17] Even if we had complete faith that our democratic institutions are currently fit for purpose, that does not mean that they are prepared to deliver the democratisation of money.

---

[16] Although alternative forms of value, such as local currencies, mutual credit systems and time bank currencies, may also be relevant here. See, for example, B. Scott (2016) The Future of Money Depends on Busting Fairy Tales about Its Past, *How We Get To Next*, 30 March, howwegettonext.com/the-future-of-money-depends-on-busting-the-fairy-tales-you-believe-about-its-past-30cbd90619e0.

[17] Money is intimately bound up with representation (something that can readily be seen, if we recognise any loan as a kind of qualified delegation of power). Democratising money therefore involves transforming those representational relationships in complex ways.

A second promising avenue is stakeholder theory. Stakeholder theory is tantalising, partly because it offers thinking about representation and empowerment that has evolved somewhat outside democratic theory. 'New Generation Co-operatives' that are '[v]ariably owned by members' and 'new "social economy" alliances that cross-cut the co-operative and non-profit sectors', to use Mitch Diamantopoulos's terminology,[18] are examples of phenomena that are difficult to understand except in terms of the intersection of different kinds of stakeholders with different needs, capacities and expectations. AccountAbility is a private firm that develop guidelines for systematically identifying and engaging with stakeholders. A prominent diagram in its *AA1000 Stakeholder Engagement Standard 2015* publication is a kind of endless loop, like an ouroboros – a serpent eating its own tail.[19] The diagram shows that, to figure out who your stakeholders are, you have to ask your stakeholders. Algocratic data-gathering techniques don't *break* this loop exactly. But they do widen the possibilities for what 'asking' might mean. As an outgrowth of corporate social responsibility, however, stakeholder theory is often a violent and unstable compromise between people who really want organisations to be morally accountable for what they do and people who just believe it makes great business sense to identify stakeholders and find out what they're thinking.[20] So as not

---

[18] M. Diamantopoulos (2012) Breaking out of Co-Operation's 'Iron Cage': From Movement Degeneration to Building a Developmental Movement, *Annals of Public and Cooperative Economics*, 83(2): 199–214, p. 212.

[19] AccountAbility (2015) *AA1000 Stakeholder Engagement Standard 2015*. New York: AccountAbility, p. 19.

[20] Have you seen that cartoon? You know the one I mean: a guy in tatterdemalion Armani sits in the corona of a camp fire.

to get lost in the storm, it may help to adopt as a kind of *focus imaginarius*, or lodestar, that old Marxist aspiration: 'From each according to their abilities, to each according to their needs.'[21]

A third and final avenue is the blurred edge of the concept of algocracy itself. That is, because any rule-governed process is in principle susceptible to algorithmic

---

Facing him are three smudge-faced children. Behind them, a soft fiery mist, suggestive of a post-apocalyptic cityscape. The cartoon's caption is: 'Yes, the planet got destroyed. But for a beautiful moment in time, we created a lot of value for share-holders.' Nowadays, there are plenty of people out there who believe, with a passion that overwhelms them, and then often overflows them, that the sole moral duty of any company is to maximise value for its shareholders, within limits set out by law. Even such people should not be afraid of stakeholder mapping. Stakeholder mapping would be a way for them to test their belief. Because if they were right – they're definitely not – then, every time you mapped the stakeholders of a company, you would come up with the same result: the stakeholders and shareholders are identical. Along the way, you might find other stakeholders, but you would gradually learn how their interests were indirectly served best by directly serving the interests of shareholders. In the cartoon, the three kids are drawn without mouths. That's just the cartoonist's style, but I like to think that they have no mouths because there is nothing left to eat and nothing left to say. (The cartoon is by Tom Toro: see www.new-yorker.com/cartoons/a16995).

[21] L. Blanc (1851) *Plus de Girondins*. Paris: Charles Joubert, p. 92; and K. Marx, (1875 [1977]) Critique of the Gotha Programme, in *Selected Writings*, ed. D. McLellan: 564–70. Oxford: Oxford University Press, p. 569 (translation altered).

specification[22] – loosely speaking, everything turns into an algorithm if you squint at it hard enough – many things we are *already* doing as participants in co-operatives and other democratic institutions,[23] as citizens and actors in civil society and as actors in communities of dissent and resistance, may provide clues to democratic algorithmic commoning.[24] What are the informal 'recipes' we're following? Can we debug them of their 'democratic self-destruct mechanism[s]'?[25] How might

---

[22] Compare what Lee Anne Fennell calls 'Ostrom's Law': 'A resource arrangement that works in practice can work in theory': L. A. Fennell (2011) Ostrom's Law: Property Rights in the Commons, *International Journal of the Commons*, 5(1): 9–27, p. 9.

[23] 'If algorithms adopt deliberative democratic paradigms, it assumes an Internet of equal agents, rational debate, and emerging consensus positions. This is not the Internet that many of us would recognize': K. Crawford (2016) Can an Algorithm Be Agonistic? Ten Scenes from Life in Calculated Publics, *Science, Technology, and Human Values* 41(1): 77–92, p. 87. As an alternative paradigm, Kate Crawford points towards the fascinating idea of a democracy that is both algorithmic and agonistic – in other words, one that recognises 'that algorithmic decision making is always a contest, one that is choosing from often counterposed perspectives, within a wider sociotechnical field where irrationality, passion, and emotion are expected': ibid. For more on agonistic democracy, see C. Mouffe (2005) *On the Political*. Abingdon, UK: Routledge.

[24] So may many of the things we are doing as market participants; see the final footnote.

[25] Diamantopoulos, Breaking out of Co-Operation's 'Iron Cage', p. 201.

they be scaled up, and made more sophisticated, adaptive and robust?[26]

(5) This chapter has sketched an encounter between the themes of *value, the commons, algocracy* and *democracy.* The last theme has more to do with the very notion of economic science fiction. The theme is *complexity and unpredictability*, especially on a grand historical scale. I didn't want the vignette to be a neat illustration of these five themes. I wanted it to be noisy. Partly this is because any radical project with designs on the future plays out in the context of *other* such projects, often embodying conflicting 'conceptions of what is ultimately good, proper, or desirable in human life."[27] (As an exercise, it might be worth trying to think through the ramifications of the realisation, and/or attempted realisation, of *every single proposal contained in this book*, simultaneously). To put it another way, just because a competing project is proved to be inferior in the abstract does not mean it can be ignored as a concrete context for whatever is pursued in its stead. To truly fix our gaze on our collective future demands extraordinary peripheral vision – 'like an emu, or whatever' (see above).

For this reason, I began Part I with an inquiry and subsequent legislation, which – debatably – may have had the opposite effect to that which it intended. Likewise, if the ending of Part I seemed abrupt, nebulous and a little underdetermined (perhaps a little convenient?), then it has come across as I hoped. It's supposed to be a comedy, after all. And, if the

---

[26] See J. Pedersen (2008) Habermas's Method: Rational Reconstruction, *Philosophy of the Social Sciences*, 38(4): 457–85.
[27] Graeber, *Toward an Anthropological Theory of Value*, p. 1.

story is messier than five themes I have laid out, and if it seems to express both more and less than those themes – well, all the better.[28]

---

[28] And, in that spirit, let's end with one last messy, open-ended – and very science fictional – thought experiment: Abiodun's MarketStarter hobby. The elevator pitch is, of course, 'Kickstarter, but for markets'. To design a market, you use the platform's mixing deck functionality. You tailor your market in almost any way imaginable. If you wanted to, you could go down to a fine narrative grain, and specify every single exchange over the entire lifetime of the market. In practice, designers usually concern themselves with more high-level, molar properties. Usually they're focused on one or two flagship features. 'This market will slow the gentrification of Easton, and the old Chocolate Factory will be developed as a technology park, not flats.' 'This market will create 100 new jobs in the steel industry in Redcar over the next five years.' OK, it's designed. Then what? People who want the market to come into existence elect to 'back' it, just as on any crowdfunding platform. People who become backers receive credits equal to the money that they pledge. These credits can be spent at face value in ways that conform perfectly to the proposed market. Depending on the design of the particular market, that may or may not still give backers a significant degree of freedom. If backers want to spend their credits in other ways, which partly conform to the market, they can spend them at a discounted value. Part of the cunning of the platform is that it can spot patterns among the different markets proposed by different designers, and suggest to them that they hybridise their markets and pool their support.

Figures

Contributors

AUDINT is a sonic research unit. Its current members include Toby Heys, Steve Goodman/Kode9, Eleni Ikoniadou, Patrick Defasten and Souzanna Zamfe. Further info can be found at audint.net.

Khairani Barokka is a writer, poet, artist and PhD researcher in visual cultures at Goldsmiths, University of London. Published internationally, she is a UNFPA Young Leader Driving Social Change, and has presented work in ten countries. Her work can be found at www.khairanibarokka.com.

Carina Brand is a writer and artist who lectures in Fine Art at De Montfort University, Leicester.

Ha-Joon Chang is an economist and author. He teaches economics at the Faculty of Economics and the Development Studies programme at the University of Cambridge.

Miriam A. Cherry is professor and director of the William C. Wefel Center for Employment Law at Saint Louis University, Missouri.

William Davies is Reader in Political Economy at Goldsmiths, University of London. He is author of *The Happiness Industry* and *The Limits of Neoliberalism*.

Mark Fisher was a writer, political theorist and a lecturer in visual cultures at Goldsmiths, University of London. He authored the K-Punk blog on mainstream and underground music.

Dan Gavshon Brady is a strategy director at Wolff Olins, London, and co-founder of the fictional consultancy PostRational.

Owen Hatherley is an author and journalist based in London. He writes about architecture, politics and culture and is a regular contributor to *The Guardian, The London Review of Books* and *New Humanist.*

Laura Horn is Associate Professor in the Department of Social Sciences and Business at Roskilde University, Denmark.

Tim Jackson is Director of the Centre for the Understanding of Sustainable Prosperity and author of *Prosperity without Growth* (Routledge 2017).

Mark R. Johnson is currently a Killam Postdoctoral Fellow in the Department of Political Science at the University of Alberta. His work focuses primarily on the intersections between play and money, such as eSports, live streaming and fantasy sports, alongside numerous other game studies topics.

Bastien Kerspern is an interaction designer specialising in public innovation. He is the co-founder of design studios Design Friction and Casus Ludi.

Nora O Murchú is a curator and designer based in Ireland. Her practice engages with fictions and narratives to explore how complex socio-technical systems are imagined, built and used. She is currently a lecturer at the University of Limerick.

Justin Pickard is a founding member of research company and consultancy Strange Telemetry.

James Pockson is an architect and studio co-tutor at the Cass School of Architecture at London Metropolitan University, and co-founder of the fictional consultancy PostRational.

Tobias Revell is an artist and Course Leader in MA Interaction Design Communication at the London College of Communication. He is a founding member of research company and consultancy Strange Telemetry.

Judy Thorne is a doctoral researcher at the University of Manchester.

Sherryl Vint is a Professor in the Department of Media and Cultural Studies at the University of California, Riverside, where she directs the Speculative Fictions and Cultures of Science programme.

Georgina Voss is an anthropologist of technology and innovation systems, an artist, and writer. She is a Senior Lecturer at the London College of Communication, and a founding member and director of research company and consultancy Strange Telemetry.

Jo Lindsay Walton is a research fellow at the Institute of Advanced Studies in Humanities, University of Edinburgh.

Brian Willems is Assistant Professor of Literature and Film Theory at the University of Split, Croatia.

Index

Index